FLYING COLOURS

Photograph by Iwao Matsuo.

FLYING COLOURS

The Toni Onley Story

As told to Gregory Strong

HARBOUR PUBLISHING

Harbour Publishing Co. Ltd.
P.O. Box 219
Madeira Park, BC Canada
V0N 2H0

THE CANADA COUNCIL | LE CONSEIL DES ARTS
FOR THE ARTS | DU CANADA
SINCE 1957 | DEPUIS 1957

www.harbourpublishing.com

Printed and bound in Canada

We acknowledge the financial support of the Government of Canada through the Book Publishing Industry Development Program for our publishing activities. We further acknowledge the support of the Canada Council for the Arts and the Province of British Columbia through the British Columbia Arts Council for our publishing program.

National Library of Canada Cataloguing in Publication Data

Onley, Toni, 1928–
  Flying colours

  Includes index.
  ISBN 1-55017-298-0

  1. Onley, Toni, 1928– 2. Painters—Canada—Biography. I. Strong, Gregory, 1956– II. Title.
  ND249.O58A2 2002   759.11   C2002-910796-2

Contents

Preface

Anatural storyteller, Toni Onley seems to have travelled almost everywhere and had one of the most eventful lives of anyone I know. We met in 1986 when I was on assignment for *Beautiful British Columbia* magazine. We made two flights that year in his Lake Buccaneer flying boat: a rained-out excursion to Harrison Lake in May and a more precarious flight to Garibaldi Provincial Park in October. While we circled Garibaldi Lake, Toni warned me over the headset, "The lake is glassy calm. I can't tell where to set down the plane." The news alarmed me. A few weeks earlier a seaplane had crashed under similar conditions. But he followed the line of trees along the shore and brought the float plane down on the water, a little roughly, but safely. Toni, fifty-eight at the time, nearly twice my age, landed the aircraft, unpacked our supplies, then painted all afternoon, setting such an energetic pace that I felt hard-pressed to keep up with him.

Watching him transform his paper and materials into a water-colour—with shapes, images, then place—fascinated me. His creative process seemed mysterious, alchemical and completely different from the process of writing and revision with which I was familiar. My interest in him took me through several magazine articles and a collaboration with Brian Ferstman on a documentary film proposal. In the meantime I wondered about the kind of form that would best suit a story like the one Toni had. Magazine pieces and short quotations couldn't do justice to his unique voice. On the other hand, a conventional biography would lose the sense of his character and the way he told his stories.

Then I read *Spilsbury's Coast* by Howard White and was struck by how well that book captured both Jim Spilsbury's personality and much of what I knew of the people living in small communities on the West Coast. There was another book as well, A.Y. Jackson's classic 1956 autobiography, *A Painter's Country*.

Events in my own life took me to many of the places Toni described. I received a two-year posting to Beijing under the auspices of the Canadian International Development Agency and St. Mary's University, Nova Scotia. Ultimately I joined the English Department at Aoyama University, Tokyo, which is where I teach today.

Paradoxically, the farther I moved from British Columbia, the more I appreciated the special character of the West Coast and the unusual people who live there. I also became very curious about the nature of art and artists as well. It astonished me that in an age of mass reproduction of texts and images through computerization and the globalization of manufacturing, artists like Toni Onley continued to create objects as singular and unique as a painting. I also wondered about the obstacles and sacrifices a successful artist faced over a long career.

Initiating this book in 1994 with Toni Onley gave me a way to explore these issues. I consulted the Special Collections branch of the University of British Columbia, where Toni has archived thirty-two voluminous boxes of papers and memorabilia, including personal correspondence, commercial records of his dealings with galleries and newspaper and magazine clippings. I interviewed fifty-three people, among them members of Toni's immediate family, relatives on the Isle of Man and, of course, his artistic contemporaries.

To complete my research, I travelled to the Isle of Man, to San Miguel de Allende, Mexico, and to numerous locations across Canada. I also visited a number of West Coast artists in their studios, among them Jack Wise and Jack Shadbolt, both since deceased.

But my primary source for the book remained Toni himself. Ultimately our project turned out to be far more difficult than either of us could have imagined. It consisted of hours of taping conversations, poring through personal papers and viewing documentaries, then additional research on the artists, places, and events he mentioned. I did follow-up interviews with Toni and others, then attempted to render the wonderful stories I had collected into a linear narrative that I hope will carry not only the drama of the stories themselves but also the force of Toni's personality and his infectious sense of humour.

The first chapter of the book is largely based on an article on his ski plane crash that Toni wrote for *Saturday Night* magazine in February 1985. While reviewing the chapters covering his youth on the Isle of Man, he recalled other childhood memories and we added these as well. Chapter 18 is in part a rendering of Toni's travel journals that made up the book *Onley's Arctic* (Douglas & McIntyre, 1989). Much of Chapter 21 concerns a trip to India that Toni made with the late George Woodcock, documented in *The Walls of India* (Lester & Orpen Dennys, 1985), a book on which the two men collaborated. Chapter 22 is wholly based on Toni's unpublished diary of his 1988 visit to Japan. His second wife Gloria, now his close friend and the editor of Toni Onley's *British Columbia: A Tribute* (Raincoast Books, 1999), contributed many editorial changes to the emerging manuscript.

As books are collaborative acts, I must also credit the encouragement of my family, and friends, in particular my wife Kathi Mitsui, my sister Lorna Strong and my friend Ian Morton. Very helpful comments came my way from John Gribble, Paul Rossiter and other members of the Tokyo Creative Arts writing group.

My work on *Flying Colours: The Toni Onley Story* has been an education in art. From a wreck on a mountain glacier, to encounters with characters like the garrulous F.H. Varley who always fell in love with his models to sojourns on the Isle of Man, in Mexico and the Arctic, it's been a wonderful journey. May it be so for you, the reader.

—GREGORY STRONG

Chapter 1

Wrecked on the Cheakamus

On September 7, 1984, I landed my ski plane on Cheakamus Glacier in the Coastal Range that stretches from Vancouver to Alaska. I was high on Mount Davidson, in the ring of enormous mountains above the ski-resort town of Whistler and about forty minutes flying time from Vancouver, forty-five miles away. To get me onto the glacier and home again, I relied on a fragile piece of technology—the Polish-built Wilga or "thrush," a small silver ski plane with canary-yellow wings.

At fifty-five, I had flown to the most remote parts of North America in search of landscapes. I had been drawing and painting for most of my life, and art remained my great passion. That day, after leaving Vancouver, a thousand feet over Indian Arm inlet, I had caught an onshore wind. As it reached Mount Seymour and the other mountains on the inlet's west side, it diverted upward and lifted my plane. On this updraft I sailed to eight thousand feet and entered the air space above Garibaldi Provincial Park. I headed the aircraft toward Castle Towers and the vast white bulk of Mount Davidson. Horsetail clouds in the deep ultramarine sky indicated a strong wind at high altitude. Sunlight burnished the broad Cheakamus Glacier as I glided to a landing on the sheet of snow.

I opened the door and stepped out. The snow felt wet and heavy underfoot. Taking off again was going to be a problem, but I kept any anxiety I felt to myself. My time on a glacier was always limited by the falling degrees of my engine temperature gauge. If the engine cooled too much, it would never start, so I carefully wrapped the engine cowl in a padded blanket.

My passenger, John Reeves, climbed out, cradling a camera in his arm, with another slung over his shoulder. Reeves, a sturdy forty-seven-year-old celebrity photographer from Toronto, was shooting a photo essay on me for an inflight magazine.

He took off his dark glasses, squinted in the dazzling sunlight, and hastily put them back on again. "What are you looking for?" I asked him.

"I'm supposed to be shooting dramatic images of Canadian landscape—misty mountains, ski plane, splendid artist, all that stuff."

"Let me guess," I grinned, "they want to call it 'The Flying Artist'."

"You've got it, Toni."

The Flying Artist—I'd dreamed of being a pilot ever since I'd been a kid running down hills and leaping into the air on the Isle of Man. At last, I'd learned to fly in 1966 while teaching at the University of Victoria and living near the airport. After my show sold out in Montreal the following year, I bought a second-hand two-seater, a Champion SkyTrac, for about $5,000 and criss-crossed North America, painting landscapes. I sold the SkyTrac in 1975 to purchase a Lake Buccaneer, an amphibian aircraft that had a boat hull and retractable landing gear under the wings. In it I could take off from a meadow, land in the sea, roll up onto a beach and start painting.

One summer I flew that plane to the eastern Arctic, an extraordinary landscape, one with only the essentials—rock, water, an endless blue sky and white, almost blinding, light. After I returned to the West Coast, I kept looking up at the mountaintops and wondering how I could reach the glaciers and find the exquisite beauty I'd seen in the Arctic. Then I read a magazine article about the Wilga 80, which could take off or land in only sixty-five yards. Outfitted with retractable skis in addition to fixed wheels, it was the perfect craft to land on the limited surface area of a glacier. In 1981, when I sold the watercolours from my book *A Silent Thunder* for about $100,000, I bought myself one. And that was why I was standing on a glacier that day.

John unslung a camera and took photographs of me by the Wilga as I got on with my painting. I placed my paintbox on the tailplane, then taped a sheet of watercolour paper onto its lid. My birchwood box opened in sections, the inside of the lid holding about fifty sheets of Arches rag paper, the rest of the box containing tubes of watercolour pigment, a mixing tray, a water container and several Chinese goat-hair brushes.

Poised over the paper as I stood in the snow, I dipped a paintbrush into the water container and then onto a squiggle of lampblack on my palette. I faced Mount Davidson and painted it as if it were part of a big still life of rock and snow. Then, after rinsing the brush, I mixed a small amount of French ultramarine blue with water and applied a thin blue wash onto the sky area of my painting.

In Canada landscape painting is one of our strongest traditions, best known through the work of the Group of Seven. I particularly like the small oil panels of Tom Thomson and A.Y. Jackson as well as Varley's windy Georgian Bay scenes and Arctic watercolours. On the West Coast, Emily Carr painted dark firs with swirling green boughs in mysterious rain forests, but where she was in the trees, I was out of the trees, looking at the forest from a distance. My landscapes depicted the mist-shrouded West Coast mountains, ragged grey storm clouds and alpine lakes so dark they appeared bottomless and supernatural, as if absorbing light.

While I painted on the Cheakamus, the wind picked up. Taking off from a glacier in a strong wind could be tricky, even dangerous, so I put down my watercolour unfinished and hurried John back into the plane. I turned the ignition key and the engine started. I faced the plane toward the downward slope. As I started my takeoff run down the mountainside, the snow began sticking to the skis. Halfway into the run, I could see we'd never reach flying speed. I chopped the power, turned the plane and headed back up the slope.

"We'll take another shot at it," I told John over the headset.

Tightening his lap belt and shoulder harness, he joked a little. "Whatever you say, Toni, as long as we're back for supper."

The tracks that I had laid down on my first try were now iced over. I swung the Wilga into the grooves. As we gained speed, I pulled full flaps, the lateral controls at the rear of the wings that increase lift to get the plane off the ground quickly. Nothing happened. We were rocketing down the glacier at fifty miles per hour. I glanced at the flaps. They were fully extended. Then I noticed the snow swirling past the window. That meant a tail wind had caught up to us and killed our lift. We careened off the tracks toward a gaping crevasse that sliced across the lower end of the glacier.

I realized it was impossible to stop. If I cut the engine, our momentum would still carry us to the edge and the plane would fall into the crevasse. My only option was to try to leap this crevasse and land back on the glacier without sliding into the next one. I left full power on.

We staggered into the air and leapt the first abyss, crunching into a narrow crevasse that ran perpendicular to the main crevasse in the direction of our descent. It was just wide enough to hold the body of the plane while supporting the wings. It minimized the impact of the crash, while preventing us from sliding into the next crevasse. Just to the right or the left, and we would have smashed into the ice and been killed. I visualized exactly how we had been saved later, for I had been knocked out by the impact.

A spasm of pain jolted me awake. Jagged strips of metal from the fuselage pinned my legs under the wrecked instrument panel. The engine had been rammed back into the cabin and had punched out the control panel. My shoulder harness had sprung open and my seat had been wrenched off its mounting. My hand still clutched the throttle. And my ring finger bled, cut to the bone.

My first conscious act had been to turn off all switches, but I could see gasoline pouring onto the hot engine and possibly still live wires and feared that at any moment we would burst into flames. As the engine rapidly cooled in the freezing air, I finally realized we would not die in a fireball.

I turned to John. His seat had been almost thrust out of the aircraft. He sat buckled into it, his head slumped forward, blood dripping from his mouth. As I struggled to free my legs, I kept shouting, "John, are you all right?" Once or twice, he flinched, indicating he lived. I thought he could be suffering from massive internal injuries. I reached over and slapped his face to revive him.

His eyes snapped open and he twisted in his shoulder harness. "What kind of a place is this?" he asked. "I hope they have a good wine cellar." He was disoriented but had not lost his sense of humour.

Through the side windows we could see only blue ice, while through the front window we had a view over the glacier surface. The narrow crevasse that the Wilga had slotted into was little wider than the body of the plane. Apparently we had skidded to a stop in it, shearing off the Wilga's skis, wheels and part of the undercarriage, before the nose of the plane nestled into the narrow end of the crevasse. Now we hung there, precariously supported by the aircraft wings that rested on the snowbanks on either side of us. With horror I realized that if the plane suddenly tilted backward, we would fall through the rear window into the eerie blue-green abyss of the larger crevasse. For some time after the crash, pieces of the undercarriage kept breaking off and falling into the crevasse, and by the sound delay I could tell it was very deep. There was a gaping hole in the cabin floor in front of the forward seats.

Fortunately, the blood trickling from John's lips came only from a bite inside his mouth. Except for a swollen cheek, which made his face resemble that of a friendly, oversized chipmunk, he seemed all right. I helped him unbuckle his harness and he shifted to the left-hand rear seat in the cabin.

I checked the ELT, the Emergency Locator Transmitter. It should have started operating automatically after the crash, but I had to switch it on manually. I noted the time on my watch, 3:15 p.m. My radio had fallen through the hole in the floor and dangled from its wires. I pulled it up along with the microphone and headset. I could confirm on the emergency frequency that the ELT was transmitting, but I couldn't call out a mayday because the cable to the antenna was severed.

I crawled into the luggage compartment in the back of the plane to stretch out my broken leg and get the first aid kit to bandage my bleeding finger. The whole fuselage trembled. Very cautiously I crept back into the cabin, sat on the other rear seat and stretched out my injured leg.

"I think one of my cameras fell through." John peered uneasily into the hole in the floor. "Toni, I suppose you realize this crash scotches our story. CP Air isn't going to publish anything that ends in an airplane crash." He turned to me. "So what do we do now?"

The crash of the Wilga.

"I turned on the emergency locator transmitter. We wait for help."

"Wait for help?" John shook his head in disbelief. "Shouldn't we do something?"

A finely grained snow started to fall outside the plane. Gusts of wind blew the snow through the wreck, and the powder settled on our clothes. I shuddered with the cold. I passed John my parka and he put it on. I remembered the sleeping bag in the luggage compartment, retrieved it and put it over myself and John's legs and feet. I wore the headpiece and I made myself a pillow from a box of John's film and a carrying bag.

For the next little while we kept shifting, trying to find a comfortable position in our cold, cramped quarters. At last I turned to him, "John, you have another camera, right?"

"What about it?"

"Maybe you should shoot some photographs of us in the wreck."

He groaned, "I'm not a crash photographer."

"To show we were alive. In case we don't make it."

"Instead of taking pictures," he retorted, "I think we should get out of this bloody wreck and bivouac on the snow!"

"With this wind, we'd freeze to death," I told him. "We've got the only shelter between here and Vancouver."

About 4:30 p.m., not long after the snow started falling, we heard the drone of an aircraft engine. A de Havilland Buffalo short takeoff and landing aircraft from CFB Comox, the Canadian Forces base on Vancouver Island, circled overhead. It must have tracked our ELT signal. I prayed they wouldn't give us up for dead because of our radio silence. The plane circled once and disappeared.

In the middle of a whiteout at five o'clock in the afternoon we heard helicopter rotors. In the gloom I could make out the grey silhouette of a huge Chinook rescue helicopter. Blindly, its glaring yellow search beams probed for life. The downdraft from its large rotors rocked our little plane. I wanted to scream, "Don't come any closer! You'll tip the plane into the crevasse and kill us!" In the end, the growing storm turned the pilot away.

In the failing light, violent gusts of sixty-mile-per-hour winds lashed through the shattered cabin. Our body heat melted the driven snow on our clothes, soaking us. Soon we were in complete darkness. John must have felt as miserable and as cold as I did, but occasionally he'd make some crack to keep his spirits up. As if we were Laurel and Hardy, he bantered, "Another fine mess you've got us into, Ollie." Talking was painful for him, but he managed to suggest that in future I pack a chessboard or at least a Trivial Pursuit game in my survival kit.

The pain of our injuries and the bitterly cold night soon reduced us to the language of cavemen. At one point I hunted in the luggage compartment for food. I offered John some. "Cheese? For strength." "Not hungry," he replied.

I tried to sleep, turning to one side then the other. I recalled some of the past year's events. Not twelve months earlier, I'd had a nationally publicized fight with Revenue Canada, which had tried to reassess the tax status of Canadian artists and collect back taxes. I came within hours of burning my inventory of prints in public to make the point that an artist is not a manufacturer, but the government relented and eventually I won the dispute. I nodded off, dreaming that a Revenue Canada ski patrol had found us. Each member of the team wore goggles and a red-and-white jacket with a maple leaf. Their leader, disguised in a woollen balaclava, opened an attaché case and brandished a sheaf of papers. He told me that if I intended to declare a loss with the crash of my plane I would have to fill out a form. I tried but had difficulty in my cramped position; besides, it was dark. I protested and asked for help but he said, "That is not the responsibility of this department."

"Would you mind calling Search and Rescue?" I asked.

"We do not communicate with any other government department," he replied.

I awoke and there was only the wind and the blowing snow.

I thought of my wife, Yukiko Kageyama, who'd fear the worst. I'd left her the telephone number of the rescue co-ordination centre in Victoria. She'd likely called them and been told they'd found no sign of life at the wreck. Desperately, I pictured her and tried to send a telepathic message: "I am alive, I am alive."

Again, I drifted off to sleep. Suddenly the fuselage creaked as if working its nose free from the snowbank. The tail dipped.

"Oh, my God!" I yelled. "We're falling!"

John gripped the back of the pilot seat. I lunged into the front of the plane, farther from the abyss beyond the rear window. Nothing happened. One of the tailplanes had dropped to the snow bank on a side of the crevasse, lodging us more securely than ever. We eased back to our places in the cramped, freezing cabin, and John tucked the sleeping bag back around our legs.

Finally the oblivion of sleep came in the early hours of the morning. Then sunrise lightened the sky above the black mountains and we woke. From a survival course I had once taken, I knew the dangers of exposure. If not rescued within two days, people who live through a cold-weather plane crash have less than a ten-percent chance of survival. Thinking of this depressing fact, I shivered uncontrollably. "I can't take another night of this," I said.

Scarcely able to speak with his aching jaw, John mumbled a reply. Morning came at last in a flash of blinding yellow light as the sun rose over the black mountains. The inside of the plane grew warmer. The snow melted from the front window. We could see Cheakamus Valley wreathed in the fog below, and we worried that the cloud ceiling might remain too low for a rescue helicopter. Even more troubling was the idea that Air-Sea Rescue might have given us up for dead hours ago.

Then at eight o'clock, I heard the unmistakable *chop-chop-chop* of a helicopter rotor. Worried that it might be only in my mind, I turned to John. He raised his eyebrows. It grew louder. We looked out the rear window. A small Bell Jet Ranger appeared above the slope of the glacier.

John described the scene as if in a movie: "They're coming, they're coming, they're coming!" The helicopter zoomed past us. "They're going, they're going, they're gone . . ."

In despair, neither of us spoke. Then we heard the helicopter again. It was returning. I realized it had been circling to gain height. Quickly I put my back against the rear Plexiglas window and shoved it out. I snatched up the yellow stuff sack from the sleeping bag, poked my head and arms outside of the plane, and frantically waved it in the air.

The helicopter circled overhead. Then it descended and hovered off the left wing of the plane, unable to land on the sloping ice. The passenger in the helicopter threw open the rear door and jumped into the snow, then floundered onto the wing of the Wilga. Breathlessly he shouted, "I'm a paramedic—Mike Johnston, CFB Comox."

I squeezed to the side of the cabin to let John crawl out first. Johnston helped him get across the wing into the snow, then onto the helicopter skid and into the chopper. With a nervous glance at the crevasse, I crawled out onto the wing and jumped into the snow. When I tried to stand, I fell over. Johnston had to drag me to the helicopter and push me up into the cabin with John pulling from above. Then he climbed in after me and the pilot lifted off.

Until that moment I did not fully realize how incredibly lucky we'd been. As we gained altitude, John and I stared at the first crevasse. A fall into that gaping maw would have killed us. But the smaller crevasse that the plane had jammed itself into was the only crevasse on the glacier that ran in the direction of our descent down the slope. It was the only one that could have stopped us from coasting on and falling into the next crevasse or off the edge of the glacier altogether, with a long drop to the valley floor.

I stared at the crumpled wreckage of my plane. Johnston looked at it too. "Usually, we pack bodies out of a wreck like that one," he said. "And you guys walked away."

Transfixed at the window, John commented, "We were incredibly lucky, just unbelievably lucky."

Then we learned that our pilot, Bob Holt, was not even part of the official rescue team, just a heli-logger who had started talking to Johnston at Squamish Airport and decided to check out the wreck for himself. The paramedic had come along but the rest of his team were still grounded because of the fog. Holt had popped his little helicopter above the clouds and spotted us.

When we landed, ambulance attendants waiting nearby strapped me onto a stretcher, piling on blankets to keep me warm. As they wheeled me to an ambulance, a young reporter from the *Province* turned up. I grabbed her arm. "Call my wife. Tell her I'm all right and I'll answer any of your questions."

She telephoned Yukiko, then called her newspaper editor. He remembered how I'd come within hours of burning my work in my fight against Revenue Canada. Apparently the editor said, "Stay with him and get the story." The reporter chased me all the way into the x-ray room where a powerfully built nurse finally ejected her. Her determination seemed an incredible affirmation of life, I thought, even if I was the victim of it.

Later that day, Yukiko arrived at the hospital with my daughter, Lynn. Shock registered on her face when she saw me in bed with a cast. Yet she politely greeted John Reeves and inquired about his health. Then she rushed to my bed, threw her arms around me and sobbed. Lynn took my hand and we all cried together.

I remembered the message I had tried sending telepathically to Yukiko. "You didn't sense anything unusual around ten o'clock last night, did you? Did you have any thoughts about me?" Yukiko shook her head. When I explained why I'd asked, Yukiko recalled that one of our friends, Inge, the wife of writer George Woodcock, had called her about ten. "She had a strong feeling that you and John were all right."

"I guess I dialled the wrong number," I said.

The three of us laughed.

The next few days were euphoric ones. In the Sunday edition of the *Province*, the reporter's story appeared with the headlines set in the bold type used when war is declared: **GLACIER TERROR SHAKES ONLEY**. Other reporters began calling. TV cameramen dropped by my house for footage of me sitting in my chair with a cast on my leg. The story went national. The painter who had defied Revenue Canada survived a plane crash on a glacier.

My parents, that tiny mismatched pair who had retired to the Okanagan sunbelt, drove all the way to Vancouver to see me. My mother tried to smile nonchalantly when she saw me. She wore an ivory-coloured silk blouse and a blue suede skirt, and with her delicate features looked every bit a graduate of Miss Farrington's Finishing School for Young Ladies. But she couldn't restrain herself and burst out with, "Toni, we were so worried about you!"

My father strutted into the room, casually dressed in a khaki shirt and beige pants. His bald, sunburnt head was shiny pink from sitting outside in his garden. He interrupted my mother, turning to me with a mischievous grin. "Florence worried. I knew you'd pull through, son. I saw the mountain on television. A superb piece of flying."

I wish I could have agreed with him that I'd flown into the second crevasse on purpose. Truthfully, I'd completely lost control of my aircraft. Some other hand than mine had pushed the Wilga into the one place that could have saved us.

"Dad, it was just luck. I was going down that slope hell bent for leather when the tailwind cut my lift. There's no way to stop quickly when you're in a ski plane, so I had to keep the power on to jump the first crevasse."

"Then you made the right choice, Toni, because you're still here with us," declared my mother. "Maybe now you'll settle into a regular job."

"Florence, Toni will never change." My father chuckled, watching me hobble into the kitchen on my crutches to make them some tea. "One thing's certain though, Toni. For the time being, that crash has put a lanket on you."

I laughed. On the Isle of Man, a lanket was a piece of rope tied between one front and one hind leg of a sheep to keep it from straying.

The kettle came to a boil and my father filled the teapot and placed it and the tea cups and saucers on the table. "Flo, did I ever tell you about the time Toni and I flew over Okanagan Lake?" he asked.

"Yes, Jim, many times."

I remembered how my father had been white-knuckled with fear while flying with me. My mother and I shared a smile.

In the weeks that followed the crash, I donated my cast to a celebrity auction at the University of Manitoba where it raised $3,500 for medical research. Then John Reeves and I appeared on CBC TV as guests of *Front Page Challenge*. Like *Hockey Night in Canada*, this program was a national institution, one of the longest running Canadian television programs. John and I were hidden behind a screen, out of sight of the panellists who had to question us and guess what our story was. We could only answer "Yes," or "No," but our survival adventure had become so well known that it took Allan Fotheringham just thirty seconds to solve the mystery.

Not everything went my way, however. Shortly after John and I were rescued, I got a telephone call from Garibaldi Provincial Park asking me to remove the plane wreck: "You can ride an elephant into a provincial park, but you have to ride it out again," the ranger said. "You can't leave anything in the park, it's littering."

I suggested a kind of a monument: "Toni Onley walked away from this one." The ranger listened patiently—for about two minutes—then replied, "Either you move it from the park, or we move it and send you the bill."

I hired a salvager with a Sikorsky S58T helicopter to haul the wreck away. He put a sling under the plane but the engine and the remains of the undercarriage broke loose from the wreck. He made a second trip the next day with a salvage crew who rappelled into the crevasse and recovered the engine. Bits and pieces of the undercarriage remain in the crevasse to this day, no doubt to emerge thousands of years from now at the foot of the glacier. It was supposed to be a $2,500 job, but he had to come back to me for another thousand.

"Hey, it's not my fault," I said. "I'm already out the price of the plane. How about a painting from the glacier instead?"

Gradually, my life settled back into a routine. Yet I had lost my ski plane—uninsured because the premium was too high—and after three years of a recession that had eventually reduced my painting sales, I couldn't afford to replace it. Furthermore, although I still had my Lake Buccaneer amphibian, I had lost some of my confidence in my flying abilities. Until I came to terms with those fears, I was a danger to myself when flying again. And months after the crash, I still had flashbacks at night, groaning as I relived the experience in my dreams. Gently, Yukiko would wake me, "It's all right, Toni."

My friends asked, "How can you keep on flying?" But there was never any question in my mind that I had to fly. My work relied on observation of nature, and the more unspoiled the nature, the better. The landscapes I most wanted to paint were almost inaccessible in any other way. It would take days to hike into remote places like Phantom Lake, which lay in an old volcano crater. And if I were ever lost in a place like that, no one would ever find me. In my amphibian, I could fly there in an hour, paint a watercolour of that lonesome lake and its amazing two-thousand-foot waterfall and then fly back to Vancouver. Furthermore, without returning from the wilderness with fresh images of nature, I would never have the inspiration or the subject matter to paint landscapes in oils when I worked in my studio over the winter.

Besides, flying challenged me to live each day as fully as possible. The first time I stepped out of my ski plane into the raw cold of an ice age, I was possessed by an animal fear of the glacier. I was out of my element, the green valleys far below, and I trod carefully in the snow, wary of a misstep that would plunge me into a crevasse or trigger an avalanche. Over two years without mishap had habituated me to a higher level of risk-taking, but after the crash, I realized anew how dangerous flying onto a glacier could be, and even how precarious any flying could suddenly become.

When the Chinese artist Kuo Jo-hsu described the act of painting watercolours with a big floppy goat-hair brush back in the Sung dynasty, he was unknowingly describing the art of flying and the projection of thought that is required to land precisely on a chosen spot. He said, "The brush must be nimble, move swiftly in a continuous and connecting manner, so that the flow of life is not interrupted as the thoughts precede the brush." The painter intends the image, just as the pilot intends to direct the plane on a certain path. Despite the overall control as "the thoughts precede the brush," there is still an element of chance and improvisation in painting a good watercolour, for not every brush stroke can be completely determined by the artist. Likewise, my aircraft is subject to the wind and the weather, so that flying it demands both forethought and improvisation. There is, however, a difference. When a brush stroke surprises him, an artist may fail to improvise successfully without losing his life.

The early Taoist sages believed that a mountain retreat was the best place to identify with nature and live in harmony with it. The ideal was to live amid the peaks, but many Taoist adepts could only visit the mountains for a short time and write about the experience. Like the Taoists, I sought the high places and returned with depictions of the beauty I found there. But where they consulted sacred texts to find out what days were auspicious for travelling in the mountains and what days were fraught with danger, I gained my confidence from a chart and from technical knowledge of the mountains.

The more I knew about the behaviour of glaciers, the more

accurately I could judge the situation and the less apprehension I felt, but the information never eliminated the risk. Glaciers change with the climate, melting in the summer and growing in the winter, their crevasses opening and closing. For many reasons, there can be no such thing as a detailed map of a glacier. A chart told me only where to find it. Once I had landed on a glacier, a map became more talisman than guide. For all my scientific knowledge, I was as reliant on good fortune as the ancient travellers.

Chapter 2

The Isle of Man

I came to Canada from the Isle of Man, a tiny British dependency in the Irish Sea, only 32½ miles long and 11½ miles wide. At the island's highest point, the top of Mount Snaefel, 2,036 feet high, you could see six kingdoms: the Isle of Man, Wales to the south, England in the east, Scotland to the north and if you looked to the west, Northern Ireland. That was five. They said the sixth kingdom was overhead: "The Kingdom of Heaven."

The island has a thousand-year-old outdoor parliament, the Tynwald, created by Danish invaders with names like Magnus the Barefoot, Sigurd the Stout and Olaf the Dwarf. They gathered clods of earth from each of the island's parishes and stacked the turf into four enormous tiers, like a big sod wedding cake, and they called the spot Tynwald Hill. To this day, every July 5 the Manx parliament meets there, albeit ceremonially now, to proclaim the new laws of the community.

The past loomed very large in our lives. One much-repeated family story concerned my mother's father, Grandfather Lord. He was a tight-fisted Yorkshireman with a walrus moustache who had come to the island to start a greenhouse and market garden business. He thought a weathered megalith, a huge standing stone marker that had likely rested on his property since the Neolithic period, got in the way of ploughing. He took a team of horses with hired men, dug it out and hauled it to a corner of the field. That night a gale smashed the glass panes in the greenhouse and ruined two fields of

Me with my mother, Douglas, Isle of Man, 1928.

vegetables. Things kept happening. Two cows were found dead. Miller, the hired hand, fell off a stone wall and broke his leg. One night they heard thunder and saw lightning, but when my grandfather took a lantern out to the barn to quiet the disturbed horses, there was no storm, only a moonlit night. The next day when he took the horses to the smithy to be shod, the smithy told him, "You'll never know any peace on that place of yours, Willie Lord, till you put that stone back." Grandfather Lord quickly had the stone replaced. As far as I know, his bad luck ended.

Many years after we'd left the island, I remember talking to my parents about my childhood in the town of Douglas. My mother told me that when I was starting to arrive my father couldn't get a cab so she had to walk all the way to the Jane Crookall Maternity Home in the middle of the night. It was half a mile to get there and she felt certain she would have me on the way. Then they met the town undertaker carrying a child's coffin on his head, which surely was a terribly bad omen, according to my father.

"And let me tell you," said my father, "we wasted our bloody time waiting for you. I stayed up all Monday night. Naturally, so did your mother. When we got to the hospital, your mother's labour stopped. You must have taken the day off, Toni, because you weren't born until Tuesday morning."

"It was the afternoon, Jim," my mother said.

He shook his head. "It had to be the morning."

One remark led to another. My mother retreated into the kitchen. My father followed her and I could hear them squabbling. At last, my father reappeared. "Toni, you were born at two-thirty in the afternoon."

"You're sure about that?" I asked.

"Two-thirty p.m.," he repeated, "November 20, 1928. You never forget your firstborn."

On Tuesday afternoon, my father had gone back to the Maternity Home. Big Ella McClellan, the Head Nurse, told him, "Mr. Onley, you have a son. Come and take a look at him." There were eight babies in the room. Instead of telling him which one I was, Ella flipped over the name cards on the babies' cribs and told him to find me. My mother had curly blonde hair so he picked up a blond baby.

"It's amazing," said Ella. "You fathers never miss. It must be instinct." He took the baby to my mother's room. She sat bolt upright in bed. "Who's that?" My father had just given her a Norwegian baby. He hurried back to the nursery. The other nurses were in on the joke and they all laughed at him.

Finally Ella pointed me out. My father could hardly believe it. I had a tiny squished-up face and tapered black sideburns. Ella said I looked like a little Italian and should be called Tony.

"That's all right," my father said, "It's my middle name. We'll call him Anthony Onley." She clapped her hands. "Right then, it's Tony Onley. Now take him to his mother for a feed."

1931, Douglas, Isle of Man.

29

In the early days, my parents lived in a row house on Albany Street in the town of Douglas, a seaside resort with a population of about 20,000. Like Brighton or Blackpool, it catered to British tourists on Labour Days and August bank holidays. Along the seaside of the town ran a wide promenade, ending at an ornate Victorian terminus for horse-drawn trams. It was serviced by green-and-yellow-liveried streetcars and red double-decker buses that rattled along, stopping now and then on the west side of the street at the Sefton Hotel or at the enormous Palace Ballroom, the largest dancehall in England, or by one of the cream or yellow Edwardian-era boarding houses. The principal attraction in Douglas lay on the other side of the promenade, the long, crescent-shaped sandy beach that stretched from Douglas Harbour to Onchan Head, a rocky clifftop several miles away. In the warmer weather, my mother brought me to that beach to play in the sand and swim with her in the sea.

My father negotiated a partnership with an electrician, Frank Openshaw, and we moved into a house at 52 Bucks Road, next to the electrician's shop. On Sundays and holidays my father tied a cushion onto the crossbar of his bicycle, sat me on it, and cycled to Elby Point on the north end of Niarbyl Bay, on the southwest coast of the island. At low tide, we hunted the crabs that scuttled into the cracks of the rocky outcropping offshore known as the Reef. We still-fished with long bamboo rods for bollen, large golden-coloured rock cod with thumbnail-sized scales that lived in a deep hole off the rock. The bollen carries in its gullet a crucifix-like bone that Manx fishermen make into a charm to protect them from drowning. I had one of these Crosh Vollan crosses once, and it worked for me, as I will relate later.

Looking back on that period of my life, every day seemed like summertime. The holiday ended abruptly when my father sent me to St. Mary's Elementary, a Catholic school that looked like a Dickensian workhouse, a grim, three-storey building of red industrial brick with dusty barred windows. A school bell hung at one end of its slate roof and a cross stood on the other.

My first teacher, Sister Mary Aloysius, wore a long black habit and kept her hair hidden under her wimple. As she walked, her nun's robe swished by our desks. We called her "Our Lady of

Perpetual Suffering" because whenever she caned a bare bottom, her eyes seemed to roll upward until only the whites showed, reminding us of paintings we had been shown of St. Teresa lost in religious ecstasy.

By the crucifix on her belt, she kept a leather pouch full of dried corn that she scattered into the corner of the room at the beginning of the class. Anyone she sent to the corner was compelled to kneel on the corn with his arms raised or outstretched from his sides. I could often be found there "doing time." I knelt so long on one occasion that I lost the feeling in my legs and a couple of the boys had to haul me to my feet.

I think that under different circumstances, I might have become more sociable with my classmates, but the shock of my early school experiences propelled me inward. I felt a sense of injustice at my treatment by my teachers. My parents had lavished so much attention on me that I hardly knew how to deal with other children, especially some of the rougher kids from large Catholic families. I realized that I had none of their ability or interest in sports. As a result I retreated from that world and spent more time by myself at home. I developed a love of drawing that helped me to deal with my loneliness.

One day around Easter time, Sister Aloysius brought in a daffodil for our nature lesson and she asked us to draw it. Thrilled to be drawing in class, I carefully noted the long rush-like leaves and the trumpet-shaped yellow flower. Yet even then, I intuited that a painting of a flower is very different from the flower itself. With a flourish, I added a seventh petal. When the sister saw what I had done she beat me for wilfulness.

My parents weren't very sympathetic about my problems at school. As a school boy my father had suffered from the same kind of tyranny. And my mother had her hands full with my baby sisters, Moira, born in 1933, and Angela, in 1935, the year after I started school. Mum found it so hard to look after us all the following summer that my parents sent me to stay with my Granddad and Granny Onley.

It turned out to be the best thing they could have done. My grandparents ran a seaside rooming house in the town of Ramsey at the northern end of the island, and I ended up spending my sum-

My grandfather Thomas Onley, centre.

mers there for the next four or five years. They encouraged me to draw and paint at every opportunity. I recall watching Granddad Onley, his steel pince-nez clipped onto the bridge of his nose, as he hammered together a sketching table for me. He placed it in a bay window that gave a view of the street. Because my grandparents allowed me to leave out my paints and papers when I wasn't working with them, that table at one end of the kitchen became my first studio.

Furthermore, Granddad inspired me to draw ships. He had served as Chief Petty Officer on the destroyer, HMS *Zulu*. Then he'd "swallowed the anchor" to run the Point Ayre Coast Guard Life Saving Station on the island. In his retirement, he served as range-keeper for the Ramsey Rifle Club. He'd wake me at six every morning and make us tea. I can still recall the whistling kettle and the popping sound of the gas lamp in the tiny kitchen. As we talked, he'd put a pinch of tobacco into the bowl of his pipe, light it, and fill the room with the aroma of a fine tobacco.

Once he told me that as a midshipman, his boat had been becalmed off the Cape of Good Hope. When the ship ran out of food and water the commander sent out a longboat for help, over fifty miles away. Before they made landfall, the starving sailors ate the cabin boy. "Luckily, I stayed on the ship," related Granddad. "We brought that longboat crew back to England in chains and the Navy hanged every one of them."

Every Monday morning Granddad and I went to the Ramsey Rifle Club to clean up the range. On every other day we went for an early morning walk, stopping at Ramsey Harbour so he could point out the different boats to me. As we walked down the streets, housewives hanging out their laundry greeted him, "Morning, Captain." He always smiled and tipped his hat, no doubt flattered by the mistake. In a small port, all the old sailors are captains.

By the time we returned, Granny Onley had risen and dressed. A formidable little Irish woman from Cobh, County Cork, she usually wore her long grey-streaked black hair in a prim bun. When we came to the table for lunch, she peered at me through her round horn-rimmed glasses. She looked owlish and very wise to me. "And what has the little man been doing today?" she asked. Granddad and I would always give her a full account of the morning.

After lunch, she'd send my grandfather off for his afternoon nap and walk with me through the glen at the Sulby River or north along Ramsey beach. I took along my paints, and Granny Onley, who had a romantic spirit, always carried a book of poetry—by Wordsworth, who had visited the island in 1833, or by Keats. When we sat down, she read to me as I worked. She claimed that my talent for painting must have been inherited from her because she had designed Irish lace as a girl.

Sometimes Granny asked me about my father. She blamed the TT, the Tourist Trophy Motorcycle Race, for bringing together my father, a Catholic, and my mother, a Wesleyan Methodist. As I grew older, I realized that wasn't much of an exaggeration. Because racing was prohibited on other public roads in Britain, the island was the only place with an international long-distance race. The thirty-eight-mile TT circuit from Douglas to Ramsey to the port of Peel on the west side of the island drew thousands of spectators. Ever since the first race event in June, 1907, riders from Britain, Italy, Spain and even Japan had competed.

In the relative affluence of the 1920s, young people on the Isle of Man went crazy over motorbikes. My father, my mother's elder sister and her two older brothers all had Norton bikes and belonged to the Peveril Motorcycle Club. On Sunday mornings when they

With my sister Moira and my dog Barney, Ramsey, Isle of Man, 1938.

should have been in church, they howled down the country roads, spooking the horses and occasioning more than one denouncement from the pulpit.

My father met my mother through his friendship with her dare-devil brothers. On Saturday nights they met at the local dance hall, and soon they were practising for the Manx Amateur Dance Championships. They got to the finals in Douglas at the Palace Hotel, which had the largest ballroom in Britain. It had a floor where a thousand couples could dance while listening to three different bands, with a foxtrot at one end, a tango in the middle of the room and a waltz at the other end. At midnight, hundreds of balloons would be dropped from the ceiling. I can imagine my parents in each other's arms in the noise and confusion, as the dancers rushed to puncture the balloons with their hairpins or break them with their heels. By that point, they had fallen in love. Grudgingly, their families acquiesced to the match.

There was another reason for my grandmother's hard feelings toward my father. Granddad Onley had paid a premium of forty pounds to apprentice Dad to the building trade when he turned fourteen. That good money had been wasted as far as Granny was concerned. Not long after completing his four-year apprenticeship, Dad married my mother and they moved to Douglas where the only thing my father ever built was stage scenery. Dad had fallen in love again—with the Gaiety Theatre, a 2,000-seat venue designed by the king of Victorian theatre architects, Frank Matcham, who had embellished it with stained-glass windows, marble stairs and an Italian-Renaissance-style gold-leaf, domed ceiling decorated with four languid rosy-bosomed women—Spring, Summer, Fall and Winter. Smitten, Dad debuted as a student accused of theft in *The Winslow Boy*. The idea of my father treading the boards further outraged my earnest, straitlaced grandmother. Dad told me he joked to his actor friends, "Don't tell my mother I'm on the stage—she thinks I'm in jail."

Granny felt that Dad had wasted his education but she recognized that he had a certain gift for creating opportunities for himself. "Your father will never amount to much," she would sigh, "but

Granny Onley, me, dog Barney, Dad, sister Moira and Mom. Ramsey, Isle of Man, 1938.

at least he'll never want." As far as Granny was concerned, I must have represented her last hope for our side of her family. She never criticized me even when I told her that I hadn't been doing too well at school.

In standard [grade] three, my teacher asked each of us, "What do you want to be when you grow up?" A girl in my class said she wanted to be a nun. That went over pretty well in a Catholic school. One of the boys wanted to drive a train. Plenty of trains ran on the island. Another boy hoped to be a fireman. One planned to be a policeman—these were all practical ambitions. When the teacher came to me I answered, "I'm going to be an artist and paint pictures." Everyone laughed. The teacher groaned, "Oh, Toni, why don't you be realistic?"

Instead of discouraging my ambition to be a painter, my grandmother praised me. She saved my drawings and tacked my paintings up on the walls to show to her boarders. Everything would work itself out one day, according to her. In Manx Gaelic, Granny comforted me, "*Traa dy liaour.*" Time enough.

Chapter 3

Once Upon a War

When Britain declared war on Germany in 1939, the House of Keys—the Parliament on the Isle of Man—convened an emergency session to decide whether or not to formally proclaim war against Germany. Then one of the record clerks discovered we were still at war with Germany from 1914.

My father commenced hostilities at Peel, a town on the west side of the island, where he'd noticed some barrels of salted herring awaiting shipment to the port of Bremen. "The Germans aren't getting these kippers," he announced at the dinner table that evening. Then he took his company van and dragged me along for a night raid. We returned with enough herring to last for two wars.

My family had moved into a four-storey row house at 124 Bucks Road, which stood higher on the hill than our previous house. A dormer window in the attic made it possible for me to climb out onto the roof. I used to sit up there and draw the gabled roofs and the chimney pots and the half-moon-shaped bay in front of the beach at Douglas. They were my first landscape drawings.

Whenever I heard aircraft engines, I'd scan the skies for Hawker Hurricanes and twin-engined German Dornier bombers. I used to draw them by copying the illustrations in newspapers and magazines. In 1940, the Germans struck close to home and bombed the shipyards in Belfast. I recall watching their bombers fly past the island, taking their navigational bearings.

In the first year of the war, there was a debate in the House of

Keys about putting an anti-aircraft gun on Douglas Head to take potshots at the passing enemy aircraft. A wise member of Parliament countered, "I think not." As a result, the Germans only dropped three bombs on the Isle of Man, none of which did any harm. One of them came from an enemy plane that had lost an engine in a night attack and had ditched the bomb on its return flight to France. The bomb detonated in a barnyard, unearthing an underground spring that soon filled the bomb crater with water. Within days, ducks were paddling in it, having a marvellous time. The farmer said to me, "I knew there was water there! I've been thinking about digging a duck pond on that spot for years." His only cost was a pane of glass and a grandfather clock. The clock had stopped at 2:00 a.m. when a piece of shrapnel flew through the window and hit it.

To aid the war effort, the government encouraged everyone to buy war bonds. They sponsored a school poster competition in Douglas. I drew a matchstick figure with a dunce cap on his head, and wrote a limerick:

> There was a young fellow called Spence,
> Who didn't have very much sense,
> One day with much glee,
> Turned his "D" into "V"—
> And saved all his pence for defence!

Spence transformed his dunce cap into a "V for Victory" by buying war bonds. My poem and cartoon won me five pounds and the Home Office made it into a poster, my first commission. For a short while, until the glory faded, my friends called me Spence.

The war I really fought, however, was at school where it took every bit of my ingenuity to outwit teachers who seemed uniformly cruel, ignorant and bad-tempered. Education should be about acquiring a love of learning but at my school, the syllabus consisted of lessons in fear, obedience and the catechism.

In an environment where teachers beat their pupils, the bigger boys always bullied the smaller ones like me. Because my marks fell so low, my standard four teacher put me into the bottom third of the class, which was at the back of the room and relatively unpoliced. To the rough, mean-spirited kids at the back of the class, my interest in drawing and painting seemed almost effeminate.

One morning Billy Cole, a tough kid with a glass eye, jabbed me in the back with his pencil. "Onley, we're going to get you," he sneered. "You're going to die." I kept my eye on Cole and his gang all day.

When the school bell rang, I dashed out of the classroom, but Billy Cole and four boys cornered me against the playground railings. Determined to make a stand, I lashed out with my fists and elbows and feet. I yelled at Billy Cole and socked him in the face.

"Onley punched Cole's eye out!" somebody shouted.

The sight of one-eyed Billy Cole on his hands and knees crawling over the gravel groping for his glass eye brought us to our senses. "Where's my eye?" he whimpered. "Where is it?"

We joined the search for it. One boy found it lying chipped and useless in the gravel. Billy stuffed it into his pocket, and with his hand covering his empty socket led the group off the school grounds. We followed, parting on the street. We even said goodbye to one another, stunned into civility. That was the last time Billy and his gang attacked me.

Mr. Manwaring, my standard six teacher, was so dull that we kept dozing off during class—much to our peril because he'd hurl his brass chalk holder at us. He threw it at me once and I ducked at the last minute, allowing the missile to break a window. After the principal made him pay for the glass, he took it out of my hide.

At the end of each school day, he made us straighten the rows of our desks, erase the boards and clean the chalk brushes. Then he stuck his foot into the wastepaper container to stomp the wadded scraps of paper into an even smaller volume for disposal.

One lunch break, a few of us emptied the paper from the container, filled it with water, and put the paper back. We waited all afternoon. Finally, Manwaring stomped on the paper as usual and almost fell over. With a shout, he lifted out his dripping wet shoe and soaked pantleg. As he ranted, we convulsed with laughter.

Manwaring's outbursts were nothing, however, compared to those of Jenny Clegg, the music teacher who taught the standard seven class. Her sharp tongue bit even harder than her bamboo cane. Even among the teachers, she had the reputation of a "tartar" with her ruddy face and cropped frizzy grey-and-red hair. While we were still in Manwaring's class, we'd whisper to one another: "Some day we're going to be in standard seven. Then we'll be in for it."

The following year in Jenny Clegg's class, a few boys and I decided that because she had no sense of humour we were going to play a trick on our stern, short-tempered teacher. She taught music with a battered upright piano that stood in a corner of our classroom. A piece of red cloth had been tacked over the back of it, and I talked a few other boys into lifting this cover during lunchtime and helping me tie some sulphur stink bombs onto the hammers in the piano. These stink bombs came in thin, easily shattered glass vials.

Jenny began the afternoon music lesson by playing a scale. The hammers struck the piano strings, breaking the glass stink bombs, and the piano erupted with the stench of rotting eggs.

"Gas!" Jenny yelled. "A gas leak! Quickly! Everybody out of the room!" Cheering, we bolted for the door.

Reasoning that I could get out of a few more classes that year, I joined the school choir. Whenever there was a requiem mass—and it was often in Douglas—we lined up in the choir loft of St. Mary's Catholic Church.

When my voice broke, Jenny assigned me to pump the organ bellows. I had to crawl behind the organ and keep the bellows full of air, particularly for her swelling "Kyrie eleison" at the end of the mass.

One Sunday, a few choir boys bribed me to sabotage the organ. I pumped just enough air into the bellows so that when Jenny struck the organ keys for the final hymn, the instrument only groaned— Unhh! She jumped from her bench and went for me. "Pump! Pump, you son of a bitch!" she hissed. "Pump!"

The following Monday she held a full-scale execution in class. She called me to the front of the room and told me to hold out my hands with the palms upward. She raised her bamboo cane above her shoulder like a whip and sliced it through the air. It struck my hands like a jolt of electricity. The school-boy code of honour dictated that I endure the caning without a murmur. That only increased Jenny Clegg's frustration. She whacked me even harder. I held out as long as I could, but the tears eventually came. Beaten and humiliated, I trudged back to my desk. My burning hands puffed up and turned purple. I sat at my desk, blowing on them, but that gave small relief. I wondered how long it would take until I could use them again to draw and paint.

I had no one to confide in at school and I spent too much time drawing. Making art seemed incomprehensible even to my best pal, a Protestant boy who lived across the street from me and attended the public school. "Bunny" had a cowlick of blond hair and a snub nose that twitched like a rabbit's.

One Saturday afternoon he came over to my house after school and found me experimenting with paint colours. I was just getting the hang of mixing pigments. I think I had just learned that I could create greens by mixing yellow and blue. "For Christ's sake, Onley," he complained, "you're always painting. Let's go to the firing range."

I readily agreed to go. Perhaps because the island had not suffered from bombing, the war had produced in us such a fascination with explosives that I liked making bombs almost as much as I liked painting. We biked over to the artillery firing range on Douglas Head. The range closed on the weekends and Bunny and I used to ride there often, sneak in and pick up unexploded trench mortar shells. We'd tie them onto the handlebars of our bikes and ride back home. I shudder now to think of what might have happened if an accident had banged the shells against the ground.

In the basement of my house on that particular Saturday, we hammered the fins off the mortar shells, unscrewed the nose cones and emptied the cordite into lead pipes. We drilled a little touch hole in the bottom of each pipe, then attached a fuse.

Remarkably, my parents never paid any attention to us. The back wall of the post office garage was just across the lane at the foot of our backyard and Bunny and I placed the first pipe bomb into a hole in the crumbling stone wall. I told my father about it and then Bunny and I ran to light the fuse.

Dad listened to the pipe bomb go off, then smiled patronizingly. "Christ, that's a baby fart. When I was your age, we made firecrackers at least ten times as big."

"Oh, yeah," I replied. "Wait till you hear the next one."

Bunny and I went back to the basement and took a large piece of steel pipe we'd scavenged. We drilled a touch hole and filled the pipe with cordite. We took the bomb outside, hammered it into the wall, then piled manganese shavings over the touch hole and lit them. We knew that when the shavings became hot enough, the heat would go down the touch hole and set off the explosion. Then we dashed back into the house.

My parents were arguing with each other about something. I entered the kitchen and Dad looked at me in exasperation. "What do you want now, Toni?"

The bomb went off with a hell of a wallop. The wall, made of river rocks, shattered into pieces. The concussion cracked the windows in the back of our house.

My father stared out the window at the smoke and dust in the alley. His face blanched. "Christ! What have you boys done?" Then another realization hit him. "This house is the first place they'll look." He turned to Bunny. "You clear out that stuff downstairs and beat it. Hide it at your place." We piled the bomb-making material into a box and Bunny rushed away. Dad looked over the basement, then hustled me upstairs. "Toni, put on your pyjamas and get into bed. If anyone asks about you, I'll tell them you've been sick all week."

Two burly policemen cycled to our house and banged on the front door. I dove under the bed covers. Dad answered and I heard him tell them, "It's done a lot of damage to our house, too. It's blown out the windows on the back."

"Did you hear anything before the explosion, Mr. Onley?" asked one of the policemen.

"Now that you mention it, constable, I heard a couple of men talking out back. It sounded to me as if they had German accents.

That did it. The headlines in the next issue of the *Isle of Man Examiner* screamed: "Sabotage at the Post Office! U-Boat Lands Germans on Isle of Man!" The news plunged the community into a state of hysteria. For a little while it even took my mind off school, but I kept cutting classes anyway. I'd become expert at running up fevers and conning my mother into believing that I was too ill to attend.

The bomb incident was an extreme case of what could happen on an island where the leisure activities of boys were, as a matter of custom, largely unsupervised. We literally ran wild much of the time, especially on the weekends and in the summer. Bunny and I got up to all kinds of mischief. One summer we staged an apple raid on the orchard of a local estate known as The Nunnery. We climbed over the stone wall, easing our bodies over the weather-eroded edges of the jagged glass cemented onto the top of it. We were busily picking apples and stuffing them inside our shirts when Bunny spotted the groundskeeper running toward us with his dogs. I managed to get back over the wall but Bunny was caught and later flogged by a policeman as punishment for trespassing and attempted theft.

The penal code of the island mandated flogging for a wide variety of offences long after the UK had abolished it, and when I was a child even young boys who got caught breaking the law were subjected to that brutal punishment. I was lucky to have escaped, and Bunny did not tell on me—he told the police that he had just met me and did not know my name or where I lived.

The island culture tolerated certain kinds of violence: the flogging of offenders, the caning of pupils and the belting of children by their parents. The reckless exploits of my childhood were partly a rebellious reaction to that system of tyranny and partly the result of a kind of institutionalized lack of supervision. Also, my father was an expert at getting away with things without getting caught, as demonstrated by his confiscation of the herring awaiting shipment to Germany and by his protection of me after the bomb incident. As a child, I must have unconsciously absorbed his attitude toward authority.

One of my recurring adventures involved lowering myself down the face of a cliff to gather bird eggs—thousands of gulls, terns and plovers nested on the island. I'd drive a stake into the ground, tie a rope to it and rappel down. In the days of severe rationing my mother was always delighted to add this bounty to the family meals. One day I was gathering eggs with Bunny when my rope suddenly broke, causing me to fall onto the rocks below. While I lay there unconscious, Bunny ran to a nearby naval station for help. They sent out a picket boat, which rescued me just before the incoming tide would have drowned me. I was taken to the naval infirmary, revived and stitched up. Across my face I had a diagonal gash that ran alongside my eye, just missing it. The Crosh Vollan charm, which I took with me whenever I was going down to the sea and which I had in my pocket when I was on the cliff face that day, must have worked to save not only my life but my eyesight.

Another daring pursuit during tourist season involved riding our bikes off the seawall. Bunny would promise we'd do this in return for a few contributions, which he'd collect in his cap. Then he'd secure the coins in a bag inside his swimsuit and off we'd go, flying through the air and plunging into the ocean below. We'd recover our bikes when the tide went out. Needless to say, my mother had no idea that her ten-year-old boy was risking life and limb for a few pennies and the distinction of being thought fearless by a handful of tourists. As for my father, he would have approved of any money-earning venture, no matter how hair-raising.

No doubt about it—my real life happened outside of school. One class I often missed was the prep class for the high-school entrance exam. It was taught by the headmaster, Mr. Lynch, a jowly heavy-set man in a tight-fitting navy blazer who knew my father. One afternoon, Lynch leaned heavily over my desk to say, "Lad, you've got to put more effort into your studies." Sounding just like a movie prison warden he added, "One way or the other, you've got to get out of here."

Lynch thought the cane inhumane so he plied the Board of Education regulation-issue black leather strap. It consisted of three or four pieces of machine-tooled leather held together with diamond-shaped studs. When I failed to show any more interest, Lynch strapped me in front of the class. It felt as if he'd hit my hand with a piece of lumber and each smack echoed down the hall. Afterward, my bruised hands were splotched with blood welts. But punishment failed to motivate me any more than his threats had. I washed out on the exam and Lynch expelled me.

My parents took it in stride. My mother had never liked the school. Even my father expressed some sympathy.

All the same, he insisted that I had to find a trade and an apprenticeship. "When I was your age, I served my time at a construction firm. For four years I was instructed by craftsmen, men brilliant with their tools." Dad needed me to start making a living. His latest business, in neon signs, had just foundered as a result of the new wartime blackout regulations and money had grown awfully tight in our household.

For a while my father kept finding me things to do. What with picking wild mushrooms and catching rabbits, I hardly had a moment to do any painting. I had a pet ferret I used for rabbiting. I would take the ferret curled up in my pocket and some small nets and go out to an overgrown, tumbledown stone wall between two fields where rabbits had their dens among and under the stones. I'd place nets over all the holes, then put the ringed ferret down one hole to chase a rabbit out into a net. During the war years, rabbits provided us with most of our meat.

My mother considered that I was entitled to some time for myself, so she would tell me to take my rucksack with art supplies and clear out before Dad came home and invented another task. Then, just when my father was almost making a career out of finding a job for me, he found himself one with the Home Office in Douglas.

Following the panic after the fall of France in 1940, the CID and MI5 scooped up all the German refugees in Britain and prepared camps for them on our remote island. In Douglas, the Home Office appropriated the forty rooming houses around Hutchinson public square along with their dishes, bedding and furniture, gave chits to the owners and evicted them all. I never found out what happened to these displaced citizens. The office erected sentry posts and twin rows of barbed wire fence around the square and called it Hutchinson Internment Camp. Then they posted my father there, outfitting him in a navy uniform with gold braid, which looked suspiciously like Salvation Army dress to me, but which he insisted resembled a Royal Navy uniform.

Dad expected to serve in a prisoner-of-war camp with a lot of smart-looking German soldiers who'd follow his orders. Instead, a ragtag mob of shabbily dressed civilians turned out at his first roll call. The sergeant-major complained to him that half the internees were not out of bed yet. "Some of 'em 'ave started growin' beards," he remarked. "It's wot you call sloth 'ere."

To his surprise, my father learned that among his prisoners were German musicians, aristocrats and professors. He loved choral music and he found the famous tenor Richard Tauber in the camp. The aging Franz von Rintelen, the German spymaster in America during WWI and the author of *The Dark Invader*, weeded the rose bed in Hutchinson Square. One of the empty houses was set aside as a university, as there were engineers and professors among the prisoners.

Thirty different lecturers in the arts and the applied sciences piled into the same room and argued about the timetable. The philosophers behaved the worst because they kept correcting each other, but finally they negotiated a schedule. They began teaching English to the internees who did not already speak it. According to one of my father's tall tales, the German pastor delivered a sermon in English on the theme: "The Spirit is willing, but the flesh is weak," which he translated as "The Ghost is willing, but the meat has gone off."

German artists were also interned, including Kurt Schwitters, the Dadaist from Hanover. Occasionally I saw him and his son picking up bits of paper litter from the ground as they trailed behind a ragged column of internees out for their daily exercise. One bored-looking guard walked in front of the line and one at the rear, their rifles slung over their shoulders.

Schwitters, about fifty-five years old when I saw him, was a tall man who always wore a bathrobe and corduroy slippers with a white rope trim. He played with a white mouse he carried in his pocket. That reminded my father of Lenny in John Steinbeck's novel *Of Mice and Men*.

My father told me that because he could not get plaster of Paris, Schwitters gathered leftover porridge and shaped it into heaps that he embellished with matchboxes, pebbles, train tickets and even cigarette butts. The quivering mounds of porridge turned the colour of Roquefort cheese and emitted a faint, sickly smell. When they dripped through the floor onto the beds in the room below, Schwitters' housemates disposed of the world's first porridge sculptures.

I would see Schwitters when I went to the camp to take my father his lunch in the wood-working shop he had set up for the internees. Dad introduced him to me one day as a famous German artist. "If you get any bus tickets or movie coupons, especially anything printed in colour, bring it in for Kurt," he said.

Schwitters began a new series of collages on the Isle of Man. Dad brought home one he'd been given as a gift. It had been constructed on top of an advertisement for Reckett's Blue, a British laundry whitener. Schwitters had folded newspaper into the shape of the crest of a wave and pasted it into the middle of the ad. He'd left the bold-lettered caption showing: "Out of the blue, comes the whitest wash." He'd mounted a cut-out black-and-white photograph of a delicate female hand so that the index finger touched the crest of the wave. Rendered into English, the title of the piece was *The Senses of the Sea*.

Though collage would eventually prove very important in my work, at that point in my experience Schwitters' collage seemed to be the oddest thing I had ever seen anyone create. I couldn't accept it as art because I understood art to be drawings and paintings of nature. I was twelve, and knew nothing of early twentieth-century avant-garde art.

After sixteen months of internment, acting on evidence offered by the directors of the Tate Gallery and the New York Museum of Modern Art, the Home Office released Schwitters in 1941, finally realizing he was a refugee from Nazi fanaticism. After I began to study the history of twentieth-century art in Canada in the 1950s, I learned that the Museum of Modern Art in New York had granted Schwitters $3,000 to re-create his most famous piece, *Merz-bau I*. *Merz-bau* was a title Schwitters had invented from the German words for "commerce" and "thing." He had begun his first *Merz-bau* at the height of the Dada movement in 1920, slowly transforming his house in Hanover into a sort of art cave so crammed with strange pieces of trash that eventually it could not be entered. He added to it for sixteen years. When Hitler came to power, Schwitters fled for his life and *Merz-bau I* was destroyed in a bombing raid. In Norway, he created *Merz-bau II*, which he camouflaged with mud and pine needles and made transportable on a sledge. When the Germans invaded Norway, he abandoned that too and escaped to Britain. Schwitters died in England in 1948 before completing *Merz-bau III*. Because of the impermanence of the materials, this last *Merz-bau* eventually disintegrated. The British artist Richard Hamilton re-created it in more recent times.

When we emigrated from the Isle of Man, Dad left behind several collages that Schwitters had given him. He thought of them as mementoes rather than valuable works of art. To me they looked like scrapbook pages. Yet a generation after Schwitters' appearance in our lives, his collages were worth tens of thousands of dollars and he was hailed as a pioneer of the kind of mixed media constructions that made American artists like Robert Rauschenberg internationally famous. *Time* magazine even did a cover story on Schwitters. Naturally, when I returned to the island for a visit in 1963, I tried to find the collages among the things we'd left with my Granny Onley.

"Oh, I burned all that the winter you left, Toni," she said. "It was awfully cold that year. But I saved all your work."

Chapter 4

The Printer's Devil

I n 1941, my father found me a job at the *Isle of Man Examiner*. The newspaper needed a "printer's devil"—a small boy to squeeze inside the press and clean between the cylinders.

Every day at three o'clock in the morning, I cycled to the printing plant to light the gas furnace to melt the lead so it could be used in the linotype machines by the operators when they arrived for work at 8:00 a.m. Then I went home to get a few more hours of sleep. About eight, I returned to the plant for the dirtiest part of my new job, which was to clean the two-storey-high Causa double revolution press that printed, cut and folded the weekly paper. I climbed up between the upper and lower levels of the press and swabbed the cylinders with rags and solvent. From the troughs underneath, I scooped out gallons of the viscous newspaper ink made of carbon and oil and poured it back into cans for reuse in the next printing run.

For about a year I slaved in this way, servicing the giant press and eventually helping the printer set it up for the weekly press run. As I was only thirteen, there weren't many other places that would employ me. Then the printer didn't show up for work one day because he had appendicitis. When I heard that the publisher had decided to cancel that week's edition, I asked to see him.

"I know how to set up the press, sir. Let me print the paper."

The publisher, J. Radcliffe, a tall, sandy-haired man, slipped his thumbs into the pockets of his waistcoat and looked me over carefully. He spoke with a clipped upper-class English accent, "All right, if you think you can do it, we'll try you."

At the Causa press, rolls of blank newsprint called webs, which turned on an axle at one end of the machine, had to be hoisted into place and threaded carefully through the dozens of rollers. Then I switched on the press. After solving a few problems along the way, I completed the press run in a few hours.

Radcliffe thanked me. He was very pleased that he hadn't lost any advertising revenue or subscription money that week. When the printer failed to return to work the following week, I refused to print the next edition unless I was given a raise and promoted to printer's apprentice.

Radcliffe agreed to all the conditions. With a wry smile, he nodded. "There's not much gets past you, lad."

The girls who tended the small presses were temporarily assigned to clean the press, while I took over most of the printer's job. About a month later when the printer returned to work, he found me in a white printer's smock. Grinning, he shook my hand. "Congratulations! I guess we'll be looking for a new printer's devil now."

Although I'd been promoted, I still dreamed of becoming an artist. I convinced my parents to let me enrol in evening classes at the Douglas School of Art. The classes were a disappointment, however. The teachers had me painting portraits and sketching plaster casts of Greek statues. I learned a little about oil painting and the theory of perspective drawing, but most of the time we practised lettering by copying reproductions of the 400 illuminated initials of the ninth-century *Book of Kells*. This exercise permanently transformed my handwriting into an uncial script like the lettering in old manuscripts; at the age of seventy-four, I still write that way.

But I just wanted to paint landscapes. Painting outdoors was how I'd become interested in art in the first place. When I found out that my lettering teacher took his older students on landscape painting trips on the weekends, I begged to go along with him.

John Hobson Nicholson, well known on the island as a watercolour painter, stood over six feet tall. A broad-shouldered man in his twenties, who carried himself like a drum major in a regimental parade, he looked "terribly British" in his hound's-tooth tweed jacket and knotted wool tie. He chewed thoughtfully on the stem of his meerschaum pipe. "Toni, you can come if you can keep up with us."

I thought he meant keep up with the level of painting in the group. I felt sure I could do that. What Nicholson actually had in mind was to match his walking pace in getting to the painting sites, and he was a champion walker. He held the record for the first lap of the TT motorbike course, which measured thirty-eight miles and which he'd walked in less than fifteen hours. Because Nicholson was almost a foot taller, I had to take two steps for every one of his, and when he moved in full stride, I had to run to keep up with him. I was out of breath by the time we arrived at the first site, Monks' Bridge, Rushen Abbey.

Our group fanned out into a farmer's field by the fourteenth-century stone bridge, which the monks had built over the Silverburn River. I sat down with my back against a tree, pinned a sheet of watercolour paper to a drawing board and began rendering the river and the bridge. In pencil, I sketched the bank and the twin arches of the bridge, its span, and the rough shape of the trees on the opposite bank. On the paper, I indicated the brightest and darkest areas of light. Then I mixed my paints and started applying them to the paper.

Nicholson came over. After studying my work for a few minutes, he took a tube of paint from my small wooden paint box. "Chinese white? You don't use white in a watercolour—the paper's already white. And you don't mix white with other colours, either. That's a different medium called tempera. Watercolour is supposed to be a transparent medium."

He rifled through my paint box and extracted two more colours—Prussian blue and Hooker's green light. "You can't use these! They're fugitive colours and they'll change on you." He threw the tubes of paint into the river.

I jumped up. "Hey! Wait a minute! I just bought them."

I stared into the Silverburn. Though shallow, the river was so swift that I couldn't see the paints on the gravel at the river bottom.

"More fugitives!" Nicholson had noticed some carmine red, sap green, and two tubes of yellow, gamboge and chrome. He flung them into the river too.

"I could have taken them back—traded them!"

"Van Dyke brown, I never liked that colour." Nicholson tossed another tube away.

"I never even opened them!" I protested. But Nicholson just laughed. "Now you'll remember not to buy them next time."

He sat down near me and placed a sheet of thick buff-coloured David Cox watercolour paper on his drawing board. As his style was built on solid draftsmanship, he began by carefully outlining the bridge and the riverbanks. He then picked up a sable brush and laid down some light washes of green pigment. Gradually, he added colours onto that base. He built up the perspective in the painting with successive colour washes, which he layered from the paler colours to the darker ones. He established the foreground, middle distance and background in the painting by using the most intense colours in the foreground, nearest to the viewer. As for the clouds, he depicted them by leaving unpainted areas where the paper seemed almost white in contrast with the other colours. Then he took a pointed brush and began adding details to the painting.

I returned to my work, glancing at Nicholson from time to time. I noticed how swiftly he worked, at times mixing his colours on the paper rather than on his palette. Less than half an hour later, he had finished his watercolour and started cleaning his brushes.

I decided that my goal would be to learn how to paint like that. I went out with the group every weekend. As the weather grew cooler, our numbers thinned until finally I was the only member of the group to attend regularly. The weather never put me off; if it rained, we rolled up torches from newspapers and dried our watercolours. In the winter, when everyone else had dropped out, Nicholson and I cycled out manfully into the cold, adding glycerine to our paints to keep them from freezing.

Nicholson kept me entertained with sly comments about the people in our little group of painters. An older man with a bald white head that looked a little too small for his body, he nicknamed "Carter's Little Liver Pill." The lady who had complained about fording a stream became "Caution." After I burst into a demonic Boris Karloff-like laugh at one of Nicholson's jokes, he christened me "The Criminal Laugh."

I learned that Nicholson's style came from the great nineteenth-century Norwich School of watercolour painters—artists like John

Sell Cotman and Peter de Wint who had painted landscapes on walking tours of Norwich, Wales and northern France. His grandfather was John Miller Nicholson, a contemporary of Turner and one of the most accomplished painters ever to come from the Isle of Man. The younger Nicholson worked in his grandfather's old studio in a building on Well Road Hill and had taught himself to paint largely through studying his grandfather's work. None of these artists used opaque pigments and neither did Nicholson.

In part because he supported himself with the family painting and decorating business, Nicholson had developed an exquisite sensitivity to colour. He could match any commercial paint. He could also look at any colour in the landscape and mix its equivalent in watercolours.

In spring, when the other members returned, Nicholson forbade us to sit too closely together. He wanted each of us to develop our own versions of a scene. Afterward, he'd give us critiques of our work. Sometimes walking to a place meant almost as much to Nicholson as painting it. Once he led a thirty-mile hike to the village of Andreas, where my mother had been born. It became known as "the moonlight expedition." We hiked under a full moon and attempted to paint by flashlight on the mountain road. When I looked up from my white paper, all was black. Since it proved impossible to paint anything, I just boarded a train and headed home.

I still worked at the *Isle of Man Examiner* during the week. Although I felt some satisfaction in seeing people read the newspaper, I'd lost whatever interest I had in printing. It frustrated me to work under the pressure of newspaper deadlines. The printing press often jammed and broke down. In the summer, we had to use harder inks or the ink would pool like melting ice cream instead of spreading evenly over the rollers. When it rained, the humidity increased and the paper curled and jammed the press. In winter, the newsprint sometimes got so cold that it contracted. I daydreamed of getting home early enough to do a little drawing, then left work too exhausted to do anything.

It didn't look as though I had any alternative to the printing trade. There were no realistic prospects of becoming a professional artist on the island. Nicholson's famous grandfather had developed a family decorating business to earn a living. Nicholson himself worked there in addition to teaching art classes. There was hardly enough room on the island for him, let alone someone else, so he constantly feuded with a second, even better-known island painter, Bill Hoggatt.

Hoggatt lived in Port Erin at the south end of the Isle of Man. He scraped together a living by selling paintings and teaching art classes at King William College. I sometimes saw him in Douglas, a gruff character in a shabby grey overcoat and a dented brown fedora. Because he had studied in Paris at the turn of the century, he possessed the academic training that Nicholson lacked.

The art magazines *The Studio* and *The Connoisseur* published reproductions of Hoggatt's paintings and he regularly exhibited his work. He had belonged to the Royal Institute of Painters in Watercolours since 1925. In all of England, there were only fifty-eight members. The quarrel between Hoggatt and Nicholson began when Nicholson asked the older man to sponsor him for membership in the Royal Institute. Hoggatt not only refused but insulted him for asking, and Nicholson never forgave him, even though in later years he was elected to the Institute.

One Saturday, our group headed to Ballacoates Pond where Hoggatt could often be found painting the water lilies—he was a great admirer of Monet. On this occasion, no gaunt figure rose from the shrubbery to challenge our right to paint his landscape.

Nevertheless, Nicholson took great pleasure in shouting out, "Hoggatt! We're painting your goddamned pond!"

As my interest in art grew I began looking for books and magazines on it. There seemed to be very little about art during the war. At the Manx Museum, however, I discovered another island artist, the late Archibald Knox who had died in 1933. His photograph hung on a wall of the Manx Museum along with several of his watercolours. He had bushy brown eyebrows, a long Roman nose, a full beard and a woolly, soup-strainer moustache. I could see that Archie was a bit of a dandy, as he wore a vest, a polka-dotted tie and a soft tweed trilby hat. On his tombstone he described himself as "a humble servant of God in the Ministry of the Beautiful."

One of the foremost designers of the English Art Nouveau movement, Knox was inspired by the complex, interlacing patterns of the ancient Celtic and Norse cross carvings found on the island. As a successful commercial designer, he created about 400 pieces of gold jewellery, silver tableware and tea services, and pewter household objects for Liberty House in London. His paintings were a private, personal form of expression, never sold and often unsigned. In his later years on the Isle of Man, Knox painted landscapes in a free-form style, quite unlike the rational, almost architectural approach employed by Nicholson, and larger as well, on half-Imperial-sized sheets, twice the dimensions of the paper we used. His watercolours were tranquil atmospheric scenes, painted with broad simple strokes and washes of various colours.

There was even a Canadian connection because the director of the National Gallery of Canada visited England in 1926, saw Archie's watercolours in an exhibition and convinced Archie to let him exhibit the work in Ottawa. A Canadian collector saw them and offered to buy the entire show. To everyone's surprise, Archie refused to sell any of them and demanded that they all be returned to him.

When I mentioned Knox to Nicholson, he laughed uproariously because he'd attended some of Archie's classes at the Douglas School of Art. Nicholson and the other boys in his high school were occasionally sent to the art school for a bit of vocational training in the afternoon and poor Archie could never control them. He had a magic-lantern-style slide projector with a carbide lamp that operated by burning acetylene gas, and he had created about 3,000 art history slides which he regularly attempted to show to the boys.

One day, Nicholson pinched some carbide from the projector and was kicked out of class. He knew that wet carbide forms acetylene gas, so as he stood on the street outside the classroom windows, he threw the carbide onto the street and urinated on it. A pungent cloud of gas billowed forth, and Archie rushed out. "Nicholson!" he shouted angrily, then chased the naughty boy down Bucks Road all the way to the Manx Museum about three blocks away. This was one of Nicholson's favourite stories about the days of his youth.

It was a long time before I realized that Nicholson was not a particularly original artist. He never discussed aesthetics or ideas of any kind. Learning to paint watercolours with him was a bit like practising piano scales but, for the time, that was all I needed. He was a highly effective teacher of colour, perspective and proportion, and of watercolour technique.

One day after a long hike, when our group had finished a particularly satisfying day of painting watercolours, he launched into a diatribe against Picasso, describing him as one of the biggest frauds in history. *Les Demoiselles D'Avignon* had been reproduced in one of Nicholson's art magazines, prompting Nicholson to complain, "Picasso can't draw people. He has no sense of perspective or colour. Nobody really likes his work—that must be why in London it's considered intellectually sophisticated to admire it."

We went along with Nicholson's view because Picasso's cubism was a mystery to us. Like so much of modern art, it lay entirely outside our experience. Abstract art was a part of that untrustworthy world beyond the island, a world at war. At the age of thirteen, I had never seen anything like Picasso's work, so it was particularly strange and ugly to me.

In 1942, the war turned against Britain. The Axis powers sank the Royal Navy's finest battleships—the *Hood*, the *Prince of Wales*, the *Repulse*. Field Marshal Rommel's Afrika Korps overran Libya, Tunisia and part of Egypt. After invading Hong Kong, Malaysia and Singapore, the Japanese Imperial Army invaded Burma and was poised to attack India.

The Isle of Man metamorphosed into an armed camp. An RAF fighter base was sited near Ayre. A bomber training field was constructed at Jurby on the west coast. Ronaldsway Airport near Castletown had a naval air base. Douglas had a radar station and, of course, Hutchinson Internment Camp.

Nicholson was fortunate to be exempted from military service because he worked in a trade associated with building, but almost all able-bodied Manxmen were conscripted early in the war, including my father. Gloomily, he marched off to a troop ship with a column of conscripts for the King's Royal Rifles in Yorkshire. As my mother and I watched the men tramp past in their "civvies," Dad walked out of step in protest, as if to say, "I'm forty years old, married, with three children. This war is none of my doing, why should I be sent to fight it?"

But just before he was to be sent overseas, Dad had an epileptic seizure and received a medical discharge. That didn't sit well with his poor brother Martin, who had a daughter and a pregnant wife and was shipped off to fight the Japanese in Burma, the worst theatre of the war. "The best performance of his life," Martin grumbled when he heard about Dad's epilepsy. "Your father always was a good actor."

All through 1942 and 1943, while working at the *Isle of Man Examiner*, I painted landscapes with Nicholson. Watercolour proved to be a difficult, unforgiving medium, for it was impossible to paint over mistakes. Yet I learned to appreciate its subtlety in capturing the transient effects of different kinds of light on landscape, as with Nicholson I followed the clouds across the landscape. I learned to fix a point in time on my paper, seeking the eternal even as the war raged, and every night I could see the distant flashes of bombs exploding on the mainland.

"Look and paint and never turn back," Nicholson said. It was worth remembering.

Chapter 5

The Family Gypsies

When peace came in 1945, a sigh of relief swept the island. Many people couldn't believe that Britain had survived the years of bombing and the V-2 rocket attacks on London. Then, on November 20, my seventeenth birthday, even though the war had ended, I received a draft notice. I was stunned. I had just begun a whole new career, which would be over if I had to disappear into the army.

In 1944, the publisher at the *Isle of Man Examiner* had told me he needed a picture. A millionaire planned to build a spa on a cove near Onchan Head, a location Nicholson and I had visited. I painted a copy of one of my watercolours of the cove, then superimposed a view of the proposed spa buildings onto the painting. The publisher printed the resulting graphic along with a story on the proposed development. The project architect, H.A. Thomas, was so impressed that he offered me a salaried articling position at his office. I then spent most of my time studying for the qualifying exam, so naturally I had a lot to lose when I received the draft notice.

But before appearing in front of a tribunal of "local worthies"— a retired army colonel, a magistrate and a village headmaster who would decide my fate—I had to pass a medical exam. This gave me a chance to control what happened to me. During the war, we had boarded a British Eighth Army officer, who had suffered a terrible case of shellshock in North Africa and been invalided home. I remembered how he had burst into tears whenever he mentioned the fighting to me. One day he said, "Dinna go, lad, dinna go. Get thee to a grocer's. Purchase a large tin of Lyle's Pouring Syrup. Drink the contents before your physical exam. When they take your blood, you'll be diabetic."

So before the medical test I drank as much syrup as I could swallow. I kept it down long enough to flunk the blood test, then dodged into the back lane and threw up. Thus I saved my career as an architect.

During this time, I still painted as much as I could with Nicholson. Our group went out drawing on Saturdays, then on Sundays we painted watercolours. After the war ended, Nicholson organized a weekend painting expedition to Liverpool and four of us joined him. I was tremendously excited. It was my very first trip off the Isle of Man.

Liverpool shocked me. German bombing had levelled the Mersey dockside. Although the rubble had been cleared to one side, warehouses and dry docks lay in ruins. Rusting hulks sat in the harbour, and I learned from a passer-by that one of them, a German cruise ship called the *Bremen* had been in Liverpool when Britain declared war. To prevent the British from seizing and using the ship, the crew had set it on fire. The burnt sienna of the ship's oxidized hull stood out against the misty greys of the sea and sky. I painted this strange beauty that had emerged from destruction.

I then moved on to the smashed concrete blocks of several submarine pens whose wrenched, twisted strips of rebar memorialized their destruction. I suddenly saw an opportunity to depict the horrors of war, and I approached the subject enthusiastically, working on it over several hours.

When Nicholson saw my painting, he exclaimed in mock horror, "You've mucked up the horizon, Toni." With a crayon, he drew a thick black line across the paper where the principles of perspective suggested the horizon should be placed. He always recommended placing the horizon according to "the golden mean," either one-third or two-thirds of the way up the paper. I'd made one of the most obvious mistakes one could make in his class, but I still resented his destruction of my work. In disgust, I stripped the painting from my drawing board and threw it into the Mersey.

While I painted at the docks on the following day, a banana

boat from West Africa docked nearby. Indian lascars wearing sarongs carried huge stalks of green bananas onto the wharf. It occurred to me that I hadn't eaten a banana since the beginning of the war. I could hardly remember the taste. I went to the ship and bought a stalk to take back to my family when we returned to the Isle of Man.

Nicholson teased me when we took the boat back to the island. "Ah, Toni, I wouldn't keep those bananas if I were you. There might be tropical spiders in there. One bite, and fifteen minutes later you're dead."

Before I realized he was pulling my leg, I started looking through the bananas. "What do they look like, these spiders?" I asked.

Nicholson and the other students all laughed. But food was still rationed in England, so when I brought those bananas home, I was a great hit. My sisters could hardly remember what bananas tasted like. In all the war years, we'd only had one shipment of tropical fruit, Jaffa oranges from Palestine, and that had been in 1944.

Unfortunately, my Liverpool trip marked the last time I ever painted with Nicholson. I upset him by showing some of my Liverpool paintings at a little framing shop in Douglas where he often displayed work. It was the closest thing to a private gallery on the island. He grew very angry when he heard about it.

Furthermore, both he and I had submitted watercolours to an exhibition of the Royal Institute of Painters in Watercolours. They accepted my painting and declined his entry. Because he was by far the more accomplished painter, neither of us could understand why his painting had been rejected. The only explanation I have for my acceptance is that the judges may have seen, and liked, a freer, more spontaneous approach in my work than what they found in some of the more technically accomplished paintings. Nicholson was so jealous that he broke off all contact with me.

Finally, Nicholson disbanded our group altogether because he started dating one of the women in it, Dorothy Kemmel, who was later to become his wife. He bought a motorbike and began to take Dorothy out on painting weekends. I couldn't have kept up with them, even if I had been asked along.

It hurt to be rejected by my old friend and teacher. Several times I spotted them while I was out painting by myself. Although I tried to catch up with Nicholson, he always sped away. I just wanted to settle our differences and wish them the best.

One afternoon I was at Langness, a beach on the south of the island at the end of a long promontory, when I noticed Nicholson's motorbike parked nearby. He sat painting on the beach and I positioned myself so that he'd have to walk past me to get to his motorbike. I painted there a few hours, patiently waiting for him to finish his work. When he walked toward me, I put down my sketchboard and smiled at him, hoping for a simple greeting, a few words that might restore our friendship. Nicholson pretended he didn't see me. He averted his eyes and went by without uttering a single word. It devastated me and marked the final break between us.

Life changed in other ways on the Isle of Man. The wartime industries were finished. In 1946, so few tourists visited the island that most of the hotels remained closed. At H.A. Thomas, we'd been doing restorations, estimating the repairs needed to restore the houses that the government had appropriated to intern German refugees and prisoners of war. That work had slowed to a trickle. I was certain they'd have to lay me off.

As for my father, the cinemas in town had completely undermined the local audience for live drama and now there were not even any tourists to attend performances at the Gaiety Theatre. Plays were only put on by a few amateur groups performing on the weekends. My father realized that he no longer had even a remote chance of becoming a professional actor, nor did he have the prospect of making a living doing anything else on the Isle of Man, so he suggested to my mother that they emigrate. My mother had always been against such a move. Now she was forced to recognize that none of her children had much of a future on the island. My sisters had no job prospects after high-school graduation and I'd probably have to move to England to work as an architect. The whole family would break up, just as her own had done when her brothers and sister left the island.

One thing held us back, however. My grandparents had helped my parents to purchase a large house on Cambridge Terrace in the last years of the war. They had moved in with us and they had no intention of going anywhere.

Granddad Onley detested change of any sort. I remember his

complaint about the contemporary Royal Navy. "Do you know they issue sailors with toothbrushes?" he said. "How ridiculous! In my time we used salt and a stick to clean our teeth."

Meanwhile everything about our home suggested permanence. It was a twelve-room house that had been built during the Napoleonic war and it had three-foot-thick walls, a dining room, a sitting room and the suite at the back where my grandparents lived.

Then one Saturday night in 1947, Granddad Onley left for the Bowling Green Hotel, which had a pub on the ground floor and was only a few blocks from the house. "I'm off to see the boys," he announced. He usually went there on the weekends when he'd meet some of his friends from his social club, the Royal Antediluvian Order of Buffaloes.

After he finished a glass of beer that night, Granddad toyed with the empty glass. He was a man of great moderation who never drank more than a single pint. That night when the bartender asked him if he'd like another pint, something came over him.

"I believe I shall, Bill," he replied. He finished the second drink, then slumped over the table, dead at age seventy-seven. The publican moved him into the back room of the pub. Someone ran over to our house.

None of us knew what to tell Granny Onley. She and Granddad had been inseparable, a regular Darby and Joan. Finally my father broke the news to her. Although Granny didn't cry, I knew she had gone to pieces inside. A few men from the bar carried Granddad's body over to the house and he was laid out with pennies placed over his eyelids to close them. Granny and I sat together for awhile beside him. She knew how much I'd loved him, too, and when we were alone she held my hand and wept. I felt incredibly sad but I imagined that if I cried, Granny might break down entirely so I kept my grief to myself.

Granddad's death altered everything. My father made it clear to Granny Onley that we were going to leave the island. The Onley family met together one last time for my grandfather's funeral. My Auntie Pat, who had become a nun in a teaching order in England, came over and my Uncle Martin was there. He still bore a grudge because my father had been discharged from the army while he had

had to serve overseas. Now he was going to have to take care of Granny as well.

Leaving the Isle of Man was common enough. For centuries, the island's chief export had been tens of thousands of emigrants. Its coat of arms depicts three armour-clad legs joined at the hip. The Latin motto reads *Quocunque Jeceris Stabit* or "Wherever you throw me, there I will stand." A Manxman is supposed to be able to land on his feet, no matter where he goes.

My father decided we'd go to Latin America because during the war he'd become friends with one of the British Latin American volunteers, an Argentinean, Nicolo Bantelo, who had served with the RAF Air Sea Rescue. Bantelo's brother managed the famous Colon Theatre in Buenos Aires, a seven-storey theatre complex where ballet, classical music and opera were presented, and Dad was offered a contract as one of his assistants.

In preparation we all started learning Spanish, then a dispute broke out between Argentina and Britain over Deception Island off British Antarctica. The British sent over HMS *Royal Oak* and the Argentines cancelled all British visas. Somebody said, "Jim, go to America." Dad tried. As an actor, he desperately wanted to get to the film industry in Hollywood. But America had a quota system. It would have taken years before we were eligible to emigrate. His next choice was Canada. Large numbers of Britons were emigrating there, which must have been why there were no tickets available.

Dad announced, "We're leaving anyway. The next boat to North America, or Africa or wherever the hell it's going, we're getting on it."

At the Gaiety Theatre, Dad had been cast in an amateur production of the Rodgers and Hammerstein musical *The Desert Song*. Set in North Africa, the show featured dancing harem girls, singing French Legionnaires and a philandering Moroccan Robin Hood called The Red Shadow. Dad played The Red Shadow's comic sidekick, Sid El Car. I remember the fire curtain they used between acts. It was painted with a desert scene inspired by Delacroix, and it always swung down with a crash. The final act was a tremendous battle scene in the desert, with drums representing musket fire and clashing cymbals for artillery bombardment, leading up to a big musical finale. Eileen Brookes, one of the prettiest women on the island, had the role of Azeera, the black slave girl, and Dad had created body makeup for her with a mixture of cocoa powder and cooking oil. Eileen had an uncle in Liverpool who was a director of the Cunard White Star Line, and to return the favour, she wrote to her uncle about getting us tickets to Canada.

Our passage from Southampton to Halifax came through more quickly than either of my parents had imagined. In May 1948, we were to sail on the last voyage of the *Aquitania*, a huge passenger liner—four-funnelled like the *Titanic*—that had been converted to a troop carrier during the war, then hastily refurbished for fare-paying passengers. It would carry 10,000 British emigrants to Canada and then sail to the Japanese port of Yokohama to be scrapped. The result was that my parents had just three weeks to raise 600 pounds. They sold our house and got rid of everything we couldn't carry in a few suitcases. They took a big financial loss, but at least we got on our way to what we hoped would be a better economic future in Canada.

As I stood at the rail of the ferry leaving the island, I was filled with a sense of adventure. I had read some of the books that

Emigrating to Canada aboard the SS Aquitania, *1948, with friend Pip.*

Granddad Onley had kept on naval exploration and now I too felt like an explorer. I couldn't have located Halifax on a map and I had very little idea what Canada looked like. I had seen pictures of moose and bears but I had never seen any photographs of Canadian birds. "What are they like?" I wondered. "How do the people live?" In school, we had studied the geography of Europe, the Middle East and Imperial India. We learned nothing about the dominions. I knew Canada had large cities like Toronto and Vancouver, but all the stories I'd read of Canada featured mounted police riding over a frozen northern wasteland. In my wilder dreams, I imagined that Dad and I would have to build a log cabin and learn how to shoot game.

The enormity of the undertaking struck me. I tried to imagine my life there. If I were lucky, there might be a position in an architect's office. I resolved that as soon as I made some money, I would rent my own apartment and buy a car. At the back of my mind lay my childhood ambition of becoming a full-time artist. I'd brought my painting kit and a portfolio of my favourite water-colour paintings.

I had no idea what sort of opportunities awaited in Canada but I had a pretty good idea of what I had left. I had only to think of Nicholson, a part-time artist, bitterly resenting anyone else who showed promise. I didn't want to be that kind of artist.

My sisters and my mother were sad to leave the island. On deck sometimes they sang *Ellan Vannin Veg Veen*, "The Dear Little Isle of Man," in Manx Gaelic. Moira and Angela missed their friends, and my mother feared that she might never see her parents alive again. Because her siblings had all left the island, she had been the only child they had left and they took our departure very badly, even as a kind of betrayal.

"My poor parents!" she would often say on the voyage over. "What on earth did we move for? We had a house on the Isle of Man, the first home we'd ever owned."

Dad, who could never really empathize with anyone for very long, was impatient with her misgivings. "Florence, you can't take it with you. What were the children going to do on the island, go fishing? Take up farming? Make beds in a hotel? There was nothing there for us. The island is mostly a holiday resort. It opens for three months, takes every shilling that comes its way, then shuts down for the rest of the year."

My father shed no tears at emigrating from the Isle of Man, for he'd spent half his life trying to break through its social and economic class barriers. He'd grown beyond his working-class Catholic roots by losing the thick Manx accent and teaching himself to use a good vocabulary. He'd learned ballroom dancing and married into an upper-middle-class Protestant family. He'd moved from Ramsey to Douglas, from half a house on Athol Street to a home on Cambridge Terrace and a middle-class lifestyle. Yet, despite his success, he always wanted to be in motion toward a better future. If you could have given him wings to fly, he would have taken off. He felt so happy to leave the Isle of Man that on the eve of departure he crowed to my mother: "We're the family gypsies, Florence! There are worlds out there to conquer—let's go and have some fun!"

Chapter 6

Painting is the Jam

At Halifax we disembarked at Pier 21 to go through immigration, and then boarded a CPR train that was shunted down a siding alongside our ship. The name of a Canadian city had been stencilled onto the side of each carriage. "By Christ, Sherbrooke—Sherbrooke, Quebec!" exclaimed the grizzled World War I veteran in line with us. "If that don't beat all. I left Canada in the same car thirty years ago." Sure enough we filed into a carriage with wooden seats with swing backs, and the porter came by and lit the gas lamps.

We headed for southeastern Ontario, to a town named Galt, known today as Cambridge. My father had been corresponding with an Englishman there who headed the local Chamber of Commerce. The long train journey across the Maritimes and Quebec took over a day and a half. Everything about Canada thrilled me and I could hardly wait to unpack my brushes and palette and start painting the landscape. My father was not so enthusiastic.

At a Union Station restaurant in Toronto, the waitress brought us sandwiches, cups and saucers, and individual pots of tea.

Dad jabbed his finger at a label dangling from one of the pots. "What's this?"

"A tea bag, mister."

"Tea—bag?" My father fished it out of the teapot and dropped it onto his saucer. "What the hell is a tea bag? I ordered tea!"

After we arrived in Galt in late May my parents put some money down on a house and my sisters started school at Galt Collegiate.

Because of the post-war currency restrictions, we hadn't been able to bring more than $2,000 from England, so Dad was reduced to whacking out frames for the local window sash factory. As soon as he had saved enough money for my mother's household expenses for a few months, he pushed off to Toronto to look for theatre work. He found a position as an actor-manager with the Straw Hat Players, a summer stock company that toured in Ontario. It was run by Brian Doherty, a Toronto lawyer who had inherited some money from his mother and later went on to found the Shaw Festival at Niagara-on-the-Lake in 1962. I remember seeing one of Dad's plays at the Red Barn Theatre on Lake Simcoe. It was *The Drunkard*, a Victorian melodrama about the evils of drink, and it was played in 1948 Ontario as a comedy. I doubt that it could be presented that way today.

In the meantime, I looked for a job in the nearest town to Galt. Getting work there would provide me with an excuse to move out of my parents' house. The next town was Brantford, where Massey Ferguson and Cockshutt Farm Equipment cranked out tractors and combines. I couldn't find anything in architecture, but architects in Britain were trained as land surveyors, so eventually I was able to get a job with a local land surveyor.

For fifty dollars a week, I hacked out sight lines from the bush so we could stake out new subdivisions for houses. The crew had in it some hard men who had done prison time, but I took their ribbing about my British accent in stride. Nevertheless, real trouble came when the boss asked me to help him out in the office. He was an outdoors kind of guy who hated paperwork, and I was only too happy to stay indoors for a few days instead of exhausting myself in the bush. One guy in the crew got jealous, took a swing at me and knocked me out cold.

The boss stood behind me and fired the guy. That surprised me a little because the boss happened to be a pretty rough customer himself, a beefy fifty-year-old brawler named Shirley King. His father had given him that name to put some fight into him and the tactic had succeeded too well. Like the guy in the Johnny Cash song "A Boy Named Sue," Shirley angered easily. Our office was on the second floor of a building on Colburg Street. One morning Shirley kicked open the door and threw a client down a flight of stairs. Noticing me, he shrugged. "I know I've got to stop doing this, Toni," he said. He seemed to find it easier to throw the man out than to argue with him any more. Yet his clients always came back, mainly because Shirley King had the only land-surveying office in Brant County.

I moved into a rooming house in town and spent my weekends painting. I soon learned that an aspiring painter was little better off in Canada than on the Isle of Man. In 1948 hardly anybody bought art. The most prominent dealer in Toronto, Douglas Duncan, operated a picture loan society and for fifty cents per week would rent out a watercolour by David Milne and then forget who had rented it. Milne was an artist with a completely original kind of landscape painting—energetic, exploding brushstrokes and fantastic colours—mulberry purples, tangerine oranges, indigo blues—that somehow hung together marvellously. But Milne, an artistic genius, sold almost nothing and, I later learned, was slowly starving to death in a painting shack in the wilderness.

Like Milne, I had always painted because I wanted to, not to make money, so I was no more discouraged in Canada by the lack of a market than I had been on the Isle of Man. From my experience of painting excursions on the island, I knew I needed to get to places without becoming too tired to paint, and that gave me the idea of buying a car. I imagined myself driving all over southern Ontario in search of landscapes. I could also use a car to get to work, saving me a little more time for my painting. Besides, there was another reason. I ate my meals at the local Honey Dew restaurant and I wanted to show off to a gorgeous waitress I knew there.

In the old-country way, I sent my mother some money every week. Because I had very little cash to put down on my first car, I had to take out a loan, which Shirley King very generously co-signed. I picked up a beautiful cream-coloured '32 Buick coupe for about $300. It had spoked wheels with whitewall tires, running boards and a rumble seat in the back. The interior had crushed velvet upholstery with tassels, and the rim of the steering wheel sported a glass knob inside of which shimmered a dancing naked lady. It was a bordello on wheels. The engine was an in-line eight-cylinder 113 horsepower, which got no more than six miles to a gallon—not that it mattered because gas sold for pennies a gallon.

As soon as I bought it, I asked the Honey Dew waitress to the Saturday night dance. It rained heavily that night and she lived outside of town in a new subdivision, so I barely made it down the gravel road to her house.

I left the car at the foot of her unpaved driveway and walked to the front porch. She stood there in a pink chiffon party dress with a crinoline. "Toni," she said, tapping one of her silver dancing shoes impatiently, "What are you doing? Bring the car here!"

"Why don't we just walk to the car?" I suggested.

She put her hands on her waist. "You can't expect me to walk through the mud."

"But I'll get stuck in the driveway," I argued.

She taunted me, "Daddy drives up here all the time in his truck."

My date would have to mention her father, a hulking football-shaped foundry worker who hated the idea of his daughter seeing an artist. He'd threatened to break me in two if I ever came calling. To avoid him, we'd planned a Saturday night date because he worked the night shift.

After her challenging remark, my hormones took over and I revved the engine, slipped the car into gear and floored the accelerator. The Buick sprang onto the driveway and sank into the mud. I pumped the accelerator. The wheels spun uselessly. I left my jacket on the car seat and took a look outside. My car had sunk to its axles.

"What a mess!" said my date. "C'mon, Toni, are we going to go to the dance, or aren't we? Forget your silly old car, I'll call a cab!"

After the dance, I sent her home in a taxi. When I came back for the coupe on the following day, her father had demolished it with his double-bladed axe. I stayed away from the Honey Dew after that. I had lost a potential girlfriend and a new car, and I still had to finish paying for the car. That was a major setback. It did, however, cause me to look around for less romantic recreational opportunities.

Without a car it was much harder to get out of Brantford, a real smoke 'n grit town with little or no theatre, music or art, so I frequented the library, which had an exhibition space called the "Canadian Room" where the librarian, Miss Bailey, hung travelling art exhibits. When she found out that I was a painter, she and I started the Brantford Art League and brought in guest speakers on Canadian art.

A few months later, I exhibited in the Canadian Room myself and acquired a reputation as the first serious painter in Brantford. Many of my paintings were from the Isle of Man; however, I had done some watercolours in Ontario, too. The *Brantford Expositor* decided I'd found inspiration "in the sunswept fields and rough-hewn farm buildings of southwestern Ontario," concluding: "Mr. Onley's position as assistant to a Brantford surveyor is his bread and butter. His painting is the jam."

The reviewer also noted that I was having trouble coming to terms with the Canadian landscape. The soft light and temperate marine climate of the Isle of Man had presented me with a variety of subtle greens and other muted colours. But the summer landscapes of southeastern Ontario confronted me with a sky that glowed a pure cobalt blue over fields of pale green, leaf green, bright yellow or gold. The intensity of the light and the monotonous colours reminded me of a remark by a disgruntled nineteenth-century landscape painter who once complained, "What's the point of painting nature? It's all green and badly lit." Later, I thought the blazing red maple trees were somehow vulgar compared to the less vibrant autumn foliage on the Isle of Man.

In time I adjusted my palette to the new landscape. I also examined Canadian art. I learned about the Group of Seven, still a major force in landscape painting seventeen years after they disbanded. They had sketched outdoors, painting with oils on birchwood panels. Afterward, they used these panels to paint larger works, which I thought sometimes overemphasized pattern through a pronounced stylization of the trees and other elements of landscape. It was the sketches, however, that really excited me, for the small panels had the spontaneity of great watercolour painting. I particularly admired the oil sketches of Tom Thomson.

The following year, 1949, I decided to spend a week or two at the Doon Summer School of the Arts in Doon Village, about a forty-five-minute bus ride from Brantford. Many of the teachers at Doon came from the Ontario School of Art, so I expected a high level of instruction. Classes were held in a quaint nineteenth-century brick house with a gabled roof that had belonged to the

Canadian academic painter, Homer Watson. His picture of the pioneer flour mill on the nearby Grand River had been purchased for Queen Victoria, an honour that resulted in Watson being called "The Canadian Constable" after the great British landscape painter, John Constable. After his death, Watson's house was taken over by a retired major, Colin Hamilton, who ran it as a summer art school. We painted on the slope behind the house or on a hill overlooking the Grand River or by the ruined mill that had been the subject of Watson's famous painting or in Cressman's Woods, a 250-acre spruce and pine forest that Watson had helped preserve.

The most famous teacher at the school at that time was Fred Varley, formerly of the Group of Seven. The magic associated with those great Canadian landscape painters still opened doors for him. That was ironic because Varley had been the least outdoorsy of the group. I remember seeing a photograph of A.Y. Jackson, the last of the hairy-chested outdoor painters, waist-deep in a snowdrift by a barn in eastern Quebec, labouring over an easel. But if you look at the pictures of the group's camping trips in 1915 or in 1920, Fred Varley is never doing anything strenuous or practical. I doubt that A.Y. would have trusted Fred to fry a flapjack.

It was Varley's work, however, that made the strongest impression on me. He surpassed the others in his talent and range, painting everything from *For What?*, a muck-filled World War I battlefield scene that depicted a lone Canadian gravedigger as he rested on his spade by a cart full of dead soldiers, to *Vera*, a lovely portrait he did in 1931 of Vera Weatherbie, an auburn-haired beauty and former student of his who became his lover. The arch of Vera's eyebrows and the faint smile on her delicate heart-shaped face suggest a sensitive, compassionate nature, while Varley's use of colour also gives her image a sensuous dimension. She is Canada's Mona Lisa. I remember how, decades later, when I was on the acquisitions committee of the Vancouver Art Gallery, Varley's *Vera* came up for purchase. The director was not interested in it, dismissing it as "just a portrait." Another Varley canvas, his 1920 *Stormy Weather, Georgian Bay* with its windswept spruce tree, became not only a signature piece for the Group of Seven, but also a national icon of Canadian landscape.

When I studied at Doon, Fred Varley was a boozy, garrulous sixty-seven-year-old with a high forehead, white hair and a putty-coloured face as appealing as an old boot. In his West Country accent, he growled at one student: "The sky in your canvas is a debauchery!" He told another, "Lighten that brushstroke. You're not a house painter, for God's sake." Yet Varley had a wonderful child-like enthusiasm for painting. I'd see him roaming through the farmers' fields, a slight, puckish figure in his rolled white shirt sleeves and baggy navy corduroy pants, with a small easel strapped onto the army pack on his back.

One afternoon I was sketching in the shade of a large tree at the Doon Lookout. Varley was close by and I watched him painting. He sat on the bank of the Grand River, in his canvas folding chair, cocking his head right, then left, working on the painting on his easel. He caught the sweep of the winding river curving toward the horizon and almost meeting the blue of the sky. In a burst of energy, he painted furiously, his brush full of paint as he blocked in some of the trees on the opposite bank. Then he stopped and rose from his folding chair to look at the effect of his colours from a distance, accidentally tipping over the flimsy chair as he stepped back for a better view. These were impatient little landscapes he was doing, painted with inferior materials that made them flat and lifeless. Despite his enthusiasm for painting he was alone and lonely at Doon and it showed in his work.

One of the students in Varley's landscape painting class was Mary Jean Burrows. I'd met her before in Galt when she was acting in a play directed by my father. Small and slender, she had a pretty freckled face, large blue eyes and short curly blonde hair. At seventeen, she had just finished high school. She immediately won my sympathy because, despite her love of the arts, her parents were determined to send her to business college. She wanted to attend art school as a full-time student in September but she'd only been allowed to go to the Doon summer school.

Mary lived in mortal fear that her straitlaced parents would see Varley's drawings somewhere and discover that she had modelled for him in the nude. They were full-length nudes in red and green chalk, highlighted in white. Varley, who could talk any woman out of her clothes, had remarked at the time, "My girl, it shows your verve." To protect Mary he did not put her name on the drawings. One of them, titled simply *Girl with Apple*, eventually formed part of the Charles Band collection at the Art Gallery of Ontario.

I noticed Mary's pastel drawings and after I talked to her, I realized I'd found a kindred spirit who cared as passionately about art as I did. She had a curfew at home and she didn't live far by bus so she came to the school in the morning and left in the early evening. I didn't stay in the dorm in the school, or in one of the guest cabins either, mainly for reasons of economy, so we rode the bus together a few times. We started painting together. I tried to teach her about watercolours although at the time she painted mostly in oils. What a great relationship, I thought to myself. Nothing could be better than two artists falling in love with each other. We soon became an item at Doon.

One night—I think the school had held a barbecue—Mary and I and a few other students wandered into the fields afterward. We paired off. I remember Mary and I rolled together in the grass in a sweet, light embrace. Suddenly we heard a peal of thunder. It sounded like something from the Old Testament. But the crash only frightened us into a closer embrace.

As far as the class went, Varley never taught me technique or anything else. You didn't really study with Varley, you drank with him. He loved partying with young people and one Friday afternoon he announced, "Now I want you boys and girls to paint in Cressman's Woods, then meet me at the Red Lion Inn tonight."

The inn was a dilapidated two-storey hotel by an abandoned Grand Trunk Railway line and a train station. The school principal had set Varley up there for about thirty-two dollars per week, probably thinking that if any scandal erupted, the inn lay a good half mile from the school.

When we ordered drinks that evening, Varley kept putting them on his tab. We could hardly believe his generosity. We all got sloshed and talked about art and love and life. Varley was such a romantic. He seemed to be going through a bad period at Doon, at least in relation to his landscapes. As if to remind himself that the artist had to be forever inventive, he kept saying "Artist awake! Or be forever fallen."

Some time afterward, Mary and I dropped by the Doon School before it closed for the winter. The principal's wife, Bess Hamilton, sat in Watson's old gallery, which served as her office, poring over the accounts. We asked about Varley.

"That man—Varley!" she sputtered angrily. "He'll never teach here again."

Varley had returned to Toronto, and the Red Lion Inn had just sent Bess the bill for his summer of drinking including the drinks he bought for the students. For the longest time, I truly believed that Gully Jimson in Joyce Cary's novel *The Horse's Mouth* was modelled after Fred Varley, until Sir John Rothenstein, director of the Tate Gallery, told me years later he definitely was not.

Later, Mary and I had to drive to Toronto to buy some moulding to frame some of our pictures. I had arranged a small joint exhibition for us at the Brantford library. Mary suggested we drop in on Varley and she telephoned him and set a time.

At his walk-up apartment building on Grenville Street, he had scribbled "V-A-R-L-E-Y" on a piece of cardboard tacked to his door. No one answered when we knocked. As the door had been left ajar, we walked into the small L-shaped room. On the table was an ashtray stuffed with cigarette butts. One butt lay smouldering, as if Varley had just stepped outside, so we waited for him. Mary sat on his sofa bed. I looked through the paintings he had stacked against the wall to see if there were any of the watercolours I especially admired.

All I found that day, however, were oil paintings, largely of the figure and in superb colours. On the wall above the sofa, he had tacked the nude figure of a woman whose florid pink skin was set off by splashes of scarlet, gold, violet and blue-green. Viridian green was interwoven among these colours. Varley felt that green was the metaphysical foundation of all colour and, according to his somewhat eccentric colour symbolism, could be used to depict the spiritual dimension of his subject.

Half an hour passed and I turned to Mary, "We've got to get to the store before it closes."

After we headed home, about halfway from Toronto, Mary telephoned Varley. "Where were you, Fred?"

"I thought about it and thought about it, Mary," he confessed. "I just couldn't face you and Toni together."

Poor old Varley always fell in love with his models.

I was never to see Fred Varley again. He was eighty-eight when he died in 1969. His last watercolours done at Kootenay Lake still show the strong influence of Turner. In the end, we come back to our beginnings.

Varley's artistic outlook, like my own, was deeply rooted in the traditions of nineteenth-century English painting. During the two years I knew him at Doon, he was sometimes distrustful of himself and unhappy with his work, as I was at that time. He was completely unlike the other members of the Group of Seven. Born in Sheffield, he came from the English romantic tradition and managed to keep it alive through the temporary decline evident in the small landscape oils he did at Doon. Once back in Toronto, he painted the masterful portrait of Dr. Hardolph Wasteneys that hangs in Hart House, and his last watercolours are fine landscape paintings. After the Doon hiatus, he had "awakened" to find the inspiration and the strength to do his final works.

Like me, Varley was also influenced by oriental art and attitudes toward painting. In a letter to a friend in Halifax, he once wrote about BC, "I often feel that only the Chinese of the eleventh and twelfth centuries ever interpreted the spirit of such a country. We have not yet awakened to its nature." Although I didn't anticipate such a change at the time I knew Varley, a few years later I was to make my home in BC and begin a lifetime of painting its many landscapes. And it all came about through my connection with Mary Burrows.

Chapter 7

For Whom the Bell Tolls

I had first met my future wife through my father in the summer of 1949. He introduced me to Mary Jean Burrows in a coffee shop in Galt near the theatre where he was directing her in an amateur production. Mary had auditioned for a part in *The Cloak* and she looked so fawn-like and innocent that Dad had cast her as the angel. When he introduced her, Dad remarked that with her curly blond hair she reminded him of Ingrid Bergman in the 1943 film classic *For Whom the Bell Tolls*. To Mary he added, "In Spanish, you're a Maria, too."

Mary and I met again later that summer at the Doon School of Fine Arts and became better acquainted. After we'd taken a class with Fred Varley and our love of art had brought us together, Mary brought me home to her parents. Her mother, Helen, must have thought I was a starving artist because soon after my arrival she slipped into the kitchen and returned with a plate of ham-and-mustard sandwiches and two glasses of cold milk. As soon as I was happily eating she asked about my religion. As a devout Christian she was really taken aback when I told her I wasn't religious.

"Sit down," said Carl Burrows, a fierce-looking red-headed little businessman, pointing to a chair in the living room. I had to sit down while he kept standing so he'd look taller, all five foot three of him. "I understand you're an artist. Not much money in that." He crossed his arms. "Do you know how I got through the Depression? Selling washing machines." Mary told me later that Carl had marketed a single washing machine nine or ten times for a local retailer.

He'd sell it to one woman for a small down payment. When she fell behind on the monthly instalments he'd repossess the machine and sell it again. The washing machine made the rounds and he kept making money from it.

He circled my chair. "Now I'm in the insurance business. And it's provided a pretty good living for us." He glanced at Mary. "Business can provide financial security and that's why Mary's going to business college this fall."

Mary, the only person in the family who dared stand up to Carl, sighed and told him once again that she intended to go to art school full-time, not just in the summer.

Carl dismissed the idea with a wave of his hand. "Art school, bah!" He turned to me. "I pay my way. Can an artist make that claim, Toni?"

"I don't make a living at painting now," I countered. "I'm a surveyor, but I hope to make a career in art one day."

Carl shrugged contemptuously. Actually, as a businessman he was more of a con artist than a successful salesman. When I got to know him better I found out how he got new clients. He had a morbid interest in rare diseases and his hobby was reading about them. He'd go to a small-town doctor, faking symptoms like headaches and fainting spells, or pain spasms in his leg. After a lengthy consultation the doctor would announce something like, "You have a rare tropical disease. I've never heard it reported outside of Kenya!" Carl would beam with pleasure. "My God! I've been through hell and high water and you're the first doctor to diagnose it."

As their conversation turned to the question of treatment, the doctor would ask Carl what he did for a living. "As a matter of fact, I am selling a new kind of insurance," he'd reply and explain the difference between whole-life insurance and the relatively new low-cost term insurance. Doctors were building family dynasties, passing on their medical practices to their sons. As a result they were more interested in reducing their expenses than in building up savings for a far distant future. Thus Carl built a network of clients among the small-town dynasts—doctors, dentists and undertakers—the only people with any money in rural Ontario.

Eventually Carl studied medical textbooks so obsessively that he began believing his imaginary ailments. He bought himself one of the first speaker phones. On one visit I made to see Mary I heard him tell the operator: "Help me, I'm a cripple." After she had made the connection without charging him, he held his hand over the mouthpiece and laughed like a maniac. His son Tom later told me that if he ever wrote a book about his father, the title would be *Help Me, I'm a Cripple.*

Mary had absolutely no support from her parents for her ambition to become an artist. Her father was a tyrant; her mother was kind but very conservative. Both parents insisted that she attend business college. One day Mary showed me a canvas she had painted of a forest in which a frightened half-suffocated figure was imprisoned by branches. That this beautiful fragile creature looked to me for help made her even more attractive to me. It wasn't long before I fell in love with her.

We were very young—Mary had just had her eighteenth birthday and I would be twenty-one in November. Because I lived in Brantford and Mary in Galt, we saw each other only on weekends. If you added up all the time we spent together over the six months of our courtship, it couldn't have been more than three full weeks. However, we wanted each other so badly that Mary soon became pregnant. When she told her parents they agreed we'd better get married right away. They didn't approve of their daughter marrying an artist but the alternative was worse.

Mary and I were ecstatic. I arranged a minister for the wedding, Father Thompkins, an Anglican priest who'd befriended me when I'd moved to Brantford. He'd invited me to high tea and asked my opinion about the Inuit art he had collected while posted to Labrador. He married us on May 27, 1950.

I recall standing at the altar while Mary and her father remained in the vestibule. Father Thompkins leaned over and whispered to our ringbearer, Mary's nine-year-old brother, Tom, "Please tell them we're waiting." Tom ran down the aisle yelling at the top of his voice—"Mary, we're waiting! We're waiting!"

Soon after we moved into an apartment, I had to leave town for a surveying job in Barrie, Ontario. The baby was due early the next year and we decided we'd need more space, so Mary started looking for a house while I was away. We didn't qualify for a mortgage, however. My parents had no money and Mary's father was too upset for us to approach him. In the end, her grandfather offered to lend us the money if we found a suitable house. One day Mary telephoned in great excitement to tell me that she'd found a lovely farmhouse on a 300-acre property near Cainsville, a village close to Brantford. "Toni, you have to see this place! There's clematis growing over the kitchen porch. It's beautiful!"

I could hardly believe they were asking only $5,000. "Is anything wrong with it?"

"It's not perfect, Toni. There's an outdoor toilet, a two-holer. And the house is heated by a wood stove. But it's been here nearly two hundred years. The people who lived here before never froze to death. We could fix it up."

"The outdoor toilet sounds like a problem."

"There's nothing like it in our price range," added Mary. "And Toni, there's a barn. You could turn it into a studio."

"A studio?"

All of a sudden, the house seemed like a great deal. It would be wonderful to have a studio. "You're right," I replied, "we better buy it."

It was an old wooden Victorian house with gingerbread trim and a concrete front porch that was flagstoned with discarded white marble gravestones. In the summer it was charming but we soon realized that buying it had been a mistake. The wood stove was too small to heat the entire house. There was no plumbing at all, not even a cold water tap. We had to use the hand pump outside and carry pails full of water into the kitchen. In the summer the shallow well dried up and we had to fetch water from a neighbour's farm and keep it in a tin bathtub. In Ontario's sub-zero winter weather we had to use the outdoor toilet, staggering through snowdrifts to the outhouse and shivering on the pinewood bench. The first summer, wasps built a nest under the seat and I nearly got stung to death trying to get rid of it.

We brought our daughter Jennifer home from the hospital into that difficult pioneer lifestyle. Mary and I were thrilled with her but a baby meant more work than either of us had ever imagined. Conveniences became more important than ever. When we could afford it we had central heating installed and a thousand-gallon oil tank buried near the house. Then we saved up and got running water in the house and an indoor toilet and a septic tank.

Mary and I were very busy. But the following year we scraped together some paintings for a joint show at the Brantford Library. A few months later, at the Western Ontario Art League Exhibition in London, I was awarded a $75 prize for the best entry for painters under twenty-seven. The judge, Clare Bice, must have expected me to say I'd buy paints with the money, because he looked shocked when I told the audience I'd put the prize money toward a second-hand Model A Ford. I hoped to drive my little family out into the country on the weekends so that Mary and I could paint landscapes.

However, our workload was such that we had almost no time for art. We both became very frustrated because we had held such high hopes for ourselves. Our parents and our friends expected us to buckle down and get on with raising a family. That meant my working full-time in the bush and Mary staying home with Jennifer. Our marriage was a disappointment to both of us. Mary had hoped that by marrying a painter she could gain the confidence and freedom to pursue her art interests. I'd thought I'd found a soulmate who'd understand that I needed time to develop my work. In fact, we were both trapped.

I was still in charge of finding the speakers for the Art League meetings at the Brantford Library. I heard that A.Y. Jackson of the Group of Seven was available to lecture to our group. Probably Canada's best-known artist at the time, he was a popular speaker and he, better than anyone else, could tell me about the life of a professional artist and whether there was any hope at all for me in that direction.

A.Y. was about sixty then, a short, stocky and slightly pot-bellied man with a friendly homely face and a fringe of white hair around the crown of his head. "I've been looking forward to this, Toni," he grinned, gripping my hand firmly.

In a warm, relaxed manner, A.Y. told the group how he had travelled from the Rocky Mountains to the Northwest Territories, painting the landscapes so that people could recognize and identify with them. "Canadians should join the big adventure of discovering this country," he said. "I never want to work in Europe again—I even discourage art students from going there because there's so much in our own backyard."

With self-deprecating humour, A.Y. confessed that for most of his life he'd never made more than a thousand dollars a year. He'd never owned a car and he'd never married. "The first time I proposed to someone, back in 1913 or 1914, the lady in question replied, 'Alec, you could never afford to keep me'." He laughed. "She was right about that."

Mary had brought baby Jennifer to the lecture and held her in her arms as we stood together near the back of the room. After the lecture Mary asked A.Y., "Don't you get lonely painting in the wilderness?"

"I have company sometimes," he said. "But nature is my friend. You aren't lonely with a friend."

I'd brought in a few of my paintings for him to look at. They were watercolours, of course, and A.Y. was an oil painter, working in a Post-Impressionist style quite different from mine. I don't remember what he said except that he tried to be encouraging. He could see that I hung on his every word. Then Jennifer began crying and Mary rocked her.

I know how trapped I felt then. I must have looked unhappy, too, because I think old A.Y. felt sorry for me. "You know, Toni, I envy you and your young wife," he told me. "The one thing I regret in life is not having a family."

I'm sure it was his way to let me down gently. A career as an artist might not work out for me but at least I would have a family.

A.Y.'s well-intentioned remarks depressed me even more. I sank further into self-pity, miserable that I had to give up so much of my painting time. Then Mary suggested that we have a second child to keep Jennifer company. I argued against it, pointing out that Mary had never got along with her sister. However, Mary felt that an only child would be selfish and spoiled. We finally made a deal that if I agreed to another child, she'd put up with my going out painting more often. She even agreed that I could spend a week of my summer holiday at the Doon Summer School of the Arts.

My week at Doon revitalized me because there I met Carl Schaefer, a teacher from the Ontario School of Art who had studied painting with Arthur Lismer and J.E.H. MacDonald, two other members of the Group of Seven. Schaefer had struck out in his own direction, developing an unmistakable style. In 1940 he became the first Canadian painter to win a Guggenheim Fellowship.

He'd also supported a family but he'd kept his sense of humour. Schaefer was a clown, a wiry man with a long Roman nose and a huge bushy moustache like the cowcatcher on a locomotive. He was full of surprises. He'd suddenly pluck off his straw hat and do a handspring on the grass. One evening that week, he donned a Confederate Army jacket, charged up Pinnacle Hill and fired off a musket.

Schaefer was always very serious about art, however. Once he marched us outside the school and pointed to the great spreading beech tree in the front yard. "Do you see this tree? How many colours do you see in it?" he asked.

"Twelve," volunteered a woman in our class.

"Twenty-seven," he replied and pointed out each one.

Later, he looked at one of my watercolours of Cressman's Woods. "Your trees look like hose-pipes." So that became my hose-pipe tree period. I could only paint elm trees decently and they were being wiped out by Dutch elm disease.

One day Schaefer set up his easel in a field near the top of Pinnacle Hill and I crossed the road to watch him work. He was painting a view of the landscape south of the hill: an expanse of farmers' fields broken up only by rows of windbreaks and a few woodlots. He had a realistic style, yet plied his brush in a forceful, expressionistic manner, laying down the colour of the fields by moving diagonally across the paper in short, staccato strokes. But I was more impressed by his choice of colours.

"Contrasts, Toni, that's what I paint," he said, painting a dark green for a field where cattle grazed, then introducing a brighter green for the foliage on some cottonwood trees. He added a distant black silhouette for a farmhouse. Then he took a larger brush and added washes of ultramarine and sepia for the threatening sky. "It's all in the contrast between light and dark colours. That's how I learned to paint a flat, almost featureless place like Hanover county." The watercolour sizzled with dramatic lighting.

I went back to my easel. Schaefer shouted across the road. "Toni, forget everything I told you. It's my style, not yours. Just paint, for God's sake. That's all any of us can do."

In the fall of 1952, I put together a show of my new paintings from Doon. Again I held it at the Brantford Public Library. The local papers reviewed it, as did the art critic of the *Globe & Mail*, Pearl McCarthy, whom I had invited to speak. That show led to a whole new identity for me. I remember Mary reading a description of me in one of the reviews as "that young painter who has contributed so much to art circles in Brantford, Norman A. Onley."

Mary frowned. "Norman Anthony Onley. It's just too long and formal. It's not like you. Everyone calls you Toni." I could see Mary's point. After that I shortened my name to "Toni Onley."

That fall was one of the last good times Mary and I had together. Then our second daughter Lynn was born on February 24, 1953. She would turn out to be entirely different from Jennifer, a real chatterbox like her father. I loved both of the girls, but everything had happened too fast. Family responsibilities seemed to be crushing our spirits. Mary and I had no time for one another at all now and I had to find a better way to support our family than land surveying.

I found a position as a draftsman with Cockshutt Farm Equipment. I knocked myself out developing plans for their new office and a design for a manure spreader that made it look like a streamlined Ford sedan. After one particularly exhausting week I came home Friday night hoping to get a little painting done. Mary snapped, "I've been with the children all week. *I'm* going out painting for a change." In six months I think I produced a single painting. And I did that one in defiance of Mary by storming out of the house, driving off in the car and painting peacefully by the roadside.

I complained about my marital problems to some of the fellows at work. "Toni, I've got the answer," one of them replied. "You take a long run at a brick wall with your head." He laughed. "End it all."

The worst thing to happen to our marriage occurred in the middle of a summer drought. The well at our house ran dry and I called in a driller to dig us a deeper one. A good-looking young man showed up with his truck and drilling rig. Every day before he started work he stripped to the waist, revealing a washboard stomach and broad, bronzed shoulders. It took him forever to find water. Whenever I came home he had dug only a few inches because he'd found salty water, hit rocks or broken a drill bit. The job cost us twice as much as he'd estimated.

A month later Mary took the car one evening and disappeared. I had no idea where she'd gone. I had to stay home from work so I could look after the kids. Frantically I reported her missing and the Ontario Provincial Police began to search for our car. A couple of days later they located it on a back road, parked near a farmhouse where a family of hillbillies lived.

A police sergeant visited me. "Well, your wife's coming home." He snarled, "If I were you, I'd beat the shit out of her."

"Why would I do that?" I asked.

"She's been living with another man."

I was shocked to hear that it was the well driller I had employed a few weeks ago. I was deeply hurt, but also furious.

When Mary returned, we argued all night. We shouted and called each other names. I blamed her for abandoning our children. She shouted that I'd never helped enough with the children. Then we never talked about the incident again. A long, bitter silence fell between us. After five years of marriage we had betrayed all our ideals and completely lost our faith in each other. In retrospect I realize that she may have been in the manic phase of a bipolar condition. Many cases went unrecognized in those days.

Over the next eight or nine months Mary and I struggled to find a new equilibrium in our relationship. Since emigrating to Canada I had never made more than fifty or sixty dollars per week. Trying to support a family and a mortgage on that kind of salary meant that we never had enough money and were always doing without something. To resolve this problem, Mary found a part-time job in Brantford, which brought in some money and got her out of the house, and I started teaching art classes at the YMCA on Saturday mornings.

As a new teacher, I relied upon my experience of teaching a little painting to Mary's younger brother Tom, and upon what I remembered of learning to paint when I was a child. Soon I had about twenty-five students aged six to twelve. The *Brantford Expositor* carried an article on how I used classical music to inspire the children. For instance, I would play Smetana's description of the Moldau flowing through Bohemia and set the children to painting ships that glided past darkened villages.

The results even fired me up a little about my own painting. My watercolours had begun to seem too cautious to me. If I could only render landscapes with the spontaneity of a child, I might be able to break through to some new painting. Through reading *Canadian Art* magazine and even a few copies of *The Studio* from Britain, I had become very aware of the abstract expressionist movement in America. Mary and I had travelled to some of the shows at the Toronto Art Gallery, even as far as the Albright Art Gallery in Buffalo, New York, but I'd found the paintings too big and the colours too strong. I'd come from a European tradition where the emphasis had been on mood, atmosphere and the subtleties of the local colour of a place. In America the focus was on colour and size, and the relationship between colours was of primary importance. It was the antithesis of what I was doing as a painter and it seemed to make any prospect of my becoming a successful artist all the more remote.

Then events took a turn for the worse again. There was a bad harvest on the prairies and Cockshutt Farm Equipment laid me off. I was unemployed for a few months but early in 1955 I found a job as a commercial illustrator with Standard Engravers in Hamilton. They had me design everything from labels for McNally's Pickles and Aylmer soup to advertisements for *Maclean's* magazine. Some of my package designs are still around, like the blue package with the white swan I created for Swan Chalk. Though I liked commercial design, it frustrated me that every assignment came with a time limit, usually of one or two hours. Paid on the basis of these time estimates, commercial illustration became a kind of production-line work, with the foreman always hovering over me to see if I had finished yet.

In the spring of 1955, I expanded my art classes, organizing adult outdoor painting classes through the Brantford Art League. That got me out painting landscapes again and cheered me up a lot. But just when I thought things were finally getting better, on the morning of June 15 I received a shocking phone call from my father-in-law.

Carl told me that Mary had suddenly collapsed and died at work, right after her boss had yelled at her for some typing mistakes. I couldn't believe it. I was certain that it was a mistake or that Carl was playing a malicious prank on me.

Mary had taken the car that day to drop off the kids and get to her part-time job, so I got a taxi to take me from my job in Hamilton to the Brantford hospital. There a doctor informed me that my wife was dead and then asked me to identify her body. He turned back the sheet and it was Mary, but her face had turned blue. Shaking, I fled from the room. Still clutching the lunch bag and the Thermos of coffee she had packed for me that morning, I stumbled down the corridor and into the hospital lobby.

The Burrows family had a plot in the Galt Cemetery and I agreed that Mary could be buried there. The funeral was held at the cemetery chapel. Helen had arranged to have Mary dressed in her wedding gown. As she lay in her casket, Carl, chain-smoking, leaned over to kiss her with a cigarette in his hand. His hand trembled and the cigarette ash dropped onto her face.

One blow fell after another. I discovered I couldn't keep our home together. I found myself in a quandary—I had to get back to work but I was a twenty-six-year-old single parent with a four-year-old and a two-year-old who needed me.

The Burrowses offered to take in the children, even to adopt them, but I quickly declined. Mary had been extremely unhappy in that home and I didn't want our children living there. By strange coincidence, just a few weeks before she died, Mary had asked me to promise that if anything ever happened to her, I would never let her parents raise Jennifer and Lynn. I'd tried to reassure her that she was fine, in good health. "Anyway," I had said, "your parents are the last people I'd leave the kids with." Now I didn't know what to do. Jennifer became silent, while Lynn never stopped crying. There was no one to look after them while I went to work and I couldn't afford to hire a housekeeper. I was too distraught to work anyway.

Then Carl started making anonymous phone calls to the police in which he accused me of poisoning Mary. Two policemen arrived at the house and began searching the property. They found a tin of rat poison in the barn, left there by the previous owner.

"Who called you?" I asked. "My father-in-law, Carl Burrows?"

"He's your father-in-law?" replied one of the policeman. He shook his head in disgust. "That's all we need to know." Carl had made crank calls to them before. They apologized and left.

Coming so swiftly after Mary's funeral, the police investigation completely unravelled me. I hardly knew where to turn. My parents would have helped me but they had left Ontario and moved out west. Finally, I telephoned my father. Dad urged me to come to

Penticton and assured me that he and my mother would help look after the girls. I quickly agreed.

When I told Carl I was going to take the children to my parents' home in British Columbia he cagily suggested we could leave immediately if I authorized him to sell the house, and he advanced us the money for the airplane tickets. Because Mary had borrowed the money for the house from her late grandfather, Carl, the only son and heir, assumed the right to collect that debt from the sale price. Nevertheless, I had some equity in the property, and with the improvements I had made I expected it to sell at a profit. I agreed to the arrangement and started packing.

When I called my father again he sounded really disturbed. "Take the girls and get on a plane to Penticton," he urged. "Settle things up, or don't settle them up, just get out of there." I found out later from my mother that he'd just received an anonymous letter, obviously from Carl Burrows, which accused me of poisoning Mary. My mother told me he was so upset he cried. He burnt the letter before I arrived and never mentioned it to me.

The autopsy and subsequent tests finally revealed that the cause of Mary's mysterious death was Cushing's disease, a rare malfunction of the pituitary gland that affects ten to fifteen out of every million people. But paranoia does not readily yield to mere science. Carl Burrows preferred to believe that his daughter was poisoned and that the autopsy report was a mistake or a cover-up.

I and my daughters were well out of there.

Chapter 8

A Weekend Painter

Dad had moved my mother and sisters out west a few years earlier. Like a character in a Fellini movie, he'd marshalled a ragtag troupe of actors, tied their props and costumes and suitcases to the top of an old school bus and toured *Julius Caesar* and *Macbeth* through every one-silo town in western Canada.

When his Shakespeare troupe ran out of money, he and Mom were forced to settle down. Dad wrote me from Penticton, BC, then a town of about 15,000, a six- or seven-hour drive from Vancouver. "I can't think of a better place for the company to go broke. It's a lovely valley and your Mom and I have a little house that some generous people have loaned us. We don't have any money for fuel but the house has a wood stove and we're collecting driftwood from the beach and storing it up for the winter. We'll make it somehow."

They made it through the winter, and the following summer Dad built an outdoor theatre and produced "Shakespeare Under the Stars." He was the director and star performer and my mother and sisters ran the box office and the concessions. The theatre landed him in another financial predicament, however, when his partners raised about a thousand dollars, then skipped town.

One of their biggest unpaid bills was owed to the editor and publisher of the *Penticton Herald*, one Grev Roland, a tall, distinguished-looking local businessman. When Dad went to the newspaper to place an ad looking for work, Roland beckoned him into his private office.

"You're Jim Onley, aren't you?" Dad admitted that he was. Roland then said, "I'm out $1,200 for all the advertising your partners did."

"There's nothing I can do about it," said my father. "They owe me money, too. In fact, I'm looking for a job right now."

In the best tradition of small-town newspapermen, Roland put his feet up on his desk and leaned back in his chair. "Sell advertising, Onley."

Dad smiled. "I've been selling myself all my life." He started at the *Herald* for $225 per month.

At that point, in the summer of 1955, the kids and I limped into my parents' lives. It was a long trip to make with two small children. We had to change planes in Calgary, where I fought with the ticket agent over Jennifer's fare to Penticton. Although my two-year-old, Lynn, could sit on my lap, Jennifer, four, was supposed to have her own seat, for which the airline wanted an adult fare. We haggled over the ticket for half an hour until the agent finally realized I just didn't have the money and relented.

When the plane landed, I staggered off, harassed and exhausted. In one arm, I held Lynn, hanging onto my neck, half asleep. With my other arm, I led Jennifer, who was quietly sucking her thumb.

For once my father didn't know what to say. He looked shocked at my appearance. My mother took Jennifer and Lynn and they sat together in the back seat of Dad's car.

On the ride to my parents' house Dad tried to comfort me. "Cheer up, Toni, you'll get back on your feet in no time. How does that saying go? When one door closes, another one opens."

At that point nothing could have relieved my misery. I'd fallen into a pit of despair. My hopes for a happy life and my ambition to become a painter seemed finished. The mother of my children had died. My life lay in ruins. I couldn't see why my father didn't recognize that and leave me alone.

Dad chuckled, "Or maybe it goes—one door closes and the other one slams shut." Then he turned to me. "Come on, son, you've got to snap out of this."

Mom piped up, "Jim, he needs time. He's just getting over Mary's death." My father sighed, "Poor Mary, it's tragic she died so young. But you've got to get on with your life, Toni. You've got children to look after. You've got to make your way in the world."

When Dad's pep talk didn't have much effect on me, he started criticizing Mary. He seemed to identify with the fox in the fable of the Fox and the Grapes, eager to demonstrate that what you can't have, you didn't want anyway. "I don't know that Mary was much of a cook," he innocently observed. "I don't think she could even boil an egg properly."

"Jim," warned my mother, "don't start that."

Dad had a knack for saying the wrong thing. "Son, listen—you have to admit your marriage had its troubles."

I burst into tears. "You don't understand, Dad, I loved her!" In their surprise at seeing me cry, first Jennifer, then Lynn, started wailing. The three of us cried all the way to my parents' home.

To my father's dismay I broke down several times that day. He didn't know what to make of it. Dad had never felt comfortable with people expressing their emotions and in no uncertain terms he indicated that I shouldn't behave like that around him. I finally pulled myself together, though for weeks afterward I had an enervating depression that occasionally resulted in crying jags.

Fortunately my mother helped me cope with Jennifer and Lynn, my most immediate concerns. The girls still couldn't understand that Mary had died. They kept asking when they were going to see her. Four-year-old Jennifer began to realize that she'd never see her mother again. It disturbed her so profoundly that she retreated into a private world. Though she had been a quiet girl before, she now became almost comatose. Mom and I tried in vain to get her to say more than a few words. Lynn, on the other hand, relieved her insecurity by hyperactivity; she couldn't keep quiet or still for a moment. Whenever Mom or I left the house, we had to reassure her that we were coming back.

The first thing I had to do in Penticton was to get back on my feet financially. Carl Burrows had promised to forward some money when he sold my house in Cainsville. I hoped the house would do well on the market because Mary and I had furnished it and made several major improvements, namely installing central heating and an indoor toilet, putting in a septic tank and drilling a new well.

Unfortunately, Carl was never at home when I called. Helen

Burrows would answer and she'd try to cheer me up. One day she said, "Toni, you'll be happy to hear that Carl finally sold your house."

We'd bought the house for $5,000 in 1950. Five years later, it was sold for $8,000. Even after Carl deducted our airfare to Penticton and our expenses there should have been at least four or five hundred dollars owing to me as well as my equity. In 1955, that kind of money could have supported the kids and me for the rest of the year.

"Can he send me the money he owes me right away?" I asked Helen.

"You'll have to talk to Carl about that," she replied. "He just left on a business trip to Mexico City."

"Mexico City? Oh, no!" I almost dropped the receiver. I could just imagine the kind of business Carl was engaged in—the destination should have tipped Helen off. But she had spent so many years in denial of Carl's extramarital affairs that she believed anything he told her. I suspected he had called up one of his girlfriends, taken the money and run off for a holiday.

Knowing Carl I assumed he'd stay at the best place in Mexico City. I called the operator and she connected me with the Hotel Reforma. Sure enough, Carl Burrows was registered there. The hotel switchboard put my call through to his room and I asked him when I could get the money owing to me from the sale of the house.

"I don't owe you a thing," he snarled. "I cleared your debts and bought your airplane tickets."

"You just wanted me out of the way so you could sell the house and keep all the money yourself," I snapped.

"You can go to hell, Toni," he retorted and hung up.

That was it. I'd lost my equity because I'd left Ontario without selling the house myself. Carl had cunningly taken advantage of my grief and lack of ready cash. In retrospect I wondered why Mary's grandfather, who had been quite well off, did not leave Mary the amount of the mortgage. But Carl had handled the estate and was certainly in a position to appropriate Mary's inheritance, if there was one. Had I been cheated twice on the house? I would never know. I could not bear to pursue the matter legally, nor was I easily able to do so, being so far from Ontario.

I had to get on with my life and find some way of earning an income. I remembered the success I'd had with my art classes in Ontario. My father got the paper to run a notice for a watercolour-painting demonstration. It proved very successful and I took on a number of art students. Every Thursday evening I met them at the band shell in Gyro Park. Sometimes we'd walk to the wharf at Okanagan Lake, sketch the landscape in charcoal, then add water-colours.

Soon I started a Saturday morning class for children. I'd try to help them find a subject they found meaningful. We discussed "spring" one afternoon. For one girl, it meant "spring cleaning," so she painted a girl and her mother sweeping the house. A little boy thought of it as a spring of water and painted a waterfall cascading down a mountain.

Out painting with my adult students, I learned about an entire-ly new landscape. Penticton lay close to the American border on the central plateau in a valley in the low Okanagan Mountains, while beyond those mountains lay higher peaks, the spectacular Coast Mountains to the west and the Selkirk Range to the east. The light and colour of the Okanagan Valley shimmered in the hot dry sum-mer. From the hillside above long, narrow Okanagan Lake I could see thousands of acres of apple, pear and cherry orchards, many of them growing near the city limits of Penticton. Sometimes if I was alone and had my father's car I'd drive farther out of town to do some painting. The sunlight in the valley gave the landscape an airiness I found difficult to capture, so I preferred the solidity and sense of per-manence of the rocks and bluffs at the edge of the valley and even up in the mountains farther away, where I could sit and paint a watercolour among the trees and the rock formations.

Slowly I regained my old sense of equilibrium as I studied the landscape before me. The time I spent painting was therapeutic in helping me come to terms with Mary's death and concentrate my thoughts upon just exactly what I hoped to do with my life. The more I examined my ideas the more I realized how untrue I'd been to myself in Ontario by neglecting my painting. I was still deter-mined to become a full-time painter.

My father asked his newspaper to help promote my art classes and the editor sent out a reporter and a photographer. In August the *Penticton Herald* printed a front-page photograph of me. The reporter lauded me as the key man behind a growing interest in art in the town and credited my students with some of the best paintings exhibited at the Peach Festival.

The art classes gained momentum. By the end of the summer, I had about thirty students who paid two dollars each and so I earned about sixty dollars per week. That enabled me to move out of my parents' house and rent an apartment. Because I wasn't paying a mortgage I fared better than when I'd been working eight-hour days in Brantford doing commercial illustration.

I met a Vancouver reporter who wrote another newspaper article on me. The *Vancouver Sun* ran "Youngsters 'See' the Wind and Paint It on Canvas" in October. In it, I argued that an art education could help children become better adjusted, even happier. I also made the somewhat exaggerated claim that Vancouver had become the new art centre of Canada and that Penticton was its satellite— more wishful thinking than reality on my part, especially when a drive I'd led in Penticton for a permanent art centre with a classroom produced no tangible results. And far from being a new centre for Canadian art, Vancouver had only one commercial gallery that dealt in contemporary Canadian artists. Without indoor painting facilities, my teaching turned out to be very seasonal work in Penticton. As the weather grew colder my students dropped out. By October my income had fallen off to nothing and a chill fell over my relations with my parents.

Although they'd been very supportive, I'd exhausted their patience. They wanted me to hurry up and find a permanent job and take Jennifer and Lynn off their hands. By turns they pressured me.

"When will you settle into a career, Toni?" asked my mother. "You have family responsibilities now. You've got to think of Jennifer and Lynn."

My father feared I'd turn into another Vincent Van Gogh and sponge off him for the rest of his life. "Next thing we know you'll be cutting off your ear," he grumbled.

At a party I cornered a local architect, Roy Meiklejohn, who had distinguished himself as the first man in BC to turn out a public school for only ten dollars per square foot. The baby boom was in full swing and thousands more children were attending school that fall. The provincial government had to construct schools at a breakneck pace just to keep up with the anticipated demand for the following year.

Meiklejohn adjusted the black tie on his crisply ironed white shirt. When I told him I'd studied architecture he offered me a job. "Toni, I have more than twenty schools on the drawing board. I'm working night and day. How would you like to come in a few evenings a week and take some of this work off my hands?"

The arrangement sounded ideal. It would leave me enough time to get out painting, yet keep me in funds for the winter. Come summer I could likely start up my classes again and quit the firm.

Things didn't work out that way. Meiklejohn grew even busier than before. He soon had five of us working full-time in the office. Even his wife Carol started coming in. The pay enabled me to buy a sleek white MG TD sports car to get out painting. Before I knew it, however, I was putting in five days a week plus overtime, and spending the weekends with my kids. This frantic schedule put me right back to where I had been in Cainsville, Ontario, with no time for painting.

Designing schools didn't turn out to be creative, either. The BC Ministry of Education had issued a blackbook of details specifying everything right down to the chalk rail. Small wonder that the new schools looked like medium-security prisons; nevertheless, Meiklejohn kept getting more work. In fact he had so much to do that he had to delegate some of the design work or he'd never have got it done.

I was assigned the working drawings for a four-room elementary school in Bralorne, a small gold-mining community in the Lillooet area north of Vancouver. Meiklejohn had visited the site himself, recorded the spot elevations, and taken some photographs, which he passed on to me. He did not consider it necessary for me to visit the site.

The school was going to be one of the most prominent buildings in Bralorne. Its appearance had been more or less fixed by the ministry. However, by special dispensation I could do what I wanted with the interior spaces. I eliminated the corridor to make the four rooms larger. Then I replaced the fixed walls between the classrooms with moveable partitions. I added a series of long laminated beams running to the exterior walls to support the roof. In this way

I created a multi-purpose community school. The teachers could turn the four rooms into one large open room for assemblies, performances or other activities. On weekends the entire school could be used by the community.

Unfortunately the "glulam" laminated beams had to come from Vancouver. The truck carrying them couldn't make it around the hairpin bends on the road into the mountains because the beams were too long. Every beam had to be sawn in half. After that, the only way to support them was to stick columns underneath them, spoiling the clear span I had intended. When Meiklejohn told me of the fiasco I refused to accept any blame. "How could I know about the road?" I asked. "You didn't let me visit the site!"

Just about the time of this setback at work I had a domestic crisis. For most of my first year in Penticton my parents had looked after Jennifer and Lynn. It had got to the point where the kids had started calling my mother "Mommy Fluffy" and my father "Daddy Jimmy." Understandably, my parents felt they'd done enough to help me get back on my feet. I took over their rented house on Vancouver Avenue and moved in with Jennifer and Lynn after my parents purchased a house in Summerland about ten miles away.

The kids were too young for school so I hired housekeepers. It proved impossible to keep any of them. We went through one woman after another. Just when I thought it would be impossible to find good help, I hired Mrs. Whitbread, a cheery white-haired grandmotherly type who looked like she'd stepped right off a Betty Crocker cake mix box. For the first time in months we had clean clothes, hot dinners and a tidy home.

Mrs. Whitbread was a grandmother several times over and she lived in an extended family with her divorced daughters and their fatherless children in a house off Main Street. One afternoon while she was at our house she noticed a motorcycle parked on the street. I don't know whether one of her ex-sons-in-law had been a biker or if she'd just seen Marlon Brando in *The Wild One*, but she flipped, seized my wood axe and attacked the bike.

The police were called. Just as they led her to their patrol car, I arrived home. When I was told what had happened I was stunned.

Mrs. Whitbread waved goodbye. "I'll be seeing you, sweetie! Supper's in the fridge."

Later I visited Mrs. Whitbread in jail.

"Don't worry, Toni," she smiled. "My daughter's just separated from her husband in Toronto and she's coming to Penticton. I'll see that she looks after you."

Her daughter arrived on the next flight. My jaw dropped as I watched a beautiful young woman disembark from the plane. She had flaming red hair and looked the spitting image of that Hollywood seductress, Maureen O'Hara. I took her to my house and walked her around the yard, explaining the housework and extolling the virtues of small-town life. My next-door neighbour Judge Washington was out trimming his hedge. He looked at me over his glasses and quipped, "I'll be seeing you in court."

On Saturday night Mrs. Whitbread's daughter asked for her first month's pay in advance. She then hurried off to an evangelical tent meeting. The next day she brought the preacher to the house. By the time I drove home from work on Monday she had run off with him to Washington State. That left me back where I'd started, trying to find help to look after Jennifer and Lynn while I went to work. Monday night I started making the telephone calls, again.

I felt I had to act quickly if I wanted to be a full-time painter. At the moment I was a part-time artist with a full-time job, a car and a life in Penticton that was, despite its difficulties, becoming too settled. I could see myself living there for the rest of my life.

I fired off applications and slides of my work to art schools all over North America. The Instituto Allende in the Mexican state of Guanajuato offered me a scholarship that covered my tuition fees for a year. Studying in Mexico was not as unusual as it might seem. The institute was one of several in Mexico accredited under the American GI Bill; it offered art courses in English. And following the revolution of 1910, Mexico had become a great centre for the visual arts. A breathtaking renaissance had occurred in Mexican art through the great historical mural painters like Diego Rivera and David Alfaro Siqueiros.

But I didn't want to go to Mexico because I was interested in its art or culture. Primarily I sought a place where I could live cheaply enough to paint full-time for a while. According to the information the school had sent me, I could stay in the town of San Miguel de

Allende, maintain a studio and spend all my time painting for a little over $1,000 per year.

At first I thought of taking both my children, but Jennifer, then six, had just started school and was learning to read. If I took her to Mexico, she would have to learn Spanish to continue her schooling and would not be ready for Grade 2 when we returned. My parents were living in Hollywood, where my father had found work, so I couldn't leave her with them. But since Carl had recently moved out to live with another woman, I asked Helen if she would take Jennifer for a year. She was delighted at the prospect of a long visit from her grandchild and quickly agreed.

However, I didn't have the $1,000. The only assets I had were about 250 watercolour paintings. Then I remembered the small town auctions Mary and I had attended in Ontario when we were furnishing our house. I hired the only auctioneer in town, Doug Smithson. On his advice I rented the recreation room in the basement of the Knights of Pythias Hall for a Friday night in early December, 1957. When I went to place an ad in the *Penticton Herald*, Grev Roland liked the story of my scholarship and the upcoming auction so much that instead of charging me for an ad he gave me a front-page story.

Shortly before the auction Doug Smithson looked around the room. I'd hung the paintings on the walls earlier that day, putting a white cardboard mat around each one to set it off from the lime-green walls and the floral drapes.

"There's an awful lot of paintings here, Toni. I don't know much about art. Tell me how you'd like me to do the auction."

"How do you handle cattle?" I asked.

"We auction off the whole pen," he replied. "The person with the highest bid takes the cow he wants. Everyone after him pays the same price for any other animal in the pen. The ones that are left over are re-auctioned."

"Then why don't you do the same here? Auction off each wall of paintings. The highest bidder gets the first choice."

The preview started about seven o'clock. About seventy or eighty *Herald* readers, bargain hunters, former art students and family friends squeezed into a basement room twenty by forty feet and examined my paintings. Half the show consisted of pieces from the

Isle of Man, including several I'd done at the Mersey docks in Liverpool. The others had all been painted in Ontario and Penticton. So many people crammed into the room that I left to make space.

When the crowd thinned a little I went back inside. Smithson introduced himself and the registrar who would collect the money from the successful bidders. Then he walked over to the first wall and explained the rules.

"Can we start at a dollar? A dollar." Smithson pointed at someone who'd raised her hand. "Do I hear two dollars?" Another hand shot up as people started bidding against one another for the particular painting each bidder had in mind. "Two dollars!" He cried. "We have two dollars—"

"Two-twenty-five!" Someone shouted.

"Do I hear two-fifty? Two-fifty per painting?" Smithson asked. "These paintings are going very cheaply, folks. The artist usually sells them for about fifty dollars apiece. Do I hear more?"

Smithson heard another bid and another. Finally, he banged down his gavel and sold the paintings on the first wall for five dollars apiece. Some still hung unsold. He moved to the next wall. The paintings went for about the same price, as did the ones on the third wall.

One woman brought her painting over to me with a complaint. "There's a tear in the corner!"

"That's easily repaired," I replied. "You just glue down the corner or you could place the mat over the edge of the picture. No one would ever know it had a tear."

"It's not fair," she whined.

"Look, you don't have to buy it." I directed her to the auctioneer who was finishing the bidding for the fourth wall. "Put it back on the wall and get another."

The bidding on the last wall had finished, so she exchanged it with one of the thirty or forty watercolours that remained unsold. These paintings, the auctioneer explained, were to be sold, too, and might go for a little less than the five dollars for paintings on the first round.

People at the auction must have been confused or a little excited, because the bidding went even higher for the leftover paintings. All the watercolours, including the one that had just been returned, sold for about ten dollars each. Soon everything in the show had been sold. The entire event had lasted less than an hour and some people left the room with armfuls of paintings.

I felt exhilarated. Although I'd received only a fraction of the usual price for each painting, I'd netted $1,350 and I'd never seen that much money in my life. More importantly, it would enable me to get to Mexico.

In mid-December I packed some clothes, children's toys and art supplies into a large steamer trunk, loaded it onto my MG and left for Mexico with Lynn, aged four. For better or for worse, I was no longer a weekend painter.

Chapter 9

La Tierra de la Mordida

I'd heard that dealing with Mexican officials required bribes. The little extra to grease the wheels was known as *la mordida*—the little bite. Indeed, Mexico proved to be *la tierra de la mordida*. To keep the border guard from ransacking our luggage I had to slip him two American dollars. *"Buenas dias, señor!"* Grinning, he stuffed the bills into his shirt pocket. I didn't get more than a hundred feet past the border before my MG stalled and I had to refill the tank. While I'd been filling out the customs declaration someone had siphoned my gas.

The stark bleached landscape of Mexico stretched ahead of us like a scorched canvas as I zigzagged the car past ghostly yucca plants and organ-pipe cactuses that erupted from the desert floor. Like any kid, half an hour into the drive to San Miguel Lynn asked, "Are we there yet?" In the heat, she eventually nodded off. The road bridged shallow muddy rivers, then jogged along cattle tracks into the burnt, blackened mountains. In one place in the Sierra Madre mountains, the road shrivelled to a gravel track with a toll rope strung across it and the local people charged us five pesos to continue driving on it. Lynn woke up and I tried to distract her to keep her from whining. We counted telephone poles together. However, she couldn't count very high. Then I started telling her that San Miguel was just over "the next big hill." I don't know how many times I told her that before she dozed off again.

Some ten to fourteen hours after we'd crossed the border, we passed Guanajuato City to where the road wound through range

country of scrub and cactus and abandoned haciendas. Descending
to an elevation of about 6,400 feet on a mountainside overlooking
the Lara River Valley, we saw rolling pasture land that proved, as we
drew closer, to be dry and stony. We turned down a road and entered
San Miguel de Allende, a colonial-era town, its architecture preserved under a 1926 law that forbade neon signs, traffic lights, even
fire hydrants. We clattered over a narrow cobblestone street and
passed a broad-domed baroque church. Dark women with berib-
boned black braids watched silently from the doorways and windows of their homes. Straw-hatted Mexicans in white cotton shirts
and trousers led a long line of burros with tinkling bells on their har-
nesses across the road. Lynn cried, "Donkeys, Daddy! Look at the little donkeys!"

I pulled into the *zocalo*, or main square, which had a Parisian-
style park, the Jardín, with trimmed laurel trees, wrought iron
benches and street lamps, and a wooden bandstand. On the east and
west sides of the Jardín were several palatial colonial residences that
had been converted to businesses. Under the vaulted arches of the
building on the eastern side was an arcade with watches and cheap
jewellery for sale and vendors offering flour, lard, cilantro and
oregano as well as barbecued chicken and tortillas. On the ground
floor of the building on the other side was the Bougainvillea restaurant, and a noisy cantina, La Cucaracha, was on the southwest corner. The most noticeable feature of the town square was the salmon-
coloured Gothic steeple of the Parroquia parish church. It rose above
the Jardín like the tower of a Disneyland castle.

Because Lynn and I were so hungry, I found us a table in the
Bougainvillea. Before I could stop her Lynn snatched a handful of
dried chilies from a bowl left on the table for seasoning. She stuffed
them into her mouth and started chewing them. A look of shock
passed over her face. She spat out the chilies and let out a piercing
wail. The other diners in the restaurant stared as Lynn screamed
louder. I forced her to drink a glass of water but it just made things
worse so I picked her up, still screaming, and carried her back to the
car. We drove around San Miguel until the effect of the chilies wore
off and we could return to the restaurant.

The letter from the Instituto Allende offering me the scholarship
had mentioned that I could stay at the Hotel San Miguel for about

$13 US a week, so we checked in there. The proprietor, Don Ramone, a pot-bellied bear of a man, couldn't have been friendlier. After the evening meal he invited me to join him for a glass of wine. He refilled my glass so often that I staggered back to our room, a difficult task because the Hotel San Miguel had no electricity. Finally I was led down the hall by someone carrying a burning torch. We gave up the hotel room after our first week. I was itching like crazy and Lynn's skin was raw from bites. The place was a flea pit!

It didn't take long to get an apartment. Of the 12,000 people living in San Miguel, only 200 were foreigners so I found out through the grapevine what apartments and housekeepers or *criadas* were available. Lynn and I moved into a small two-floor apartment with a tiled kitchen and a red-tiled roof on Santo Domingo hill above the town. My landlord was Padre Mercidio, a priest. It was illegal in Mexico for the clergy to own property, but no one was complaining. The entire month's rent was only about $13. For another two dollars a Mexican girl named Lupi kept an eye on Lynn and cooked our meals—tamales, corn soup and fruit salad. We particularly enjoyed the food after we'd built up a resistance to the local stomach bugs. For a few dollars more I enrolled Lynn in the Santo Domingo elementary school run by nuns across from our apartment. Our expenses that month came to less than $45.

At first I tried to be very selective about Lynn's food. Then she started learning Spanish and began playing in the streets with her school friends. My blond, freckle-faced Spanish-speaking daughter soon grew so popular in the neighbourhood that the Mexican women would fill her up with God knows what—unwashed fruit, unpasteurized milk, black beans, even wine! It proved impossible to enforce my precautions. After a while, when she came home I hardly dared ask what she'd eaten.

Lynn often slept in my bed at night, so I was terrified one morning when I found a scorpion on the sheets. I quickly flicked it onto the floor and crushed it under my heel. Then I found another scorpion on the bed the following morning. My neighbour, a writer named James Norman, told me that scorpions were almost as common as spiders in San Miguel. He once forgot to knock his shoes together and empty them before he put them on and a scorpion had stung him. Frantically he drove to the doctor to get an antihistamine shot. He never made it because he grew so dizzy he had to pull his car over. Luckily a friend passing by found him slumped over the steering wheel and drove him the rest of the way before it was too late. I reasoned that our scorpions were climbing up the legs of the bed so I filled four empty paint cans with kerosene and placed one under each leg. When I checked them later the cans were empty but I found another scorpion on the bed. Finally I found their nest high above the bed in the curtains of a piano window that levered open on a metal rod. Because the window was so high I'd never bothered to draw the curtains. I shook them and about two dozen scorpions dropped onto the bed.

San Miguel de Allende, Mexico, 1957.

On Sundays, as the twenty-eight different pealing church bells in town called the faithful to mass, I liked to take Lynn to the big Calle Mesones market. It was a jumble of stalls in heavy canvas tents and lean-tos with corrugated steel roofs where we could buy oranges and bananas for eight cents a dozen. I found it intoxicating to wander among the *rancheros* with their sunburnt leathery faces and handlebar moustaches and the broad-hipped Mexican women in embroidered blouses and billowing red cotton skirts, some with babies slung into the black *rebozos*, or shawls, on their backs, and then to hear a vendor call after me, or a beggar proffer blessings and a reward in the hereafter for a donation of a few centavos. Five- and six-year-old children sold pastries, three for a half-peso and as tasty as Christmas shortbread. Lynn always had to have some.

After Lynn started school, I attended art, Spanish, even Mexican history classes at the Instituto Allende. The school was housed in a faded eighteenth-century colonial mansion that had once been the summer palace of the Duke of Canal. Enclosed by a high wall of plastered brick, it stood on the outskirts of town on the Celya Road. Within it were administration offices, classrooms, studios and a gallery. Stone arcades led to the different wings of the mansion, and at the rear of the building were several patios. A carved stone fountain cooled the air in a garden of violet bougainvillea, white calla lilies, yellow irises and exotic purple orchids.

During my first week of classes, I sketched outdoors with an advanced landscape class, recording my impressions of the fields and buildings near the school. I tried to render the landscape with a free, supple line, then added texture by rubbing the crayon over areas of the drawing. An American tourist watching me told me how much he liked the sketch. "Seven bucks and it's yours," I said. Though a little surprised at the quick offer, he dug out his wallet and passed me the bills. I peeled the paper off my drawing board and gave it to him.

The other students watched a little enviously. The instructor, Kent Bowman, who later became a good friend, was a Clint Eastwood type, a tall, handsome ex-Navy SEAL who had married a Mexican woman and lived in San Miguel for seven years. "How did you pull that off, Toni?" he asked with a self-deprecating chuckle. "I've been trying to do that ever since I got here."

I laughed, "I don't think I even finished the picture before I sold it."

Jim Pinto, who had studied in California at the Schon Institute, was the chief painting instructor at the Instituto Allende. He had emigrated to America from eastern Europe in 1939. He was about fifty and had a kind of weathered Russian-steppes look to his lined square face and a tough wiry Charles Bronson-like build. It surprised me that someone as tough as he appeared to be was so completely browbeaten by his wife. I'd see Pinto in the Jardín, trailing Ruschka, a large hot-tempered Russian woman who marched ahead with a leashed brood of yelping dachshunds. "Tell me, Jim," I asked when I knew him a little better, "does Ruschka ever smile?" He rolled his eyes. "Only when I'm in pain."

Later, after Pinto helped me find a studio to rent in town, he told some of my friends, "You can stay at the instituto and take classes but what you really need is your own studio space." He kept shunting people over to the same building, then telling Ruschka, who worked at the institute as a secretary, that he was going over to check in on us. It was strange because I'd never see him for more than a few minutes on any of his visits. The mystery was soon solved. The door between two of the studios in another part of the building didn't close properly. I heard from my friend that upon investigating the noise from the next room, he saw our instructor in bed with the Mexican landlady, so I guess Pinto managed to out-manoeuvre Ruschka.

In class, Pinto was a fine teacher. He didn't have much to work with because of the amateur level of most of his students, but he inspired his classes because he loved painting so much. He'd survived in California, working for Disney along with Rico LeBrun, then come to San Miguel and enrolled at the institute. When the director, Stirling Dickinson, saw his work he asked him to teach there instead.

While Pinto explored semi-abstraction in his own paintings, he'd often try to work the class up to a state of excitement by initiating grand discussions on art inspired by nature versus abstract art that emphasized the two-dimensional picture plane. Though scarcely sure of my ground in abstract painting, I was outspoken in my opinions and could handle myself in an argument, so he often called on me.

One morning he placed one of his recent paintings on an easel at the front of the class. At first it appeared to be a series of squares and triangles. On closer examination it reminded me of the view of San Miguel from the hill on the road to Celaya and Guanajuato, the view I'd seen driving into town.

"This is an abstract piece, Toni," Pinto motioned to the painting. "But it comes from somewhere." He asked the class. "Does anyone recognize it? It's the view from El Mirador, the lookout above Moctezuma Hill."

"Abstract painting shouldn't represent anything," I countered. "It's just supposed to be itself."

Pinto took a few paces at the front of the room as if thinking something through. "No, I don't believe that. Every image comes from somewhere, from some place. Ultimately it all comes back to nature. What I do in abstract painting is exaggerate some elements of the landscape to create an effective composition." He turned to his painting again. "In this case, I'm interested in the general shape of a town in the mountains in Mexico."

"Maybe we shouldn't talk about your painting, Jim," I said. "What about 'automatic painting'? Or 'gestural painting'? The abstract artist just works in his studio. It has nothing to do with nature and everything to do with the nature of the artist. The ideas just flow from the associations he makes while painting his canvas."

Pinto had been one of the first artists to come to San Miguel after the war. That gave him respect in the local artistic community that would never be granted to a newcomer like me, so I felt pleased to be scoring a point against him. A few of my fellow students smiled and nodded their heads in agreement. They thought I'd cornered Pinto. "Let's talk about 'action painting' and the art of Franz Kline," I continued. "He paints entirely in black paint on big white canvases, just using black lines and shapes like huge fragments of Japanese calligraphy. You can't say he's painting from nature."

"But I can," insisted Pinto. "What about the fundamental aspects of nature such as energy, weight and gravity? The dynamics of motion, the interplay of light and darkness, all these are natural. Aren't these the concerns of abstract art?"

"But that's such a broad definition of nature!" I objected.

"It's still nature," he replied. Then he turned to the class as if summing up his argument. "I leave it to you to decide whether abstraction comes from nature or not. For me, there are no absolutes—only questions—which is exactly how it should be if an artist is truly to be a discoverer." He sat on a corner of one of the student's desks. Meditatively, he clasped his hands together. He lifted his arms and rested his chin on his hands. "The abstract expressionist movement is one of spontaneous personal expression—an improvisation free from perspective painting that has dominated Western art from the time of the Renaissance. I don't think abstract painting precludes responding to the landscape in an abstract way. I don't believe we should replace one dogma in art with another."

Despite the brave talk I had trouble coming to terms with abstraction myself. When I first arrived in San Miguel I painted watercolours. I also drew extensively in charcoal and Conté crayon. My first attempts at abstract painting were through gestural or action painting. Mostly I used acrylic paint because it dried more quickly than oils. That forced me to work quickly and think less. It all came down to the act of painting. As Kline said, "The artist paints blind." The abstract artist had to paint blind—blind in the sense that he worked without any preconceptions about what the painting would become. Yet at the same time he had to be able to move back from the work and look at it objectively as a composition. I was trying to introduce spontaneity and improvisation into my work. It proved very hard, however, to abandon the painting skills I'd spent so much time learning on the Isle of Man. I'd start with a line or shape, then respond to it with another line or shape but my sense of design kept taking over. Everything I painted formed into regular rounded shapes. Instead of painting freely I kept moving toward the same shapes.

At the same time, I tried to expand my palette by introducing new colours into my paintings. But the colours in Mexico seemed overwhelming, almost shrill to me. It started with the intensity of the colours in a Mexican market. The sun played on tall yellow stacks of bananas and splashes of orange on the cobblestones from crates of fruit dumped onto blankets and mats. Nut-brown Mexican women shelled green peas, braided cloves of white garlic and sold sap-green sticks of sugar cane. There were rush baskets with mounds of crimson chilies, leafy green corn ears, brown beans and fiery red

Mexico, 1958, with friend Rita Derju.

tomatoes. Then there were the whitewashed buildings in San Miguel, gleaming in the sunlight, and the starkness of the desert and the dusty range country surrounding the town. Even the sky overhead seemed too rich a blue compared to skies in British Columbia or the Isle of Man, where the sunlight was diffused and filtered through cloud and vapour. I had to learn to see things in an entirely new way if I were ever going to come to terms with the environment in which I was now living.

Unfortunately my classes at the Instituto didn't help much at all. The school had more or less been a post-war outgrowth of the GI Bill in America, when veterans with government tuition money swamped US colleges. A few universities in Mexico had been accredited, like Guanajuato and its affiliate, the Instituto Allende. The school offered bachelor's and master's degrees in fine arts, but if any graduates had presented these credentials anywhere they would have been laughed off the premises. Scholarship students like myself had just been seeded among the hobby painters, the amateurs I called "pale lady watercolourists," to give the program some credibility.

Some of us had taken to calling the institute "Menopause Manor" because so many rich middle-aged women studied there. They stayed in apartments and cottages on the school grounds. A handful of the richest of this "blue rinse set" lived in the "American colony" at the Atascadero Ranch outside of town. One of them had a husband with a shipping line. Another woman owned a family publishing business. The colony was a walled estate with tropical birds on the grounds. Sometimes you could see a beautiful Mexican girl with a guitar under a tree there, playing romantic Spanish songs.

Yet for all my reservations, living in San Miguel gave me the opportunity to spend my days painting. I'd never had that chance before. Sometimes when I started a new painting I'd feel as if I'd entered another world. Moments like that were pure transcendence, rare at first, then occurring more frequently as I learned how to get in touch with my creativity. It kept me painting.

Because I had enough money to live on and a housekeeper to look after Lynn and prepare our meals, I had a social life, too. I spent some evenings pursuing a children's book illustrator, a svelte beauty with long brown hair. Martha Bolling never walked—she floated. I just loved to watch her move in her long rustling skirt. "Are you listening to me, Toni?" she'd ask. "Toni, you haven't heard a single thing I've said." That much was true. When I did pay attention to what she told me, I got the impression that she lived in a different world.

One time she started complaining about her ex-husband, who had been in the air force. They had lived in Kodiak, Alaska, where he'd been stationed. When he heard he'd be transferred to New York the following summer, he started building his own airplane. Even during that early period of my life when I'd never flown in a small plane, the idea excited me tremendously. It was something I would have loved to do. I enjoyed a great deal of freedom as a painter living in San Miguel. But flying—that had to be the ultimate achievement. "An airplane!" I exclaimed. "His own airplane!—what kind of an airplane was it?"

Martha grew a little impatient. "That's not the point of the story, Toni. His airplane came between us in the end," she explained. "He spent all his time in our garage, building it. He never had time for me any more."

"No kidding. He actually built and flew his own airplane. That's something I'd love to do someday," I said. "Did he ever fly it?"

"I'm getting to that," she snapped. "He flew it to New York and I had to drive the car all the way from Alaska."

Her ex-husband took on mythic proportions for me then. I had to hear more about him; I even wanted to meet him. Martha was furious.

Between getting Lynn off to school in the morning, painting for most of the day, then seeing Martha in the evening, my hours seemed very full those early months in San Miguel. I'd always had a lot of energy, but as the weeks passed I grew weaker. By April I felt certain there was something wrong with me. Doctor Dobarganes at the local hospital couldn't find anything. That shouldn't have surprised me though; the Americans in town claimed that if you pooled all the medical knowledge in San Miguel you couldn't match a single country doctor back home.

Then one morning I didn't wake up at all. Terrified, Lynn called the maid, who looked in, then ran to tell my neighbour, an American woman who had been a nurse. She took one look at my jaundiced colour, then drove me to the hospital and had me admitted—against the objections of Dobarganes who was concerned that I might die there and scare off American patients.

The diagnosis came as a double blow: malaria and hepatitis. In the hospital, I dropped to about 105 pounds. The staff consigned me to a ward with patients dying from multiple diseases—hepatitis and tuberculosis, tuberculosis and malaria, or even hepatitis and dysentery, the most miserable way to go. Because the culture in Mexico was very fatalistic everyone at the hospital spoke of death as the will of God. A more lugubrious image came to my mind. A few weeks earlier I'd seen a tile-maker in his coffin. He was the father of Martha's *criada*, a man so fat the undertaker had great difficulty closing the coffin lid.

Luckily the head nurse at the hospital put me on a regimen of antibiotics and intravenous feeding. After a week I began to slowly regain my strength. I recall Lucha, a sexy dark-eyed nurse, very well-endowed, who checked my pulse. Noting my swiftly beating heart, she giggled, *"Bueno, rapido! Rapido!"* Back in the world of the living, I thought. Maybe I should have myself neutered while I'm here so I can get more painting done.

After that, Dobarganes, who had been more or less out of the picture, dropped in on me occasionally. His favourite remark in English was, "I want from you, today—a stool!"

Soon I could stagger up and down the halls. Seeing I was recovering and a little bored, the head nurse suggested that I might like to watch an operation on a Mexican boy. I found it to be the bloodiest thing I'd ever seen and I almost fainted halfway through. The head nurse was worried that I might suffer a relapse but within days I was well enough to leave. The hospital must have only made money whenever a foreigner fell ill because as soon as I paid my bill for the treatment and ten days' stay, about 500 pesos or forty dollars, one of the nurses rushed out and bought some medical supplies.

Back at the institute, I learned that Kent Bowman had gone over the wall of the municipal cemetery, and among the crumbling tombstones and caved-in graves had found a perfectly bleached white skull. He'd brought it back to draw it. Perhaps a little haunted by my scrape with death and my protracted stay at the hospital, I drew that skull for a while myself. My interest in the subject also resulted from my reading of philosophy—there's nothing like the loss of a loved one, poverty and the study of Nietzsche to evoke a sense of the tragic. I had rejected Catholicism after spending my boyhood in a Catholic school, so I had been poring over books on existential philosophy that I'd borrowed from friends. Everybody in my circle was talking about Jean-Paul Sartre's *Nausea* and *Being and Nothingness* and even Zen Buddhism, and I struggled through those books as well, trying to fill in the gaps in my education. Reading such books strengthened my resolve to become a painter; art seemed the only purposeful act in a meaningless world of pain and suffering.

One afternoon I drove a few miles out of San Miguel to find the potter's field in the mountains. Corpses were left there because their families could not afford the price of a coffin and burial in the municipal cemetery. The buzzards circling overhead pinpointed the place for me. I found it beyond a ridge in a natural hollow in the earth. After I parked my car, I ran from one skeleton to another, picking up, then discarding the bones. The initial excitement passed as I realized the field contained bones of all sizes. I looked more carefully for a subject. The buzzards began swooping at me and I threw rocks to scare them off. Then I discovered a pair of skeletons entwined in an embrace: a broad-shouldered male and a shorter female recognizable by its wider pelvis. The female skeleton was missing its skull, which made my discovery appear all the more strange and pathetic. Could this be a suicide pact or a double murder? Or was it just the wind tossing the skeletons around? I strung the bones together, put them on the seat of my car and drove back to the institute.

Much to the horror of the "pale lady watercolourists," I hung them on the wall of the studio. A lady friend of mine observed, "You could at least have found a woman's skeleton with a head, Toni."

In retrospect, taking the skeletons seems a bizarre, macabre thing for me to do. But I think I may also have looked at them as a sort of memento mori, a reminder that life was short. If I wanted to be a serious artist there was no time to waste. I had lost nearly a month of painting time while in the hospital and then recovering, and I'd spent at least a month's supply of cash on the costs.

I decided to organize a show for May to replenish my funds. Jose Torres, the owner of the Vista Hermosa Taboada Hotel, gave me permission to hang the paintings in his patio. I framed ten paintings, put aside a lot more for sale, had about 300 invitations printed, hired some mariachi players and ordered cocktails. Very soon, I'd run up some substantial debts—I had to sell the work.

Two weeks before the show, I left Martha's apartment about two o'clock in the morning and found a barefoot, mangy-looking cop sitting on the hood of my MG in what looked like half a uniform: a khaki shirt and a battered peaked cap with a badge. *"Buenas noches!* He hopped off the hood of my car. *"Estaba vigilando su coche."*

I nodded, thanked him, then climbed into the sports car. He leaned over the driver's side of the car and rubbed his thumb and forefinger in my face. He expected a tip. I shook my head. I'd never asked him to guard the car and protecting property was supposed to be his job anyway.

"Do you mind clearing off?" I told him.

When he ignored me, I revved the engine and pulled out from my parking spot. He sprang aside and shook his fist at me.

A few days later I found my tires slashed. I had to order new tires in Celaya, then pick them up in a friend's car. My cash reserves dwindled even further.

The next time I drove downtown I saw the same cop I'd found at my car that night. He was directing traffic on the south side of the Jardín. He stopped the other cars so I could make a turn and then hailed me: *"Veo que compraste nuevas llantas?"*

Angrily, I raced around the block and pulled into the police station behind the *Presidencia* or Municipal Hall. A few unshaved, scruffy policemen with shotguns in their arms stood on duty outside the front door. After I demanded to see *el jefe de la policia*, one of the men disappeared inside. I wondered if I'd made a terrible mistake.

The police in San Miguel de Allende were a law unto themselves. Earlier, some Mexican boys from Queretaro had come to town. In the Jardín, one of them had tried to pick up an American woman who had discouraged him, even slapped him, but failed to drive him away until she complained to a local cop. There was some pushing and shoving and the kids finally took off in their car.

The cop flagged down some other policemen in a passing jeep and they chased the car up Santo Domingo hill and shot out one of the tires. Terrified, the kids kept on driving up that steep hill on the flat until the tire shredded right off the wheel and their car lurched to a stop. When the cops came to the car, the traffic cop found the boy who had started the trouble and shot him in the head. He told the others. "Take your buddy back to Queretaro. We don't want your kind here." The story of that murderous encounter had come back to San Miguel from Queretaro and everyone in town knew about it.

The policeman returned and led me to Captain Zavalla. Like a South American dictator, he wore a pair of sunglasses and a dark green uniform with gold braid on the shoulders. The scent of his heavy cologne filled the room. He motioned to a chair in front of his desk. *"Sientese, señor."*

I told him about the policeman and my slashed tires.

Zavalla leaned back in his chair and smiled. *"Tienes un problema. Cuanto dinero tienes?"*

"Look, I don't have any money." I replied. "I'm just a poor starving artist."

The captain feigned a bored expression and shrugged, *"No es mi problema,"* and pointed to the door.

I had to think quickly before he had me thrown out. I realized I had said all the wrong things. In a country that ran on bribes, like

Mexico, the greatest crime was poverty. I had to come up with some cash for Captain Zavalla. I suddenly remembered that as a tourist I was about to do something illegal by selling some paintings, and realized I might be able to turn that to my advantage.

"I don't have any money now," I remarked, "but I'm having a show at the Vista Hermosa Taboada Hotel. I'll give you a ten percent commission on everything that I sell that night. *Seria un placer para mi si usted esté mi patrocinador por favor.*"

"*Perdone?*" He sat up in his chair. "*Puede usted repetir, por favor.*"

I repeated the offer. "I would be honoured if you would be my patron for this art show."

We shook hands on the deal. Shortly afterward, word went out to the policemen on the street. The harassment stopped and I also didn't have to worry any more about my illegal art sales.

When the show opened, I looked for him. A trio of musicians wandered among the guests. The guitarist strummed and the two other men shook their maracas as they sang and tapped out a rhythm with their metal-capped shoes. The captain entered wearing a formal black cap and white gloves. He swept into the room and gallantly kissed the women's hands. Then he circulated among the guests, most of them American tourists.

I sold out the show that evening and paid Captain Zavalla his ten percent. The next morning I met an American woman in the street. She told me she had been pressured by the captain into buying one of my paintings. He asked to see her tourist visa and told her it was unfortunately not in order. If she bought a painting, however, he would overlook it. Because my prices were very low and she did not want to risk being deported, she did buy one, as did several other guests under the same pressure.

I was appalled. I had not foreseen this happening, although I realized that I might have expected the captain to inflate his bribe in whatever way he could. I decided to visit the coast and live on the beach for a while until things cooled down for me in the foreign community.

Later I joked to fellow artists that Zavalla was my first art dealer. He was crooked but he had no pretense about being anything else. That is more than one can say for some Canadian art dealers.

Chapter 10

The New Design Gallery

O ne summer afternoon in 1958 I had lunch with Bob Murray at the El Patio restaurant, an outdoor café off the Jardín on the ground floor of the Vista Taboada Hotel. We'd both dropped out of the classes at the Instituto Allende and rented studios in an old building on Calle San Francisco, a few blocks away. As we sat at a table with our beer and a plate of tortillas, beans, enchiladas and rice, I told him I was running out of money.

"Toni, if you've got cash problems," he said, "why don't you apply for a grant of some kind?"

Although mornings in June were cool enough to work until noon in San Miguel, now the sun was blazing hot. My back prickled with the heat as I picked at the rice on my plate and thought about what Bob had suggested. "The only grant I can think of is a Canada Council grant and I already got turned down three times on that one."

Bob drained his glass of beer and wiped his mouth on the back of his hand. At twenty-three, he was a tall, lean prairie boy from the Regina Fine Arts College. He'd arrived in San Miguel recently with a little cash and a copy of D.H. Lawrence's Mexican novel *The Plumed Serpent*. Now he shook his head in silent sympathy. Many artists here were in the same predicament. Although it cost very little to live in Mexico, obtaining that little was often a huge problem.

Bob and I, along with Kent Bowman, whom I knew from the Instituto, Kent's friend Jack Wise, an artist I'll call Adrian Smith and a few other painters in San Miguel, used to meet regularly in each other's studios. We traded issues of *Art News* and *Art Digest* looking for reproductions of paintings from the New York art scene. We were especially interested in works by abstract expressionists, including the late Jackson Pollock, whom critic Clement Greenberg once described as "tossing paint like a cowboy throwing a lasso." One of Pollock's paintings, *Autumn Rhythm, No. 30*, reminded me of a Canadian fall, with its tracery of paint spatters evoking whirling red and gold leaves.

Inspired by Pollock's drip paintings, a young artist in our group dripped and splattered paint onto a colossal canvas. The result never satisfied him so he kept flinging on more paint. We kept coming around to discuss his painting until it grew so heavy with paint that no one could lift it. When he finally announced it was finished, he said, "Now comes the hardest part, I have to think of a title for it."

"That's the easiest thing in the world," I observed. "There's more Winsor and Newton paint on it than anything else. Call it *Winsor and Newton.*"

One of my fellow artists, Jack Wise, was an intense, mystical character with a full red beard. He'd studied at universities in New Orleans, Washington and Florida, then run off to San Miguel, both to paint and to live out a Wild West fantasy of riding a horse into the hills and packing a six-gun. He claimed he wanted to be an artist even when he was a kid on his parents' farm in Wyoming and the only Art he knew was the farmer in the next quarter section. Jack argued this proved the transmigration of souls. "Where did Mozart come from? Where do people come from who have no choice and very early know what they want to do with their life."

I remember Jack was doing collage—the art of the random discovery of spatial relationships. Collage had come into its own in abstract expressionism with the work of Conrad Macarelli, who'd start a canvas with gobby lines of black paint, then stick different shapes onto it, squirting the paint in all directions and tracking his fingerprints across the work. For his collages Jack varnished charred pieces of paper onto pasteboard with Duco, a cheap lacquer found almost everywhere in San Miguel. He was fascinated by the visual paradox of creation and destruction, and out of that fascination came these beautiful burnt-paper collages. I've never seen anything like them.

Adrian Smith had been in advertising in New York. He drew

pointy designs on pieces of metal, then enamelled them. They glittered like junk jewellery.

Adrian and his wife Betty were gourmets who hosted elaborate dinners for us. They reminded me of the nursery rhyme couple, Jack Sprat and his wife. Betty had pudgy arms and wide hips; Adrian was thin as a cigarette, a leaner version of David Niven, with a pencil-thin moustache and a long nose.

Our group of artists went to Mexico City for the day for the opening of a United Nations Exhibition of Painting and Plastic Arts, and that evening we had a few drinks at a nearby cantina that turned out to be a hookers' bar. Adrian was puffing away on a cigarette when he was approached by one of the women. He followed her to a room upstairs. Shortly thereafter he returned to the bar looking angry.

"What's the matter, Adrian?" I asked him. "Wasn't it any good for you?"

He snorted, "She wouldn't take American Express."

The worst thing Adrian did was to kick out his wife. When Betty went on a trip back to the US, he started having an affair with their *criada*, a good-looking woman who was their gourmet cook. Returning unexpectedly, Betty caught him in bed with her. "Either she goes, or I go, Adrian! I mean it!" Within an hour, Betty was out on the street with her bags, where Bob Murray and I found her crying and heard her sad story.

Adrian's affairs raised eyebrows, but no one said anything because we met only to make constructive comments on one another's art. If anybody started making personal attacks, someone would jump on him for ignoring the ground rules.

The group sessions in my studio were extremely helpful because through them I recognized I had to change the way I painted. None of my abstract paintings captured the spontaneity and sense of freedom I was after. I realized that although I had abandoned imagery my style was still heavily influenced by my early training as a watercolourist on the Isle of Man. I failed to convey any sense of tension between the shapes in my paintings. My paintings were large, decorative and symmetrical, filled with honeycomb shapes.

Bob pointed to one of my paintings. The too-obvious pattern looked like the rosette in a stained glass window. "You've got to break free, Toni," he said. "You're in a loop here."

One afternoon I became so frustrated with my efforts that I tore a painting on paper into pieces. Then I ripped apart another. Months of work lay in pieces on the floor. One painting after another I destroyed.

Then it hit me—something in the way a few scraps of paper lay on the floor. I walked around the room, studying them from different angles. I tacked up a large sheet of white paper, picked up a few pieces and tacked them onto the paper, and then stepped back to get a better look. The pieces of paper formed asymmetrical patterns and I could move them around to increase the tension between the shapes. With growing excitement I found several more pieces that worked together and tacked them up as well. Further relationships developed. I moved the pieces around into a strong contrapuntal relationship. I went from there, finding new pieces to collage against the ones I had just put up. In less than an hour I had assembled an energetic and even powerful abstract piece that I would have given my right arm to paint earlier. Through collage I'd found a powerful tool for creating a whole new vocabulary of shapes and relationships. I could paint, tear up the paper, then collage the pieces into a fresh painting.

As the summer passed, my funds shrank. I couldn't believe the bad timing. After fumbling for months I had finally produced a work that was solid and personal. Every painting seemed to count now because each one was a progression from the last. I had found my direction and I realized that the further I pursued it, the more solid and personal it would become, so that eventually I wouldn't be associated with any other painter or school. But right after this breakthrough it looked as if I was going to run out of money and have to return to Canada and find a job. To prevent this from happening I tried to find new ways of selling my work.

In July, when I had to renew my tourist visa at the Mexican border, I took a side-trip with a girlfriend to San Antonio, Texas. We visited, with no luck, what seemed like every collector in town, but I arranged for a December show at the city's Witty Museum and shipped seventeen paintings to Coste House in Calgary for a winter show there. We also met members of the San Antonio String Quartet who were planning a Mexican tour and persuaded them to include San Miguel.

Braving the traffic and the smog, I then drove to Mexico City where I convinced the owner of Decorama, an interior design gallery, to take some of my paintings on consignment. Playing up my British origins, I arranged an exhibition of ten collages at the Anglo-Mexican Institute for September, and then got the Canadian cultural attaché to agree to pay for the opening night cocktails and string quartet. However, no sales came my way while I was there, and it was nerve-wracking to drive in Mexico City where there were no stop signs and I had to bluff my way like a bull fighter.

In late September the Canadian ambassador, Lionel V.J. Roy, who had contacts at the Instituto Allende, organized a gala reception and exhibition for the five Canadian artists, including me, who held the 1958 Instituto scholarships. On the day of the opening the ambassador called us into the exhibition room. "Now, people—people, I want you to listen to this!" He clapped his hands. "I want you to hang all the big paintings at the bottom of the wall and put the smaller ones above them, getting smaller and smaller as the eye travels up the wall." He outlined a pyramid shape with his hands and arms to emphasize what he meant.

I shook my head. "I've never heard of a show hung like that in my life."

"Of course, you haven't!" the ambassador replied. "Nobody has ever done it before."

I groaned. "There's a reason for that—"

"I want the show hung in pyramids!" insisted the ambassador. And he stayed in the gallery to make sure we did just that.

As soon as he left, I turned to the other students: "Quick, let's hang the paintings properly before the show opens."

We finished rehanging our work just as the first limousine pulled up to the embassy. The Spanish ambassador and his wife entered, he in formal black evening dress with tails and she in a floor-length yellow gown with long white gloves. The British, Italian and Indian ambassadors arrived. Mexican dignitaries came too, like the finance minister who wore a crimson sash across his dazzling white shirt. I saw one of Mexico's top military men, General Ignacio Beteta. A short man as broad-shouldered as a fullback, he was known as the "Painting General" because he had studied art in San Miguel.

When the ambassador saw that we had rehung the show, he was shocked. But he carried on diplomatically making small talk with the guests and giving every appearance of enjoying the evening. He avoided me, no doubt suspecting that I was the one who had countermanded his order.

He scarcely spoke to me after the show, though I gave him one of my paintings. He must have liked it because later I heard that he had hung it in the ambassador's residence. A few years later he took up art himself, moving to Paris for his retirement. I saw him there in 1963 at an embassy function and he was friendly to me, evidently not one to bear a grudge. The last I heard of him, he had drowned in a punting accident.

Although the embassy show had been a wonderful event I hadn't sold a single painting through it. No one else had, either; in my case, however, the situation had turned critical. By late October 1958, I was reduced to 2,000 pesos, about $160 at the time. I was completely beside myself. In desperation I held an open house at my studio. I'd sent home dozens of Mexican watercolours for my father to flog in the Okanagan. Now I mailed others to him. I heard back from Penticton that some of my work went up in

My daughter Lynn with her friend Mike, Mexico, 1958.

Hugo Redivo's camera shop. Other paintings went to friends like Ethel Joslin in the Penticton Unitarian Church, who bought my work and sent money to help me stay in Mexico.

Most of my friends in San Miguel faced a similar problem so they were all sympathetic. None of us had much money. Jack and Kent plied the tourist trade by selling souvenirs. They created batiks of jaguars and Mayan pyramid motifs. Jack felt ashamed that he had sold out so he signed the fabrics "Vacci"—a bit like leaving "the mark of Zorro" because it didn't fool anyone in San Miguel. It was easy to tell when Jack and Kent were dying batiks in the fountain in Jack's courtyard. His house was on Chiquitos, only a few blocks from the Jardín, and his Mexican hairless dog was always drinking from the fountain and running about the square, its skin dyed in the day's colour.

Jack grew so frustrated that when he visited Kent and his wife one night, he drew the six-shooter he often carried and shot a batik hanging in their home. Another night he went drinking and driving. He drove toward an unlit railway crossing on a curve in the road about two miles from town. The last thing he noticed was a strange blur and then his car drove into the side of a freight train. The impact threw him out of the car with a fractured skull. For five days he lay in a coma and the doctor said he could do nothing. It was cold at night during the winter so his wife and some friends filled empty milk bottles with hot water, packed them around Jack and gently massaged him and talked to him until he finally regained consciousness, much to the doctor's surprise.

Jack had damaged a train. This was a federal offence in Mexico and he had to pay a very large fine. He didn't have the money so I had to go to his bedside and get him to sign over his car to the police chief. The vehicle had been all smashed up and dragged forty or fifty feet down the tracks. Jack shrugged. "He can have it." A few weeks later, to his amazement, he saw the car on the road again. The police chief's brother-in-law was driving it. He'd started a new taxi service.

While Jack, Kent and I struggled to make a living, there was an artist in San Miguel who did live off the sale of his art. He was a smartly dressed Spanish-speaking Filipino named "Romeo" Tabuena, who latched onto every beauty who came to town. We'd watch them eating in the best restaurants. He even charmed the famous British actress, Merle Oberon, and she left with a suitcase packed with his paintings. The odd thing was that Romeo Tabuena only painted water buffalo, and the only ones extant in Mexico were in his paintings. Jack Wise joked: "Did you hear? Tabuena has changed his style. Now the water buffalo in his paintings are walking from left to right."

The laughter helped us through this difficult time. It also made me realize just how much I was going to miss San Miguel. I'd done more painting in Mexico than at any other point in my life. Still, I hadn't had enough time. A lot of precious painting time had been used up by settling in, then by my long illness.

Jim Pinto came over to my studio. "I heard through the grapevine that you were short of cash, Toni," he told me. "You really stirred things up in class. We could use someone like you at the *instituto*."

However flattering the offer, the pay for teaching a painting class was only about 400 pesos per month or thirty-five dollars. That was not going to support me in San Miguel. Besides, I hadn't come to Mexico to teach. I didn't want to be sidetracked into a hand-to-mouth existence in San Miguel.

One night at an opening, I'd heard Kent bragging to Pinto about his next painting. Kent was a superb colourist whose patron saint was Pierre Bonnard. Hanging in his house was an incredible grass-green canvas shot through with yellow-green and blue-green in light-drenched layers of paint that shimmered like a swatch of jade green silk. Kent left Pinto in a sweat over his description of the colours he planned to use in his next painting.

The next day Pinto arrived at the gallery with a canvas so fresh the paint was still wet. Kent went white when he saw it. The painting was just like the one he had described. Kent told me that when he explained what had happened to his wife Cassie she exploded: *"Ni hablar! Ni digas nada. Siempre me cuentas lo mismo."* Apparently, this kind of thing had happened before. She cried, "Don' tell me Pinto come back with your painting again! Kent, when you gonna learn. Don' give 'way your ideas." Kent tried to laugh it off to me. "It's all right, I have lots of other ideas."

I was too busy to spare much sympathy for Kent. I dropped out of the social scene in town and retreated to my studio. I was always up early to see Lynn off to school, so I had already put in a few hours by the time most of the other painters in town were just rolling out of bed. Now I put in ten-, twelve-, even fourteen-hour days, painting from dawn to dusk.

By November I had so little cash left that I could either stay one more month in San Miguel or gamble the money on a trip to Vancouver to sell some paintings and finance a few more months, perhaps another year, in Mexico. I loaded up a car trailer with about 200 paintings. Then Lynn and I left for Canada. It was a seven-day drive and we crossed the Canadian border at night because my licence plates had expired. My parents had returned from Hollywood to Summerland, so after a brief visit I left Lynn with them and headed back to Vancouver.

It was a miserable Sunday afternoon, overcast with the steady, drizzling rain typical of Vancouver at that time of year. I ducked into a telephone booth and thumbed through the directory to find the number of the one place in town that handled contemporary Canadian art, the New Design Gallery.

When I reached Alvin Balkind he was very abrupt. "Sorry, I can't see you now, I'm hanging a show. Besides, we can't take on any more artists. We've got all the people we can handle."

"Would you mind just giving me an opinion, then?" I asked. "Just your professional opinion of my work."

"Maybe some other time," he replied politely, and hung up.

I had nothing to lose so I drove to the gallery. It was in a modest brick building a block north of the Vancouver Art Gallery on West Pender Street. I knocked on the front door. Alvin peered through the window.

"I'll just show you one of my paintings, that's all," I said. "I'll hold it up to the window. You won't even have to open the door. All you have to do is shake your head, then I'll go away and won't bother you again."

I rushed to the trailer and untied the tarpaulin over the paintings. I pulled out one of the thirty unmounted paper collages I had brought from Mexico and carried it to the window. I think it was *Collage No. 7*, one of the first I'd created, a powerful three-foot by four-foot piece in which I'd telescoped a series of rectangular shapes painted in warm Mexican oranges and reds along a vertical axis made with thick lines of black paint.

Curious, Alvin opened the door slightly. "How many of these have you got?"

The rain had slicked my hair against my forehead. My jacket was wet and I stood in front of the door, dripping. "I've got a trailer full."

Alvin swung the door open. "The paintings are going to get wet—let's get them inside." He wedged open the door, then we hurried to the trailer. We carried the collages inside and Alvin spread them out in the gallery. He really liked them. No one in Vancouver was doing anything like this. Unfortunately, he had already committed the gallery to a full year of exhibitions. He couldn't offer me a show until a year from January.

When I told him that I was going to have to leave San Miguel unless I sold some of my work, he telephoned the young director of the Vancouver Art Gallery and asked him to come over and take a look. The two galleries were so close together that Bob Hume walked out the back door of the Vancouver Art Gallery, crossed a parking lot, and appeared at the New Design Gallery a few minutes later. Hume walked up and down the room looking at my collages intently. Finally he remarked, "I want to give you a show at the Vancouver Art Gallery, Toni."

"That sounds great," I replied, trying to conceal my disappointment. I was excited about the opportunity, of course, but I'd hoped to sell him something immediately—anything to keep me going. "When are you thinking of for the show?" I knew that art museums planned their exhibitions far ahead of time, so I expected an offer of one too far in the future to affect my present condition.

Hume chuckled. "How about next weekend?"

My jaw dropped. "You mean Saturday?"

"Actually, we need it by Thursday because we have to hang it." Hume smiled happily. "To tell the truth, Toni, you're manna from heaven. I just told Alvin the other day that I had a cancellation and I was going to have to put up work from the permanent collection. So you've got yourself a show, if you can get this work framed and down to the gallery by Thursday."

I quickly agreed to the conditions, then drove back to my parents' house in Summerland and told them the good news. Because Dad knew how to do carpentry he offered to help me frame the art. He built the supports for the hardwood panels on which I mounted the collages, then stood by to cut the edging strips that would provide the effect of simple frames.

When I passed him the first one to add the framing he stared at it in bewilderment. He turned the painting to the right, then left. He squinted at it. "Toni, I'm not going to ask what it is. I know the kind of smart answer I'll get."

I laughed.

"All right, Toni, I give up," he said. "I'm asking, 'What is it?'"

I passed him the measuring tape. "If you've got to ask, Dad, you'll never know." Those were the famous words of Louis Armstrong when asked by a lady to explain jazz.

He silently framed the work, then held it up for inspection. "Anyway, this one's number one—whatever you want to call it."

We mounted and framed the works in three days and then I drove them to Vancouver. The thirty paper collages filled the entire south wing of the gallery, and the show opened to great critical success. The gallery even bought one of my collages for $250, the most I'd ever been paid for a single work. I left some of the collages with Alvin Balkind, who promised to try to find some buyers.

My landscape paintings were now in Penticton, where the previous year I had raised the money to go to San Miguel. I hired the same cattle auctioneer and rented the Legion Hall. I drummed up some publicity for the sale in the *Penticton Herald* as the artist who had just successfully exhibited in the Vancouver Art Gallery. Then I thought of another angle. The premier of British Columbia was in town to address a dinner given by the local Board of Trade. I called him at his hotel to suggest that the publicity of appearing as a patron of the arts would definitely enhance his image in this art-conscious town.

A photographer from the *Penticton Herald* met me at the hall. W.A.C. Bennett, a stout pear-shaped man in a dark suit with a white shirt and narrow tie, pushed open the door to the hall. He shook my hand then steered me toward the paintings. "Now, c'mon, Toni, tell me what they're all about." Then he turned his broad face with double chin toward the photographer and gave his famous big toothy grin. The flash went off. "Got your picture, lad? Okay, I'm on my way." He thumped me on the back and bolted out.

Despite the publicity in Penticton, I sold only ninety of the 150 Mexican landscapes I had done. People came to the Legion Hall expecting picturesque Mexican ruins and baroque Catholic churches. My semi-abstract landscapes were a surprise, but still they sold well at a price of five to ten dollars each.

At the end of the night I counted my earnings. I was a bit disappointed not to have sold out the show, especially at my rock bottom prices. However, with my sale to the Vancouver Art Gallery as well as the auction, I'd earned enough money for at least five or six months in San Miguel, enough to continue working on my collages. In December I drove back to Mexico with Lynn.

Chapter 11

La Cucaracha

After I returned to Mexico in December of 1958, my new Vancouver art dealer Alvin Balkind began selling my collages for $250 apiece to a few public galleries and wealthy clients. I even bought my friends in San Miguel de Allende a few rounds at the expatriates' bar, La Cucaracha. We often met there and anyone new to town put in an appearance there, so it was easy to have a social life just by dropping in—

> *La cucaracha, la cucaracha*
> *Ya no puede caminar*
> *Porque no tiene, porque le falta*
> *marijuana que fumar*

Que sorpresa!—Surprise!—the jack-in-the-box tune of La Cucaracha often ran through my head:

> The cockroach, the cockroach
> It can't walk any more
> Because it doesn't have, because it lacks
> Marijuana to smoke.

Although the substance abuse of choice was alcohol, marijuana was also widely used. A little old lady had a pot stand among the fruits and vegetables at the Hidalgo market. Joints circulated at most parties and if anyone had ever piped up, "This is illegal!" he would have been laughed out of the place.

But the drinking in town was something else entirely. A whole section of the San Miguel municipal cemetery was filled with World War II veterans who had drunk themselves to death on the cheap Cuba Libras at La Cucaracha.

One night, a ranchero with a wagon-wheel-sized brown sombrero and a black Pancho Villa moustache entered the bar and took the place beside me. I nodded a restrained greeting. I'd dealt with rancheros before. Once an American woman vacationing in San Miguel had been entertaining me in her hotel room. Suddenly her ranchero boyfriend pounded on the door with his pistol butt and roared, *"Abre la puerta! Quien esta allí!"* "It's Pedro!" the woman whispered in terror. Pedro bred bulls on his property. I stumbled into my undershorts, grabbed the rest of my clothes and desperately squeezed through the narrow window in the bathroom, dropping into the courtyard of a Mexican family who were eating their dinner. They stared in astonishment as I apologetically yanked on my trousers, mumbled *"Buenas noches,"* and then sprinted to my car.

The ranchero at La Cucaracha had a bandolier of bullets slung over his shoulder and a six-shooter in his leather belt. He ordered two shots of tequila. Tiny, the 300-pound bartender, waddled over to the counter with two glasses. The ranchero seized one in his fist and slid the other across to me. *"Oye, amigo, tomate un trago conmigo."*

Smiling, I tried to decline the drink. "It's kind of you to ask, but I've been here all evening. I'd better go home now."

The man pulled the gun from his belt and slapped it down on the counter. It was a rusty Colt pistol, so ancient and dangerous-looking that I thought it might go off as it lay there. The ranchero downed his tequila. *"Acabate esa copa. Tenemos que irnos."* He demanded that I drink up.

Eyeing the gun, Tiny hissed, "Do it! The man is crazy."

"Bueno, muchas gracias," I replied to the ranchero. Then I gulped the drink. We drank another round of tequilas. Then another, and I swayed as I drank the third toast. On the fourth round I crumpled to the floor. The next morning I woke up in bed. One of my friends had driven me home. Tiny told me later that when I collapsed everybody in the bar laughed, and that had made the ranchero's night.

The rumour among my friends back in BC was that I'd decided to become a permanent expatriate in San Miguel. It was true. The following February, in 1959, Helen Burrows brought Jennifer down. Now that the three of us were reunited, I was determined to stay in San Miguel de Allende. I knew that if I returned to Canada, the expenses of keeping my family would increase a thousandfold. Only in Mexico could I afford to keep a housekeeper, send Jennifer and Lynn to school and spend my days painting.

At the time I couldn't imagine a much better life than the one in San Miguel. I tried to work blind—blind in the sense that I approached my collages without any preconceptions about the finished piece. I painted without a conscious plan, then tore up the paper and placed the resulting shapes on new paper, linking them with new brush work. In *Collage No. 2*, I placed a series of squared shapes at the intersecting lines of an imaginary triangle. With *Collage No. 7*, I'd turned the shapes along north-south and east-west axes. Strong reds and blues and greens pulled the areas together.

Initially I'd been numbering my collages like musical compositions, avoiding names because I was working in a non-representational mode. Then I realized that most viewers preferred names to numbers if only because they were easier to remember, so I finally started naming my collages after places near my studio. I called one of them *Hidalgo* for the market not far from Calle San Francisco.

The act of painting had the effect of a drug on me. I lost all track of time. I soared through another plane of existence—the world of the spirit. These moments were rare at first but more frequent the longer I stayed in San Miguel. Whenever anyone asked me why I painted, that was the only reason I could give—that I loved doing it.

Circumstances were to change. By the end of 1959, my parents hadn't seen their grandchildren for nearly a year, and so they came down to visit at Christmas, the biggest *fiesta* in Mexico. Reluctantly, then with growing enthusiasm, I showed them around San Miguel. These were the *posadas*, nine days when local people re-enacted, with noisy processions of trumpets and drums, Mary and Joseph's search for an inn. In the evenings there were fireworks: fiery pinwheels, sputtering rockets and brilliant roman candles, all launched from rickety wooden towers or *castillos* set up in the Jardín. Afterward someone would release the *globos*, paper balloons with candles inside, and they would sail above the town. The wind would tip them and the paper would catch on fire and the *globos* would come fluttering down in flames, and everyone would cheer.

To surprise me Dad had studied a little Spanish. Though I thought my mother could hardly speak a word, one afternoon a few weeks after they'd arrived, she startled me. Dad and I were supposed to meet her and Jennifer and Lynn at the Bougainvillea, a restaurant near the Jardín. We were late and I was walking a little ahead of my father. When I saw them a waiter was approaching my mother. I stopped, turned to my father and raised my hand to signal him to watch quietly. The waiter bowed to my mother. Looking up at him, she pronounced *"Una cerveza, por favor, Dos Equis,"* as if she'd lived in Mexico all her life. Lynn must have been coaching her.

My parents stayed in Mexico for about six weeks. My father and I spent a lot of time together. We drove to Puerto Vallarta, then a sleepy coastal village, where we caught up with a week-long religious pilgrimage to San Juan de los Lagos. Later we visited Mexico City where I introduced him to one of my old girlfriends, a photographer, Belle Romaine, who had moved there from San Miguel.

Belle was an elegant little lady, always quick to smile, who wore her black hair swept high into a bouffant arrangement. She had an infectious laugh and was a tremendous flirt. I remember how I'd gone to her apartment with her shortly after we'd met and started making out with her. Suddenly she'd cried, "Stop, stop! This is not working. Do you want me to give you lessons?" I buttoned up my shirt, replying sarcastically, "Fine, you do that." I'd been married for five years and I'd had two kids. I didn't think there was anything she could teach me, but she was from New York and she was very sophisticated. One of her favourite jokes was that she was going to go to the Virgin Islands for recycling. Belle taught me everything she knew and I graduated *summa cum laude*. However, Belle soon moved on to Mexico City and a new lover.

Dad and I spent a great afternoon with them but as soon as we left their place he remarked, "You'll never get married again, Toni, if you keep on seeing women like that."

The more time I spent with Dad, the more I realized that he and my mother would never approve of my lifestyle in San Miguel. I remember one terrible incident that confirmed their misgivings. Dad and I were talking together one evening at the El Patio restaurant. I noticed an expatriate I knew sitting alone at a table and looking as if he were in a foul mood. He was a moody, mean-spirited type at the best of times and a local girl had just jilted him, as I found out later. He was drinking heavily, and tucked into the back of his belt was a black Luger pistol.

We gave him a wide berth. When he was refused service, he started shouting abuse at the barman, finally brandishing his gun. The manager called the cops and two of San Miguel's finest swaggered in. One of them tried to take the Luger away from him. It went off in the struggle. The cop slumped to the floor with a bullet in his head. The second policeman dashed out the door. The guitarist in the restaurant stopped strumming. The other diners gasped in horror. As Dad and I looked over, the dead man lay on the floor, blood oozing from his head. The bullet had entered his chin and blown off the top of his head.

Dad and I were afraid that because we were foreigners we might be implicated in some way, so we decided to get out of there. The owner of the lethal weapon, who had been standing above the dead man, drunk and glassy-eyed, tottered back to his chair and sat down. As we left the restaurant the guitarist resumed playing. People started talking again. Within two minutes it sounded as if nothing had happened.

Outside, we ran into the second cop. He cowered by the wall, so frightened he could scarcely speak.

"Mataron a tu companero." I told him that the other policeman was dead and asked him what he was going to do about it.

The cop mumbled, *"Nada . . . Tiene una pistola."*

A week or two later, I saw my acquaintance on the street. I couldn't believe it—he was a free man. "Good God! What happened?" I asked. "You're responsible for a cop getting shot and the police didn't throw you in jail?"

He bristled, as if I had said something outrageous. "Jail? What do you mean—jail? It was an accident. The goddamned sons of bitches fined me forty dollars. The bastard wasn't worth it."

Forty dollars, I thought to myself. That was the price of a policeman's life. It was one more reminder that you could buy your way out of anything in Mexico. The only crime was poverty.

Not long after the incident in the bar, I came home late one night to find the lights still on in my parents' room. They usually turned in if we had nothing planned for the evening, but tonight I found them waiting up for me.

"Toni, your mother and I have been thinking about the way you and the children are living here," began my father.

It was one of those rare occasions when my mother dared to interrupt my father. "We're leaving Mexico and we want you to come back with us, Toni," she said.

The news came as a surprise although it shouldn't have. I knew that my parents didn't like the way the children and I were living in San Miguel. Some of the recent incidents, especially the shooting at the restaurant had confirmed their opinions. And just the other day my mother had been shocked when she'd found lice in Lynn's hair. I'd tried to remind her that I and my sisters had sometimes had lice in our hair while we were growing up on the Isle of Man. She'd used a "biddie comb" on her own children then. But she felt that Lynn's infestation was just another sign of a generally bad situation.

My father rose from his chair. "It's high time you went back, son. Lynn speaks better Spanish than English and Jennifer's so confused between the languages that she can't read properly."

Lynn, who had been in Mexico longer than Jennifer, spoke both languages quite well. I thought the idea that Jennifer was confused was an exaggeration. "Jennifer's learning Spanish," I argued. "That's far more valuable than anything they could teach her in Grade 3 back home."

My father raised his eyebrows. "Come on, Toni, I think reading and writing are pretty important, don't you?"

"I just need more time, Dad," I answered. "I've applied for a Canada Council grant and if it comes through, I'll take the kids and we'll move to Mallorca, maybe even England." I had more or less decided to continue living as an expatriate in Latin America or go to another Spanish-speaking country, perhaps Spain or the Canary Islands—I'd heard that the Canary Islands in particular were very cheap. And as the kids spoke Spanish, they could attend school there with no loss of time.

My father crossed his arms. "You've been in San Miguel three years, Toni. It was supposed to be a year."

My mother added, "I think you should get a proper job. You could go into architecture again. I'm sure they'd take you back in Penticton."

"Oh, mother!" I said in exasperation. "That's the last place I want to go to. I've made some breakthroughs here. I have an art dealer now. I had a show at the Vancouver Art Gallery. Things are really turning around."

My mother sighed. "Toni, you've got your blinkers on. You're not paying enough attention to the children. They're at school all day, then the *criada* looks after them when they get home, and you're usually out in the evening again."

I lost the argument because I had the kids to think about. I promised to return within a few months. My parents offered to take Jennifer back with them to Summerland as it would be difficult for me to drive all the way there with both children. In February 1960, they left town with Jennifer. Unfortunately my Canada Council grant never materialized. I didn't let my parents know but I had barely enough money to hang on until the summer when I would have to return to the Okanagan. Nevertheless, I felt that the most important thing was to keep painting in San Miguel as long as I could.

That spring seemed especially bittersweet in San Miguel. The buds on the trees covered the hillside around the town with a soft green haze. The bougainvillea and the potted plants in the town began to bloom. The evenings in March were still cool, so I'd light a fire and Lynn and I would curl up by it as I read her a bedtime story. Then I'd carry her to bed and sit with a book myself. All I could think about for weeks was that I would have to leave Mexico.

Eventually I came to terms with the necessity of it. I saw the value for Lynn and Jennifer and began to realize that there was possibly some benefit in it for me as well. Perhaps I had done everything I could do in San Miguel. I might have done only a handful of paintings in which I had achieved some of my aspirations, but that was enough to provide me with a sense that I was moving forward into the future.

My work had been gaining critical notice in Canada. Alvin Balkind had submitted two of my pieces for the BC Artists Annual show at the Vancouver Art Gallery in 1959. The jurors' selections shocked many artists who had submitted their work. One juror, Tony Emery, a history professor at the University of Victoria who went on to become the director of the Vancouver Art Gallery in 1967, maintained that it was time for national standards to apply. Although more than 300 pieces were received, the jury chose to exhibit just one sculpture and twelve paintings, among them my two collages. Alvin sent two more to an exhibition in Winnipeg. He gave me my own show in December 1959, and submitted three of my collages to the National Gallery in Ottawa which, in turn, selected them for their big biennial show.

Whatever it would take to keep painting in Canada, I was prepared for it. I had a growing sense of conviction that it was time to move on from San Miguel and establish more connections with art dealers and with the rest of the art community in Canada.

As if hastening me along, things began to unravel in San Miguel. It started with a private bank known as the "Bean Bank" in a little store at the south end of the market. The store sold machetes, saddles and riding tack and sacks of beans, hence the name. To use the bank you placed your money in a paper bag with your name on it, and the clerk, a member of the family that operated the store, locked the bag into a steel safe. I never banked there, but many rich American widows did because it offered the best rates in town and it seemed very solid because the Mexican family who ran the store had lived in San Miguel for many years. One morning the family was gone and the safe was empty.

Then a little later, all hell broke loose over the news about Gaby, "the Haitian Princess." She'd got her nickname because she came from a rich family in Port-au-Prince, who had gotten rid of her by sending her on a trip around the world. The first time I saw her she was stoned and was dancing stark naked on one of the tables at La Cucaracha while everybody clapped in time. Far from well-proportioned, she was pear-shaped with an enormous bottom. She had fallen in love with a handsome American tourist and, by her good cooking, had enticed him into living with her. When he left her she was devastated.

I had driven to Gaby's house with a girlfriend the morning after this happened, to recover a handbag that she had left at a party there the night before. I went into the house to retrieve the handbag and found Gaby sprawled naked across a bed, apparently dead. From the bedside table, I could see that she had swallowed a bottle of Seconal tablets with some gin. After checking for signs of life and finding none, I found the bag and left, quickly and quietly.

The police investigation found heroin in her apartment. I never really knew the dealers and drug users among the Americans in San Miguel but Gaby had a list of her suppliers and of everyone to whom she'd ever sold drugs. The Mexican authorities shipped a few addicts to Mexico City for questioning by US narcotics agents, and San Miguel was emptied of a few more gringos.

Two or three weeks before Lynn and I planned to leave, she woke one morning with terrible stomach cramps. She groaned and cried as I carried her to the car and rushed to the Union Medica, a private clinic operated by a Dr. Olsina, a small, compact Spaniard with a shock of white hair who spoke several languages and gave readings of Garcia Lorca's poetry at the institute. At first I drew some comfort from the fact that I knew Olsina, who had taught me Mexican history at the institute, breaking into his native Castilian with excitement whenever the lecture came to the subject of revolution.

But at his clinic the doctor was very different, surprisingly insensitive to Lynn's suffering and my anxiety. After a brief examination he informed me that Lynn needed an emergency appendectomy. Lynn squirmed in agony as she sat with me. I knew what would happen if her appendix burst, so I asked him to operate on her.

As the nurse readied his instruments and prepared the operating table the doctor turned to me. "Toni, you have other children, right?" he asked.

I'd once introduced him to Jennifer. I reminded him of that.

"Yes, yes, I remember now," he replied absently. "Good," he said, "that's very good."

"What do you mean?" I asked.

Doctor Olsina scrubbed his hands at the sink. Then he shook them dry and towelled them off. "It's just that sometimes these operations don't work out."

"What are you trying to tell me? It's just appendicitis, for Christ's sake," I sputtered angrily.

"And this is just a primitive rural hospital in Mexico," he replied icily.

"But this operation is done all the time," I retorted. "Every doctor knows how to do it."

"Hey, Toni, don't worry." He raised his hands to stop me from saying anything further. "I have done the operation many times."

The nurse walked Lynn to the operating table. She was almost hysterical with fright. The nurse and doctor tried to pin her shoulders down on the table so that they could buckle her onto it. That was when I realized that they weren't going to use any anaesthetic. I covered my eyes. I couldn't watch it. I dropped into a chair in the corner of the room and gritted my teeth.

He and the nurse struggled to hold Lynn's arms down. He turned to me. "Toni, you're going to have to come here and give us a hand."

I dragged myself to my feet and walked over to the table. But it didn't matter. Lynn fainted. I felt like fainting myself. "I can't watch you do this to my daughter," I said to the doctor.

He nodded. "Go down the street to the *tienda* and get me a packet of cigarettes."

Although I was gone for less than fifteen minutes, the nurse was already sewing up the incision. The doctor lit a cigarette. He inhaled deeply and blew out a smoke ring. Then he asked for his money.

"I want two thousand dollars," he told me.

"Pesos?" I asked. "You must mean two thousand pesos." That was about $160 and more than three times the cost of my stay in the hospital when I'd had hepatitis.

"No," he said, "two thousand dollars."

My stomach started churning. "Two thousand dollars!" I exclaimed. "That must be four or five times what the operation would cost in America!"

The doctor took another drag from the cigarette. "Many of my patients are very, very poor." He butted out his cigarette. "Often they can't pay their fees, so when I have an American here, I have to charge him more."

I pleaded with him, "Look, doctor, I haven't got two thousand dollars. I've never seen that kind of money in my life—but I can give you four thousand dollars worth of paintings, instead."

He raised his hand to object. "No, no, I don't want any paintings. I want two thousand dollars."

"I can't do it, Dr. Olsina. There is no way I can get that kind of money."

"Go to your family and your friends." He raised his index finger as if lecturing me. "I've met your parents. You know a lot of foreigners in this town. Someone will help you out. You go figure it out, Toni, then bring me the money."

Feeling as if I were trapped in a nightmare, I carried Lynn out of the clinic. God, I thought to myself. Two thousand dollars. That's a death sentence, I can't raise that kind of money. And if I don't get it he'll send someone to break my arms so I can't paint any more. More likely he'd get someone to kill me. Every life had a price in San Miguel.

That night I packed all our clothes and belongings into my steamer trunk. I tied my paintings together and put them into the car trailer. Then I woke Lynn up and we fled San Miguel at two o'clock in the morning.

Up to that time I'd been using a tourist visa to stay in Mexico, renewing it every six months. I'd cross the US border, ship off a few paintings, shop a little, renew my visa and return to Mexico. The last time I returned, I wore a serape and huarache sandals because most of the clothes I'd brought from Canada had worn out. One of the Mexican border guards at Juarez had joked, "Boy, you look like a wetback headed in the wrong direction."

When Lynn and I arrived at the Mexican border on the day of our escape from San Miguel, I handed the border guard my tourist visa. Lynn was listed on the visa as my daughter.

The Mexican border guard stared at Lynn. As she sat in the car she kept speaking fluent Spanish, which she knew better at that point than English. He carefully re-examined my visa. "Is no your daughter. This young lady, she come from Guanajuato."

I switched off the car engine. "We've been living in San Miguel for three years," I explained. "That's why she speaks Spanish so well."

The guard's face flushed with anger. "I come from Guanajuato state. I know how they speaking. I tell you, she from Guanajuato." He snorted, "You tell me she is a *gringa—no es gringa!*"

I was worried that Olsina might have already learned that I'd skipped town. If he got word to the border, I could be arrested. Again I insisted that Lynn was my daughter. I showed the guard my Canadian passport with Lynn's name recorded inside it.

He brushed it aside telling me I'd faked it. *"Diablos!"* he snapped. "I know a forger man when I see him."

Only one way out remained. I took out my wallet, opened it and slowly counted out the bills. The guard took everything I had, stuffed the bills into his pants pocket and waved us across the border.

Fortunately I had anticipated the possibility of a shakedown by the Federales at the border and I'd stashed a little money in the door panel of the car. I had money for gas but nothing for hotels and only a little for a few meals. I'd bought some "va-va voom"—Benzedrine tablets that Mexican drugstores sold over the counter—and I kept taking them so that I could keep driving day and night until we reached Canada. By the time we got to Oregon, my eyes felt scratchy and my head spun. I fought to stay awake. On top of that Lynn and I were freezing, but when we pulled over to raise the roof of the sports car, I discovered that the canvas had rotted. I bundled Lynn into some warm clothes, then started driving again. My BC licence plates had expired, so I crossed the Canadian border at night.

For the last part of the trip Lynn had been in agony again. Suspecting that there might be some complications from the operation I drove straight to Vancouver General Hospital. They quickly admitted her and whisked her off to an operating theatre. Afterward the surgeon asked me, "Where did she have her appendix taken out?" I told him about Dr. Olsina.

"God Almighty!" he exclaimed. "Anyone who did an operation like that shouldn't be practising medicine. Your daughter's insides were left open. Only the skin outside was closed. She would have died if you hadn't brought her in."

They gave Lynn antibiotics and she had to stay in the hospital for a few days. I had to be careful with her diet for a while. Fortunately the medical costs were covered by the government under a new hospital insurance plan that had been introduced nationally. It was a forerunner of BC's Medical Services Plan.

Now that I was back in Canada I had to sort out my affairs and look for work. The way I'd run from San Miguel de Allende meant that I couldn't go back to Mexico any time soon. That didn't matter though because I was determined to make my way in my own country, living on my own terms.

Chapter 12

The Naked City

By the late spring of 1960, I was so broke that I had to let the car dealership in Penticton repossess my MG. The front wheel fell off as the dealer drove it away from my parents' home. Leaving Jennifer and Lynn with my parents, I moved to Vancouver where I hoped to get my art career moving. Alvin Balkind at the New Design Gallery had promised me another show in January.

In the meantime I shared a room above a camera store with a couple of other artists who had as little to live on as I did. Kerry Wald slept in the walk-in closet and Maurice Joslin and I each had one of the single beds in the one-room apartment. The building on the 500 block of Granville Street had once housed a brothel; sailors kept knocking at the door and asking for "Suzy."

We all had a difficult time living in grimy surroundings and not eating properly. When Kerry and Maurice were feeling down I'd tell them, "Try to keep in mind that what we're doing is really important, even without recognition. Many people believe that artists are always important because they help define a culture. Everybody has heard of Toulouse-Lautrec," I pointed out, "but who remembers the name of the French prime minister in 1901?"

I had no studio space, so I salvaged a few wooden packing crates from the alley and made them into a bench and worktable that I set up on the roof of the building. Then I started making paper-on-paper collages again. If it rained, I rushed everything back down-stairs into the little apartment.

My art at that point consisted of the all-over collages I'd begun in Mexico. I filled each collage to its edges with tightly interlocked paper forms. At first, I still brushed warm Mexican colours in acrylic paint onto the work, integrating the collaged fragments, but then I started painting in oil for its richer, more subtle colours. I no longer used the names of Mexican places, but instead references to feelings and states of mind, or to Canadian places. I named one of my oil-on-paper collages *Night Hawk*, after a small town near my parents' home. When I scraped together enough money, I created canvas-on-canvas collages such as *Skagway*. Primed canvas was more durable than paper and it held the oil paint better.

In Vancouver I lived hand to mouth for a few weeks until the day I ran into Hugh Redwood, an architect with whom I'd worked in Penticton. He landed me a temporary assignment at Gray, Stillwell and Loban. That big Howe Street firm hired me to produce the working drawings for an extension to the Vancouver Lawn Tennis and Badminton Club. The employment enabled me to buy a used green Volkswagen, and to take Jennifer and Lynn off my parents' hands and enrol them in a Catholic boarding school in Maillardville on the other side of Vancouver. It was the only boarding school I could afford.

I shipped some collages to Dorothy Cameron, who ran the Here and Now Gallery on Cumberland Street in Toronto. She put three of my works into a group show in October with eleven other western Canadian artists. Then the Art Gallery of Toronto chose some of my work for "Four Canadians," a group exhibition at the O'Keefe Centre. The growing interest in my work led Dorothy to promise me a show in the spring.

I tracked down a studio in the same block as my room and talked the landlord into a bargain. I promised to leave the FOR RENT sign up in case someone came by who was willing to pay a higher rent. It was a 1,600-square-foot, well-lit, high-ceilinged room with a sink, a toilet and storage space, perfect for an artist. It had once been the studio of Lawren Harris, one of the surviving members of the Group of Seven and a past president of the Canadian Group of Painters. And it cost me just $25 a month.

Sometime later, Alvin Balkind took me to lunch with Harris at his West Point Grey mansion. In classic Canadian paintings like *Maligne Lake, Jasper Park, 1924*, Harris had sensitively expressed the grandeur and harmony of nature. That piece, based on a trip he'd made to the Rockies, showed ethereal snow-capped pyramid-shaped mountains reflected in the lake's tranquil waters.

As we entered his house we saw the tall white-haired, seventy-six-year-old artist standing on a cream-coloured wool carpet and painting on an easel in the front room without splashing a drop of paint. Harris, a theosophist, had apparently been working all morning on symbolically coloured shafts of lights—yellow representing intelligence, and blue, religious feeling. In his attempt to depict spirituality he had abandoned any references to mountains or the supernal northern landscape and was pursuing pure geometric form.

As Harris painted with his brush in his right hand he rested his left hand in the trouser pocket of his three-piece tweed suit. I think he even had a fob watch in his waistcoat pocket. This must be the immaculate art process of a gentleman, I thought. Even Winston Churchill had painted in a cotton smock.

Putting the brush down, he greeted us amiably and led the way to the dining room. A Chinese houseboy wearing white gloves carried in a bottle of white wine and then the serving dishes. Throughout the meal, Harris's wife, Bess, some six years younger and also a painter, chatted gaily about how she would renovate their house after her husband's demise. Harris just smiled, as if in the amusing presence of a harmless eccentric.

Obviously he kept quiet to keep the peace between them and to avoid straining both his heart and his guests. A few years after the visit, I was a juror for a group show at the Vancouver Art Gallery and among my fellow jury members was Harris, one of the gallery's board of directors. A painting came up by his wife. It was mediocre. Furthermore, since Lawren was on the jury, Bess should never have submitted it. It embarrassed everyone, especially him.

When Harris raised his hand to vote for it he saw the puzzlement on my face. He cleared his throat, "Toni, I'm married to the lady."

Sighing, I raised my hand. "I see what you mean."

The entire jury voted for it. Given Harris's age and his heart condition, it seemed unthinkable not to support him in his relationship with his wife. Ironically, despite Bess's plans, Harris outlived her by several months, dying in 1970.

Of great help to me during that first lean year back from Mexico was Gloria Knight, an MA student in the English Department at UBC. I met her at a party, soon after I returned to Vancouver. She was slim, with brown hair and eyes and an ivory complexion. She sparkled with intellect, had been writing for years, and had recently had two of her plays produced by CBC Radio. We hit it off so well that I borrowed a pen from my date that evening and scribbled down her telephone number.

As a teaching assistant Gloria taught a section of English 100 at the University of British Columbia, earning a monthly salary of $200. She rented a bachelor suite at First and Vine in Kitsilano and after seeing her for a few months, I moved in. She paid the rent and bought the groceries, while I paid for the car, my studio rent and supplies, and the girls' boarding school.

While we lived there Jennifer and Lynn visited on the weekends. Instead of baseball cards, the nuns at their boarding school gave them holy cards with pictures of Jesus Christ, the Virgin Mary and assorted saints. I remember watching the kids shuffle through the deck of them. Lynn liked the idea of praying to the Virgin because she had the same name as her late mother. Now we had a family of sorts. All that Gloria and I lacked was a formal relationship.

That changed the following year in 1961. Long before we'd met, she had separated from her first husband, leaving him in Spain and returning to Vancouver to make a new life for herself. Now he also had returned to Vancouver and wanted to remarry. To get a divorce in those days you had to go to court with proof of infidelity. The only way to clear the decks for our own relationship was for him to sue for divorce, naming me as the respondent. After the divorce went through, on September 12, 1961, Gloria and I got married. We then moved to a slightly larger apartment in the West End and continued to have the children with us on the weekends.

After that first year, I took the children out of boarding school. We now lived in houses, first in West Vancouver, where we rented the ground floor of a large white house behind a sea wall at the foot of Dundarave, then high up on the mountain in a house we looked after for a friend. Every day I drove the children to school, Gloria to the university for her teaching job, and myself to my studio in downtown Vancouver. Gloria would take the bus to the studio in the afternoon when she had finished teaching and attending graduate seminars, and we would drive back to West Vancouver. Jennifer was old enough to babysit Lynn after school until we arrived home. It was difficult but we held things together. Furthermore, Gloria appreciated my work and that helped me, too. I remember one day in early 1961, she came to the studio while I was working on a large oil painting. She told me how much she liked it and I named the piece after her—*Joie de Gloria*. In September of that year it was chosen to represent British Columbia in the Paris Biennial.

Overall though, relocating to Vancouver after San Miguel was discouraging. No matter how hard or long I worked at my art, I still couldn't make much of a living from it. At 32, I despaired of my future prospects. I wondered if I should have left San Miguel de Allende and gone to New York City like my friend, Bob Murray.

In 1959, he had completed *Fountain*, a design for an abstract sculpture for the new city hall in Saskatoon. He'd hired a San Miguel tinsmith to make him a model and crate it, and I'd driven it to the border and shipped it to Saskatoon for him. Once fabricated in welded steel plate, the sculpture stood eight feet high and consisted of two graceful curves of steel mounted on two upright pieces of cut-out plate. It was finished in a black-green paint to suggest the patina of old bronze.

The following year Bob received a study grant from the Canada Council and moved to New York. There he continued his friendship with the abstract expressionist painter Barnett Newman, whom he had met at an Emma Lake artists' workshop in Saskatchewan. Newman introduced Bob to some of the most important painters in modern art. Bob told me that in New York some artists actually supported themselves through painting, not by teaching art.

One night he and the Newmans were on their way upstairs to an opening reception at the Poindexter Gallery. William de Kooning, the hard-drinking painter with the movie-star good looks whom the New York art critics were hailing as the next Jackson Pollock, was coming downstairs with his wife Elaine. He greeted and kissed Barney and Annalee. Then Newman introduced him to Bob, who was waiting below them on the stairs. De Kooning gave him a hug and said, "If you're still here a year from now, I'll kiss you, too."

Northwest, canvas collage, 46" x 56", 1961

In March 1961, I travelled to Toronto to meet Dorothy Cameron as well as a prospective client who was interested in commissioning a mural. Then I took a bus to New York City.

Back then, the art world was still anchored between Tenth Street and Broadway. One afternoon, Bob brought me to Newman's studio on Front Street. The fifty-six-year-old painter, a lively barrel-shaped man with a friendly face, greeted me warmly and shook my hand. "Call me Barney," he said. With his trademark monocle and waxed moustache, he looked more like Colonel Blimp or a British India army officer than a celebrated New York artist.

Yet Barney quickly put that association to rest with one of his famous impromptu tours of Manhattan. Talking with the cab driver about popular science and God knows what else, he steered us past the site of an Indian war on Fourth Street. He had the cab stop at Balens so we could look at some Chinese bristle brushes. We dropped in on Lennie Bocur at his fine arts paint factory on Tenth Street. Then Annalee met us for dinner near Fraunces Tavern on the corner of Pearl and Broad streets where George Washington had said good-bye to his officers in 1783. On top of it all, Barney turned out to be a bit of an insomniac, so the day did not end until the wee hours of the morning when we ate at a Fulton Street seafood restaurant just as the trucks were pulling in with fresh fish.

Another night Bob took me to Barney's Park Avenue apartment. The living room was as sparsely furnished as an art gallery. Huge paintings covered the walls and the only furnishings in the room were a round table, 1920s oak chairs from a lawyer's office, and a black baby grand piano.

"I'll play you something I've written," Barney suggested. He pulled out two office chairs for Bob and me, then launched into the crashing opening bars of an atonal piano sonata. As he pounded the keys he grinned at the discordant sounds. As much as I liked Barney's art I could not appreciate his music.

Barney hadn't had an easy life as an artist but he always believed that if an artist kept on working there was at least a chance that eventually what he did might be recognized. He had come to a turning point in his career between 1945 and 1947 when he'd invented "zips"—sharp, vertical bands of intense colours. Then he explored the impact of size and dimension through works like *The Wild*, a 1958 canvas 6½ feet long but only 13 inches wide.

While Bob and I were at his apartment that night he asked us to restretch a finished canvas with him. We had to wash our hands and put on white cotton gloves before we stretched the painting over the beautiful stretcher bars he had put together with carriage bolts. Unlike Pollock or Kline, Barney believed in using only the best equipment and paint supplies. The painting we helped him with that night was an early work in his monolithic *Stations of the Cross* series, large black-and-white works later exhibited at the Guggenheim Museum, and now housed permanently in a special round room in Washington's National Gallery. He had brought it from his studio to hang in the apartment for viewing.

In that work and others, Barney used themes and names from the Old Testament, a practice that culminated in pieces such as *Voice of Fire*, 1967, an allusion to God speaking to Moses from the burning bush. He created that work for the US pavilion at Expo '67, the World Fair in Montreal at which I also had a work. Nearly eighteen feet high and eight feet across, *Voice of Fire* consists of three enormous vertical stripes. The two on the outside are the blue of the American flag and the centre stripe is an angry volcanic red, perhaps Barney's protest against the Vietnam War. Because of its connection with Expo '67, the National Gallery of Canada acquired the piece from Barney's widow in 1989 for $1.76 million. A controversial purchase at the time, it cost half of what Annalee could have got for it on the international market. She felt it should go to Canada because of the historical association, his fondness for the country and the workshop he'd done at Emma Lake, as well as his friendships with Canadian artists like Bob.

When I met him, of course, his work sold for much less. He lived in poverty for most of his early life as a painter until he married Annalee and she began to work as a school teacher. He didn't have his first one-man show until 1950, and wasn't recognized as an important artist until the late 1950s and during the 1960s. Yet when I met him in New York, he already felt that he'd passed the apogee of critical notice. "I'm still alive," he complained, "I'm doing my best work and nobody seems to care any more." In fact his reputation and his prices were later to soar, reaching astronomical heights after his death in 1970.

Despite the stimulation of living in New York, the place made me nervous. Even back then, the city could get pretty rough. One night at Connolly's Bar in lower Manhattan, Bob and I sat watching a black-and-white TV police drama, *The Naked City*. The narrator ended every episode with the words, "There are eight million stories in the Naked City. This has been one of them."

Just as we were watching a particularly violent scene, two hoodlums who were beating the hell out of each other crashed through the Western-style swinging doors of the bar and fell against me, knocking me off my stool and continuing their fight on top of my body. Reacting instinctively, Bob karate-chopped the man on top of the pile in the neck, felling him temporarily. One of the Irish bartenders hustled the other man outside and whistled down a passing police car.

I stared at Bob, "What are you doing?"

Bob massaged his hand. "Ow-w, what *am* I doing?"

The man on the floor jumped to his feet and shook his fist at

Bob, yelling, "I'll be back with the Weissberger gang!" He stormed out of the bar.

The Weissbergers, who had taken their name from a nearby warehouse, were drug dealers on Manhattan's lower east side. Later Bob heard that the fight had been caused by a drug deal gone bad.

The two Irish bartenders took out their shillelaghs, the hickory clubs they wielded in fights. The people who had been drinking near us paid up, then quickly left the bar.

Jimmy the bartender, who knew Bob, said, "In the future, let me deal with these guys. Stay out of it unless I ask for help."

I turned to Bob. "We better get out of here while we can."

"I don't want to get cornered in some back alley by those guys," said Bob. "I think we should sit tight here." He looked worried.

I heard the bartenders drumming their shillelaghs against the counter. I slipped off my stool and put on my jacket. "Bob, you're making a big mistake, I'm leaving."

I hurried outside and for the first time in my life the first cab I hailed stopped for me. Through the window I thought I saw a group of men in the distance. When I got back to the YMCA near the Penn Street station, I called Bob's apartment. The telephone rang and rang. Bob finally picked up the receiver, breathless but unharmed. He had left shortly after me but had gone blocks out of his way to make sure no one followed him back to his apartment.

Despite the many attractions of New York's art scene, I was rapidly disenchanted by the gritty, crime-plagued urban environment that the city struck me as being at that time. Bob did not feel that living there was dangerous, even though there were two break-ins at his studio. After leaving New York for Pennsylvania, he joked that the worst thing that had happened to him personally was being mugged in Central Park by a grey squirrel that tore holes in his pant leg while looking for a handout. However, in addition to the enormous practical and financial difficulties of relocating, I felt that I could never enjoy living there. And so I decided I would have to take my chances on the art world in Canada. But I would make my permanent home in Vancouver, where I could live beside the ocean, among the mountains and evergreen forests, for I realized that I did not want to lose the intimate connection with nature that I had in British Columbia.

Chapter 13

The Mystery Mural

O ver the next few months, I acquired a reputation as one of the leading contemporary Canadian painters. In 1961, I won the Purchase Prize at the Vancouver Art Gallery's annual juried show of BC artists. Furthermore, my exhibitions attracted substantial critical attention. Commenting in the *Toronto Daily Star* on the *Four Canadians* show at the O'Keefe Centre in the fall of 1960, Robert Fulford described my collages as "[comprised of] tensely locked shapes" and "filled with spontaneity." Of my spring show in 1961 at the Here and Now Gallery he wrote, "Onley's way of handling overlapping shapes, gently and harmoniously, is most evident in his collages."

Not everyone felt that way, of course. Pearl McCarthy, the art critic at the *Globe & Mail*, had been an early supporter of mine when I lived in Brantford and did watercolour landscapes, but she detested any form of abstract art. Not only did she avoid my spring show in Toronto but, as a slap in the face, she sent her husband, the paper's music critic, to review it. He arrived at the gallery with a white cane. He was blind, so I had to lead him to the collages and describe them.

Nevertheless, with the attention I received back east, and with art dealers in Vancouver, Toronto and, later, Montreal, things began to look up. My spring show at Dorothy Cameron's gallery just took off. It was like dropping something into a cauldron, causing it to bubble over. The art scene was hungry for a Canadian answer to American abstract expressionism.

In the summer of 1961, the *Penticton Herald* carried a story that I found encouraging. Alan Jarvis, the director of the National Gallery of Canada and the editor of the magazine *Canadian Art*, was in Penticton to open the new Okanagan Summer School of the Arts. He told the newspaper that he admired my work and had acquired two of my paintings for the gallery and one for himself. He revealed that a few artists in Canada, like Harold Town in Toronto, were now able to make a good living from the sale of their paintings. The starving artist was becoming a thing of the past, according to Jarvis.

Then, in the fall of 1961, I was awakened by a phone call in the very early morning. I mumbled into the receiver, "Do you know what time it is?"

The caller announced, "It's the Canada Council!"

Thinking it was an artist prankster, I groaned.

But to my astonishment it really was the Canada Council, calling from Ontario at 9 a.m. eastern time. I was to be awarded a Junior Canada Council Grant on the strength of my sell-out show at the Here and Now Gallery earlier that year. It came as very welcome news because I'd applied many times and had given up any hope of ever getting a grant.

In due course, the official announcement came in the mail. The Canada Council would give me $2,000, paid in three lump sums four months apart, as well as a return trip anywhere I liked. I was delighted. The money would keep me painting for months.

As for the trip, my friend Bob Murray told me about the University of Saskatchewan's upcoming 1962 summer workshop at Emma Lake, near Prince Albert National Park, in northern Saskatchewan. The university ran the workshop annually at the cabins and studio at the lake. Barnett Newman had been the guest lecturer in 1959 and had done a great deal to encourage Canadian artists to pursue their own directions. Hoping to repeat the success of that workshop, the organizers had asked Bob to invite the famous art critic Clement Greenberg.

With great anticipation, I registered for the workshop. As Greenberg saw it, modern painting had begun when painters gave up any attempt to depict ordinary reality and to create an illusion of depth through perspective, but focussed instead on the materials of art and the surface of the painting. He had championed Jackson

Pollock and even claimed to have given Pollock the name *Lavender Mist* for one of his most beautiful and lyrical paintings.

Unfortunately, because I needed the money, I had agreed to teach a two-week painting course at the Okanagan Summer School of the Arts and therefore had to arrive late. I took Gloria and the kids to Penticton and spent some time there with my parents while teaching. Then I drove to Emma Lake at the end of the first week of the workshop.

I had some fantastic discussions there with other Canadian artists, some of whom became very well known a few years later. In particular, I remember a ferocious debate with one of the leaders of abstract painting in Quebec, a founding member of the *Association des artistes non-figuratifs de Montreal*, the pale, skinny twenty-nine-year-old Guido Molinari. His thick, wavy black hair, prominent nose, beady eyes and exaggerated gestures gave him a somewhat fanatical air, appropriate for the revolutionary he had become in the Canadian art scene by painting hard-edged abstracts. "We must stop doing the painting that has already been done," he announced in his heavy French Canadian accent. He was just beginning to experiment with colour and vertical stripe painting. In *Equilibrium*, 1961, he employed four colours—red, yellow, black, and white—in broad rectangular bands travelling vertically across the canvas, with two bands moving horizontally. His work at this time may have been inspired by Newman's.

An author of painting manifestos, Molinari had experimented with automatic writing and had even painted blindfolded in his efforts to create wholly new abstract images. I had thought I was a purely abstract painter, but Molinari went much, much further. He insisted that even Jackson Pollock's art failed to measure up because he'd created his drip paintings while standing over his canvases. Accordingly to Molinari, he should have worked with the canvas in an upright position, on an easel or tacked to a wall, so that the artist's view was the same as that of viewers of the finished work. I argued that Pollock couldn't work that way because instead of drying in place, the drips would have become vertical streaks, pulled downward by the force of gravity.

As for my meeting with Greenberg, it was a disaster. I went out onto the porch of the studio and found "Clem" standing there smoking a cigarette, his shoulders slightly hunched. He was casually dressed in a cotton dress shirt with rolled-up sleeves, black pants and canvas sneakers.

Eager to make up for lost time, I introduced myself and asked him what I'd missed. Ticked off that I'd dared to arrive late he just stared at me with heavily lidded eyes. Then he tossed his cigarette and butted it out with his foot. "I'm not going to repeat myself," he said. "I think I pretty well shot my bolt last week. There's not much to talk about now." He shrugged and walked back into the studio.

The workshop required each artist to present slides of his or her work to the group. In Vancouver and Mexico, I'd explored the "all-over" type of composition typical of American abstract expressionism. I'd stained the spaces between the collaged figures with oil paint. The rectangular and ovoid shapes were broken by the edges of the canvas and so carried the eye right off the borders, just as the spattered paint on Pollock's canvases never ended at the edges and Barney Newman's zips seemed to roll past the frame.

In the spring of 1962, I'd started my *Polar* series of canvas-on-canvas collages, the antithesis of "all-over" abstract expressionist painting. "What would happen if the edges of the painting made a big container for everything inside the picture?" I asked myself. Then I scissored shapes from strips of canvas painted red, blue and black, and collaged them around a kind of axis or pole in the centre of the painting. The pieces formed a roughly circular shape that suggested an enormous ice crystal in some paintings, and a vortex in others. Already the series had attracted critical and commercial attention. One collage won the Jessie Dow prize in a group show at the Montreal Museum spring exhibition in April 1962. Later one of the *Polar* collages would be acquired by the Vancouver Art Gallery, and *Polar No. 1* would be selected for a purchase prize by the director of the Tate Gallery in London, England. It is now in the Tate Britain collection.

Seated at the back of the room, Greenberg leaned back in his chair against the wall. While I described my work the other artists kept glancing at Greenberg, who acknowledged them with a nod or a smile. On my fourth or fifth collage, Greenberg raised his arm and held up the thumb and forefinger of his right hand as if editing a section of my painting.

Gradually the other painters in the audience turned to watch him. Finally, I couldn't stand the disruption any more and I called Greenberg on it. "What's the matter, Clem?"

"Nothing, nothing at all, Toni," he answered, feigning surprise.

I insisted, "Clem, what are you looking at?"

He cleared his throat as if preparing for a speech. "Since you've asked, Toni, I see your painting in the bottom corner of that canvas." He pointed to a corner of the picture. It had a tiny detail. "You blow that up and you've got yourself a painting."

I could see the other artists nodding in agreement. After all, Greenberg was the best-known art critic in America. With disgust, I realized that almost everyone else there would have dropped everything and gone out and painted what Greenberg had suggested. In fact I heard later that some artists were offering to pay him to look at more of their works and advise them how to paint.

The thought of this blind conformity made me even angrier. "Clem, that's your painting. It's not mine," I replied.

A shocked silence fell in the room. Everyone stared at Greenberg. He stared at me but said nothing.

Then they looked back at me, practically shaking their heads at the terrible mistake I'd made. They must have thought that I'd ruined my career. A similar idea crossed my mind. But I didn't regret the remark and I had no intention of apologizing. Greenberg never spoke to me again, and the rest of the Emma Lake workshop more or less degenerated into drinking and carousing.

As far as I was concerned this eminent critic had abandoned his earlier position supporting contemporary art. Now "Pope Greenberg" told artists what to paint. Around the time of the workshop, he was trying to promote a movement he'd named "Post-Painterly Abstraction." He saw its large abstract designs, lightly stained onto canvases, as the successor to abstract expressionist painting. Meanwhile, a new generation of artists in New York were moving in an entirely different direction—Pop Art. From Andy Warhol's Campbell's Soup cans to Roy Lichtenstein's large comic strip panels, they were making art, not by avoiding mundane reality but by enlarging it and revelling in it.

I think I was right about Greenberg's dictatorial attitude. He later shocked the art world when he was appointed an executor of the estate of sculptor David Smith. He travelled up to Smith's acreage at Bennington, Vermont, with Bob Murray and ordered stripped to bare metal the sculptures that Smith had painted, an act bordering on vandalism. He'd gone far beyond giving advice by that point. He'd gone from promoting his own view of what art should be to enforcing it.

However, the biggest event in my career that year occurred earlier than the Emma Lake workshop. On February 20, 1962, the Queen Elizabeth Playhouse (now the Vancouver Playhouse) theatre opened in Vancouver and my collage in the mezzanine was unveiled. The commission had come from my dealer, Alvin Balkind. He had shown my "all-over" collage, *Joie des Enfants*, to Fred Lebensold, one of the architects of the new 650-seat civic theatre. After almost a year of negotiations, Lebensold selected me to paint an abstract mural, 10½ feet high and 21½ feet wide.

For three months in my studio I pinned up shapes I'd cut from painted canvas, decided where they should go, then glued them into position. From time to time, I'd step back to see how the enormous composition was developing. The burnt reds and electric blues of the prominent shapes came from Mexico, while the background suggested the patina of an ancient hacienda wall, stained with red and yellow ochre from the soil and slowly crumbling into oblivion.

It was the largest art work I'd ever done. It was an exhausting effort and I still had to cut it into three panels, take it out through the rear window of my Granville Street studio, load it onto a delivery truck in the alley below, transport it to the theatre and then join the pieces together on the wall.

I received a whopping $3,000 for the mural, out of which I had to pay the expenses of executing and installing it. At that time in Vancouver, this was an unheard-of price for contemporary art of any type, let alone abstract art. As soon as the theatre opened to the public I faced a storm of criticism. A columnist at the *Vancouver Sun*, Jack Wasserman, dubbed it "Bad Night at the Box Office" and claimed it would make you woozy on 7-Up. Two thousand people toured the theatre the first weekend, many of them asking why I hadn't named the mural. That went into the newspapers, too, and I was asked to comment.

I pointed out that modern art should be enjoyed the way

classical music is enjoyed—for itself. The mural didn't have a name because it didn't represent anything tangible. I told a reporter from the *Vancouver Sun*, "If people can't understand it, I'm sorry, but I can't help them. You have to interpret it for yourself. It's contemporary art in a contemporary building." The headline in the newspaper the following day read "Playhouse Mystery Mural Even Stumps the Artist."

Angrily I wrote to the editor, explaining that the reporter had missed the point. The mural was non-representational. If I named paintings during that period in my art, the titles were simply references to some personal or historical event that, in retrospect, after the work was completed, seemed to bear some meaningful, if mysterious, relationship to the particular work. For example, in 1961 I titled one of my collages *Homage to Gagarin* because the work to me expressed a sense of curiosity and a drive to explore, a feeling of soaring and daring.

For a while there seemed to be no end to the complaints about the mural. Other newspaper articles followed, even a denouncement at a City Hall council meeting. One alderman demanded that the name of the commissioning architect be revealed to the chamber. Letters to the editor followed. The weirdest claimed the mural was part of a communist plot to uglify the western world. I guess there was more red in the collage than blue.

Even my father was interviewed. He spoke to a reporter at the *Penticton Herald*. "My field is the theatre, but I'm beginning to understand what Toni's trying to do."

"How about Toni's mural at the Queen Elizabeth theatre?" asked the reporter. "It's very controversial."

"It's way out," said Dad, "but it's catching on."

Queen Elizabeth Playhouse (now Vancouver Playhouse) mural, 1961.

Chapter 14

The London Paintings

I n January 1963, a record-breaking 3,500 people attended the gala opening night of the Royal Canadian Academy's annual exhibition in Toronto. Confronted by so many abstract paintings, Pearl McCarthy of the *Globe & Mail* was to complain bitterly the next day that modern art in Canada had fallen into "a big black hole with no door out." From the 600 pieces submitted, the RCA chose fifteen sculptures and 108 paintings, among them two collages from my *Polar* series, the breakthrough work I'd started in 1961. Elizabeth Kilbourn of the *Toronto Star* had described one of the pieces in the series as a "whirlwind of dynamic force" held together in "a tense equilibrium." Abe Rogatnick, in the March/April 1962 issue of *Canadian Art* magazine, had said that each of the works seemed to be "a product of a burst of power from a mighty engine." He found the best of them "lyrical" and "joyful."

Public interest in the show ran high because Samuel Zacks, a millionaire Toronto stockbroker, and his wife, Ayala—philanthropists with a superb collection of Braque, Gaugin, Leger and Picasso—offered a $2,000 purchase prize for a painting to be selected from the exhibition by Sir John Rothenstein, the director of London's Tate Gallery. He selected *Polar No. 1* for the Tate Gallery.

Dorothy Cameron, who'd entered the collage for me, called to congratulate me later that night. Not only was there prize money but my painting had become part of the permanent collection at the Tate Gallery, so I joined the handful of Canadian painters who were represented there. The last one I knew about was A.Y. Jackson of the Group of Seven, who had done a painting of wartime Halifax that had appeared in the British Empire exhibition in Wembley, England, in 1924. Thrilled at this new development, the following night I took the red-eye flight to Toronto.

The Zacks purchase prize became a tremendous asset. For one thing, it got me a kind of apology from the Vancouver City Council. After all the public controversy over my mural at the Queen Elizabeth Playhouse, they had planned an investigation. The city's Community Arts Council brought the Zacks award to their attention and on February 6, the city clerk wrote to congratulate me on behalf of the mayor and city council. The fact that one of my works had been acquired by the prestigious Tate Gallery told the art-buying public that my art was worth something. Before this recognition, although critical notice of my work had grown and I had paintings in the Otto Seligman Gallery in Seattle and the Point Gallery in Victoria, greater exposure hadn't translated into increased sales. My

Reach, *collage, acrylic on canvas, 50" x 62", 1963.*

December show at the Here and Now, renamed the Dorothy Cameron Gallery, had not resulted in any sales because many of her clients already owned one of my paintings. My sales had stopped, just when I'd convinced the Galerie Camille Hebert to represent me in Montreal. But after I won the Zacks purchase prize, my sales picked up again, and I felt I could tell my dealers to raise their prices to six hundred dollars for a collage.

In Toronto, I appeared on TV with Sir John Rothenstein, an eminent curator whose father, the principal of the Royal College of Art, had been befriended by Edgar Degas and Toulouse-Lautrec. Sir John was a small man of about sixty. His neatly trimmed moustache, carefully parted greying hair and immaculate navy suit, even his royal title, belied his inherent feistiness. In England he'd been nicknamed "the battling Rothenstein" for his early defence of a generation of post-war British artists.

After the show, he took me aside, "Toni, you're not painting in an American style," he declared. "Yours is an English sensibility. You're an English painter."

"But—I've lived in Canada for fifteen years now," I replied.

"That doesn't mean you've adopted the American approach to colour," he said, wagging his finger at me. "You've got to spend some time in England again and get back to your roots."

I later realized that he was right about my painting. The collages in my *Polar* series used muted landscape colours rather than the sharper colours of many American abstract painters. Also, I incorporated the white areas of untouched canvas around the collaged shapes into the composition, just as I had done while painting watercolours. Depending on its relationship to the painted areas, a white area of untouched paper or canvas could occupy many spaces, from deep to shallow.

I asked Sir John to recommend me for a Canada Council grant. He quickly warmed to the idea and repeated his advice that I spend some time in England.

With his endorsement, I easily got a $7,000 travel and study grant and made plans to spend a year in London. The connection to Rothenstein and the Tate Gallery might prove a valuable link to private galleries in London and possibly to a permanent relationship with one of them. Furthermore, my wife had started writing her

FARM, CREG-NY-BARR, ISLE OF MAN *1944. Watercolour, 11" x 15", collection of the artist.*

FARM, ISLE OF MAN *1946. Watercolour, 11" x 15", collection of the artist.*

OLD SHIPYARD, PEEL, ISLE OF MAN *1946. Watercolour, 11" x 15", collection of Mr. & Mrs. William Hodgson, Vancouver.*

PORT ST. MARY, ISLE OF MAN *1946. Watercolour, 11" x 15", collection of the artist.*

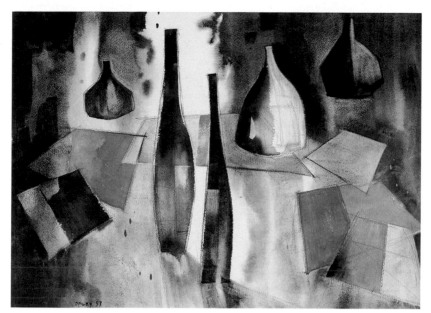

STILL LIFE WITH BOTTLES *1957. Watercolour, 21" x 29".*

HIDALGO *1959, Mexico. Acrylic collage on paper, 35" x 45".*

163

JOIE DES ENFANTS *1961. Oil on canvas collage, 70" x 91", collection Vancouver Art Gallery.*

POLAR NO. 14 *1962. Oil on canvas collage, 44¾" x 49".*

CELT *1962. Oil on canvas collage, 36¼" x 45¼", collection Canada Council Art Bank.*

CHASE *1964, London. Acrylic on paper collage, 35½" x 45".*

BARRENS *1968. Serigraph, 11" x 15".*

FORT RODD HILL *1968. Serigraph, 11" x 15".*

HEELSTONE *1968. Serigraph, 11" x 15".*

SILENT RIVER *1970. Serigraph, 11" x 15".*

OUTPOST *1971. Acrylic on board, 20" x 25¾".*

KILNS *1972. Acrylic on board, 20" x 25¾".*

BEECHY ISLAND *1974. Watercolour, 11" x 15", collection of Paul Wong.*

CONVERGING ROAD *1974. Serigraph, 11" x 15".*

EDGE OF A DARK FOREST *1974. Serigraph, 11" x 15".*

CASTLE ROCK, JAPAN *1978. Serigraph, 11" x 15".*

STONE STEPS, JAPAN *1978. Serigraph, 11" x 15".*

CARFURY FARM, CORNWALL, **1981.** *Watercolour, 11" x 15", collection of the artist.*

CUDDEN POINT FROM STOCKHOUSE COVE, 1981, *Cornwall. Watercolour, 11" x 15".*

EVENING SKY, LAKE PALACE, UDAIPUR, INDIA, 1982. *Watercolour, 11" x 15".*

LODI TOMBS, DELHI, INDIA, 1982. *Watercolour, 11" x 15".*

THE GOD NANDI, BHUBANISWAR, ORISSA, INDIA, 1983. *Watercolour, 11" x 15".*

BAFFIN BAY, MIDNIGHT *1986. Watercolour, 11" x 15".*

EASTERN ENTRANCE, LANCASTER SOUND *1986. Watercolour, 11" x 15".*

In the Eastern Lead, Baffin Bay *1987. Oil on canvas, 66" x 96", collection of the artist.*

Chehalis Lake *1990. Oil on canvas, 30" x 40", collection of the artist.*

BLACK ROCK, CORTES ISLAND, 1994. *Watercolour, 11" x 15", collection of the artist.*

STANLEY PARK AND POINT GREY FROM AMBLESIDE, WEST VANCOUVER, 1997. *Watercolour, 11" x 15", collection of the artist.*

master's thesis on Henry James, the expatriate American novelist who spent most of his working life in England.

I arranged to spend a month before sailing to England as the artist-in-residence at the Doon Summer School of the Arts in Ontario. We drove east, leaving Jennifer and Lynn in my parents' care. Then Gloria and I travelled to London by boat, shipping our Volkswagen along for an extra fifty dollars.

We found the city in the throes of Beatlemania. In August, the Beatles released their first million-selling single. "She loves you, yeah, yeah, yeah!" sang all the young women in beehive hairdos and mini-skirts, while every male under thirty wore Beatle boots and sported a basin haircut.

We spent the first night in London in a cramped attic room in a bed-and-breakfast place in Bloomsbury behind the British Museum. The next day we contacted some Canadians living in London and were directed to a Georgian townhouse on Redcliffe Road, South Kensington, where a third floor flat was shortly to become available. The front of the building had been blown out during the Blitz and the owners had it replaced with big studio windows. The more desirable second-floor flat, which even had a balcony with French doors, would be available later in the year. We decided to take the smaller flat at once and move into the larger one later. We'd planned a visit to the Isle of Man, so we went there while waiting for our flat to become vacant.

From the ferry, the island appeared as pleasant, green and rural as ever, and the serried boarding houses and hotels on Douglas Bay still looked to me like rows of iced cakes. Though it had been fifteen years since I'd left, nothing seemed to have quickened the snail pace of change. As Gloria and I drove through town, I showed her my old school and the houses where my family had lived. We booked into a bed-and-breakfast on the sea front, then headed to Ramsey to visit my grandmother and my uncle and his family.

Now that he was older, Uncle Martin looked like my father more than ever. He was a lean, bald, ruddy-complexioned man, the Deputy Grand Primo of a social club, the Royal Antediluvian Order of Water Buffaloes. Solidly working class, he drove a tanker truck for the same Ramsey Gas Company that had once employed my grandfather. When he later took me to the pub of the Swan Hotel, some men there even remembered Granddad Onley.

"Young fellow, I knew you, too," cackled an ancient retired post-man. "I got me gammy leg delivering mail to you!"

He reminded me that instead of putting a letter into the mail-box one day, he'd handed it to me through the window in the base-ment—I was painting at my table there—and then he'd lost his foot-ing, fallen and broken his leg. I remembered running for help.

My grandmother was still alive and living with my Uncle Martin and his family on Cronk Elfin, a cul de sac where they rented a coun-cil house. "Cronk" is Manx for hill, so she was living on Elfin Hill. Partially deaf, living in a room upstairs, she'd bang her cane on the floor when she wanted one of my young cousins to bring her up a pot of tea. Visiting her when she was so much older almost felt like meeting a stranger. But she surprised me by presenting me with the drawings and paintings I'd left behind, which she had carefully saved. Again I saw my *Freighter and Tug, Mersey River,* 1945, a realis-tic watercolour I'd done while on a sketching trip to Liverpool with my painting teacher. The angle of the ship cruising the Mersey River drew my eye into the composition. Though I'd been only seventeen then, the painting held up almost as well as my more recent land-scape paintings. It also reminded me of my teacher, John Hobson Nicholson.

In Douglas, I learned that Nicholson had quit the house-paint-ing business and become a shopkeeper on Strand Street, exhibiting his pictures in a tiny gallery on the second floor of his art supply and souvenir shop. I suppose it was the only thing connected to art that he could have done on the island, except for teaching art classes in the public school.

Gloria and I found him behind the cash register, ringing up a sale. Though his hair and moustache had turned white he was dressed very much the same as before with a Manx tweed jacket and wool tie. When he saw me his eyebrows arched in surprise. "Toni, what are you doing on the island?"

I explained our visit. In turn he told me how he was doing. Even at fifty-two, he walked fifteen miles a day in the summer, waking at 3:30 a.m. so that he could hike to a location and start painting at dawn. In three hours he'd finish a watercolour, walk to Douglas, frame the picture, then hang it on the wall of his gallery before he opened the shop at nine o'clock. When he showed me a recent seascape off Douglas Head it surprised me how little his work had changed over the years. He didn't seem very interested in discussing art, or my collages for that matter. Only when I reminisced about the past did he show any enthusiasm.

"Toni Onley, you were quite a joker," he chuckled. "And if I remember rightly, I called you 'The Criminal Laugh'."

We both laughed at that and I thought the ice had been broken. Just then someone else entered the shop. Nicholson introduced us to him. "You remember Toni Onley, don't you? He's living in Canada now."

Straining to see if I recognized him, I studied the man's small white face. It was Carter's Little Liver Pill. He offered me his hand, "Toni, nice to see you again."

Nicholson sold him some art supplies, then busied himself about the shop without continuing our conversation. Forgetting that we had not parted on good terms, I had hoped to spend some time with my old teacher. I had imagined that Nicholson would invite Gloria and me to dinner at his home or at least to join him for a drink. After all, we'd been very close and I'd gone to school with his wife. Besides, I'd come so far to visit the Isle of Man. We hung around the shop for a while longer but Nicholson didn't seem to have anything more to say to me. A few more customers dropped by. Feeling a little self-conscious and embarrassed we finally left.

Gloria tried to console me afterward. "Nicholson was very important to you at the time. But you were one of many students, Toni, and I guess you didn't make as big an impression on him."

Despite my disappointment I wrote to Nicholson a few times after our visit. Much later I offered to purchase one of his paintings for my 1980 book *A Silent Thunder*. Graciously, he gave me *River Glass, the Tromode*, which he had painted in 1946, about the time I'd known him. I reciprocated with a painting, several prints and a copy of the book.

In the years since I'd left the island Nicholson had been designing currency and postage stamps for the Manx Government. During his lifetime he designed over 170 stamps and has been identified by the *Guinness Book of Records* as the most prolific stamp designer of the twentieth century. He was the only British artist in the century to have designed coins, stamps and banknotes. Twenty-five years after our visit, on a black night in February, a wild shrieking winter storm swept the south end of the island where Nicholson lived in Port Erin. I heard that the wind reached hurricane force and tore some of the slates from his roof. Nicholson had always hated and feared storms. It must have found him in despair, for on that terrible night he killed himself at the age of seventy-seven. The last four stamps he designed were awaiting issue at the time of his death, and formed part of a memorial cover issued by the Isle of Man Post Office in May 1988.

After a pleasant week exploring the island Gloria and I returned to London and moved into the South Kensington flat. Each morning while Gloria did the cooking and housekeeping and worked on her thesis, I left the house, crossed Hyde Park and walked to Knightsbridge where I'd sublet a studio from a songwriter who was a night owl. He wrote in the room all evening, leaving it free during the day. The space was what was known as a sub-basement flat. The only natural light in the room filtered through some glass bricks set into the sidewalk overhead. In the dim light and the moist atmosphere, which I added to by scrubbing my canvases with water to prepare them for use, fungi started growing on the carpet. My cold dark quarters were inadequately heated by a small coin-operated gas heater.

Sometimes I visited the Print and Drawing Room at the British Museum, where Rothenstein had arranged a free pass for me. I examined the collection's wonderful nineteenth-century watercolours by Peter de Wint, John Sell Cotman, David Cox and J.M. Turner. I held them in my hands like old friends: little watercolours filled with light, space, and spirit—Turner's paintings exploding with light; John Sell Cotman's solidly built compositions, wash built upon wash; the loaded brush of David Cox—and I felt I had come home. While examining Turner's painting *Loch Coruisk, Skye*, I realized anew that the physical size of an art work didn't matter. Only 3½ inches by 5⅝ inches, this tiny landscape is described in the exhibition catalogue as a "great whirling vortex," a "meteorological and geological *tour de force*." Two tiny figures in the foreground establish the scale of a monumentally vast landscape that is actually no larger than a postcard.

Back in my studio, on rough unsized canvases, I created big airy collages with large areas of untouched off-white canvas between the figures. As I had done before, I moved around pieces of painted canvas until a spark of tension ignited between the shapes. Then I took away as many shapes as I could, one by one, while still retaining the dramatic relationship between those left on the canvas. In one large 52- by 60-inch piece I tilted the shapes toward the corners of the canvas and glued them down. Then I brushed in zones of grey, shading the areas behind the shapes to link and amplify them. In these works, everything floating in the off-white space of the canvas was black, grey or white.

I called this series the *Zone* and *Limit* paintings. Simple powerful compositions of forms balanced in space, they were monumental in their absolute minimalism. Eventually they received some positive critical attention, though initially the lack of art sales seemed to be an echo of the sparseness of the paintings.

One night in London, however, one of these new paintings drew considerable attention. We had moved to the second-floor flat in the townhouse and I had hung some of the canvases on the living room wall. They could be seen from outside the house through the large window. Someone in the street below started tossing pebbles at the window.

A derelict in wire-frame spectacles and a shabby navy raincoat waved his arms at me. "You're a painter," he squeaked, "come out and have a drink with me!"

Worried that he'd either break the window or disturb the neighbours, I joined him. The stooped, emaciated character before me with thinning hair and a haggard, unshaven face looked at least seventy, although he was actually twenty years younger. He was Roger Hilton, recognized today as one of the most important abstract painters of his generation.

Roger, who lived in the neighbourhood, took me on a pub crawl. At times quarrelsome, he was given to shaking his fist and making grand pronouncements. In one bar, he proclaimed, "Art's a blood and death battle. You've got to throw everything you've got into it." In the late 1940s he'd done nothing but abstract art. A decade later, when everyone worked that way, he started painting figures, mostly nude women. When we went into the Hollywood Bar he propositioned a French woman sitting near us. Like many British artists of his generation, he'd studied in France in the 1930s. His French must have been pretty good because she hit him with her handbag.

The bartender, a moustachioed ex-India army type, seized Roger by the collar, saying sternly, "Now, now, Mr. Hilton, we'll have none of that here." He frogmarched Roger to the door and gave him a really hard push through it. Sheepishly, I followed Roger outside. He got up from the sidewalk where he had landed and calmly dusted himself off as if getting thrown out of a pub were an everyday occurrence.

"Be a good lad," he told me. "Go back inside and get me mac."

I returned with his raincoat and we walked to his squalid quarters in a decaying Edwardian house. Dirty dishes jammed the sink. A jumbled stack of his work was surrounded by piles of magazines and newspapers, scraps of paper, and scattered dishes and cutlery. I saw witty charcoal drawings of gawky, grotesque-looking nude women with stiff flying hair, and canvases with broadly outlined childlike depictions of candy-coloured dogs and striped circus animals.

He swept some papers from a chair and pulled it over for me. Next he rummaged through his cupboards until he found a bottle of whiskey. Clutching a paintbrush and the bottle in one hand, he sifted through the debris on the cluttered floor with the other and came up with several tubes of oil paint and some blank paper. Then he drank at length from the bottle. When he had finished he offered me a swig. When I declined he snarled, "You don't know what's good for you, man. Now I'll show you some real painting." He squatted on the floor, daubed his brush into some paint and then dipped it into the whisky bottle. He set the bottle down and made a line on the paper with the brush. "Look at that, would you?" He turned the paper in my direction. "Have you ever seen such a beautiful line in your life?"

I started toward the door. "It's late, Roger. I'm going home."

"Wait a minute—wait a minute!" He threw down his brush and trailed me out of the room. As I started down the stairs, he stood on the landing, shouting abuse at me. "You'll never amount to anything. You're not an artist!"

"Good night, Roger," I replied.

I discovered an art form that was new to me in the Print and

Drawing Room. One month, they exhibited Goya's masterpiece *The Disasters of War*, a set of etchings depicting Napoleon's invasion of Spain. The tonal qualities of these anguished images of pain and death were created by Goya's use of aquatint (a technique in which nitric acid creates texture on a copper plate), and they instilled in me a burning desire to do some printmaking. I contacted Rothenstein and he referred me to a printmaking studio on Charlotte Street in Soho run by a Swedish artist, Birgit Skiold.

A small woman with short, wavy blonde hair and high cheekbones, Birgit exuded energy as she led me through her workshop in the basement of artist and war hero Adrian Heath's home. Her etching press stood in a corner by some wooden shelves crowded with tins of ink.

By that time I understood how etchings were made. A steel press bed, carrying a dampened piece of paper on top of an inked etching plate, moved between adjustable top and bottom steel cylinders when the cylinders were rotated by a wheel turned by the printmaker. The pressure of the cylinders forced the paper and plate together, transferring the ink to the paper and producing the etching.

But when Birgit heard that I'd never actually made any etchings, she exploded. "What do you think this is, a school? I'm not running art classes, you know. I do my work here and let other printmakers use the studio in return for a fee. I don't have time to teach you how to etch."

I pleaded with her. "I won't get in your way. I'll just watch you and pick things up for myself."

Birgit could never stay angry with anybody for very long. She liked people too much. She uttered a great sigh and her stern expression melted into a toothy, cherubic smile. "All right, pay the fee and you can use the press."

In spite of her initial refusal to teach me anything, I learned a great deal at her atelier. Both of us could be very sociable, and as we worked on our projects we talked for hours and became good friends. Birgit had admirers dropping in to see her from time to time and she'd discuss them with me while she taught me about printmaking techniques.

Gradually I developed an approach. With a stylus, I'd cut a few

The etching press, London, 1963.

lines into a copper plate, then ink the plate, place a piece of dampened paper over it, cover it with a felt cloth and crank it through the press to make a print. I'd take the print, examine it and then work on the composition again. I'd place some paper shapes on top of the etched lines of the print and move them around until I liked the new composition. Next, I'd etch these additional shapes onto the plate. As I became more skilled I used aquatint on the plate to create some of the shapes, giving them a grainy partially solid texture. I composed each printed image of black lines and areas or shapes of grey and black against the white paper, contrasting shapes that were just outlined with shapes filled in with texture.

"I've never seen anybody print like that," commented Birgit. "You don't plan at all. You improvise as you go along."

"It's the same way I make collages," I replied. "I don't try to produce a preconceived image. I discover the image by working on the plate."

My idea was to employ the subtle contrasts between shapes in the same way that a painter would use different colours. Only black-and-white etching interested me. At this point in my printmaking career, I felt that colour diluted a line's impact and that lines had so many possibilities: drawn lines, lines etched in hard and soft grounds, lines cut as in a collage. For me the line carried content and held my forms together in the right relationships between the figures and the plate's edge.

I sent some of my new etchings to Dorothy Cameron. "I'll be frank—I must be, in fairness to us both—I was not gassed by the prints." She stored them awhile at her gallery, eventually returning them to me in Vancouver. At about the same time, however, the curator of prints and drawings at the Victoria & Albert Museum dropped by at Birgit's invitation and bought copies of the first prints for the museum's collection. Though Dorothy's lack of enthusiasm disappointed me, I moved on, using my connection with Rothenstein to get introductions to some of London's private galleries. Annely Juda at the Hamilton Gallery in Hanover Square arranged to tour some of my collages to Leeds and a few other cities. Although I had few sales, the reviews were very good considering that I was virtually unknown in Britain.

At that point Gloria and I had been in England for ten months and we had to return to Canada to pick up Jennifer and Lynn after they finished school in June. Hoping for permanent representation at a London gallery, I asked Annely Juda to commit to a show. She finally arranged an exhibition at the Commonwealth Institute on Kensington High Street for July 1965, the following year. The venue disappointed me because I'd already shown there as part of the fifth Biennale of Canadian art. For the most part, the institute, which featured a scale model of a lumber mill, a display of fur pelts and some projected slides of Inuit fishing, only drew Commonwealth tourists and school children on geography class tours. Consequently, although the show was mentioned by the *Times* and the *Observer*, it never captured the attention of London art critics. Predictably, there was little to show financially for the effort. Afterward, Annely wanted to freight everything back to me—forty collages on paper and canvas—but I had nowhere to store them, nor did I have the money to pay for the shipping of large art works.

Fortunately, I had befriended Bob Duffy, the press attaché at the Canadian embassy. In a letter to him, I suggested the embassy mount an exhibition of its own rather than "coasting on the public relations work of the Canadian Pacific Railway." I pointed out that the US embassy had one of the best gallery spaces in the city. On the other hand, the Canadian High Commission in London, which was at Canada House in Trafalgar Square right across from England's National Gallery, had an even better location. "We can put our best foot forward there," I argued when offering him my show.

The Canadian High Commission took about thirteen of my largest *Zone* and *Limit* paintings and hung them at Canada House. I pictured one of my huge abstract collages hanging in the lobby opposite the wall-sized engraving of the Fathers of Confederation, who would have been shocked at modern art, and found the contrast somewhat amusing. After the show someone at the Canadian embassy arranged for the works to go into storage. The administration changed and my largest canvas-on-canvas collages just disappeared. No one could tell me where the missing paintings had gone. The smaller works, not in this show, were eventually shipped back to me in Vancouver.

Twelve years later, Doug Cole, an acquaintance visiting England, tracked down the paintings in exchange for his airfare. He located them in a leaky warehouse and shipped them back to Vancouver. I'd left my minimalist period behind by then, and when I uncrated the shipment I was amazed by the size and impact of some of the work I'd done in London. I restored the canvases that had water damage and in 1977 had an exhibition at Presentation House in North Vancouver, called *The Lost London Paintings*. Works that had once been almost impossible to sell at $600 because they were so simple and restrained, sold after that exhibition for as much as $30,000.

Chapter 15

Counting the Cost

When Gloria and I went to London in 1963, we left Jennifer and Lynn with my parents in Summerland, BC. Jennifer was thirteen and already showing signs of adolescent rebellion. Shortly after we had settled in London she and her girlfriend put on eye makeup and lipstick, put their hair up in beehive hairdos and ran away to Vancouver with some money the girlfriend had obtained from her father's bank account. The police picked them up a week later. My father was absolutely beside himself with frustration when he telephoned me. "She's your responsibility," he said. "You take care of her."

In desperation I called an old friend of mine living in Ottawa who had a daughter about the same age as mine. She agreed to take Jennifer for the school year and enrolled her in her daughter's school. After a short time Jennifer was expelled for bad behaviour but her grandmother got her into a convent boarding school in Combermere, a small town outside of Ottawa.

On June 26, 1964, my friend, Doris Titus, and her daughter, Patty, left Ottawa for a cottage in the country. They picked up Jennifer en route, planning to drop her off at her grandparents' home in Galt. A terrific hailstorm struck that evening while they were driving. About fifteen miles from Ottawa, a young man heading to the city went around a curve too fast and skidded on the hailstone-covered road. The rear end of his car swung into the oncoming lane, and Doris's car broadsided his. The impact pitched Jennifer through the windshield and she was instantly killed. Doris was crushed against the steering wheel and also killed. In the back seat, Patty was protected by a mattress intended for the cottage, and survived with minor injuries. The driver of the other car was only slightly injured.

Gloria and I were sailing back from England to meet up with Jennifer when the ship's purser told us the news. Gloria tried to console me but I was numb. I could hardly listen to her. At that moment nothing could have got through to me. I kept thinking of Jennifer. To encourage her at school I'd been sending her cards and letters in which I'd tried to help her to see beyond the loss of her mother. Mary's death had clouded her young life, contributing to the rebelliousness that any teenager felt at her age. I'd tried to amuse her with riddles. What's purple and hums—An electric plum. How do you get four elephants into a Morris Mini Minor?—Two in the front and two in the back. How do you get four giraffes into the car?—You can't, it's full of elephants. I sent her one of the paintings I'd done when I was just a few years older than she was. I tried to inspire her to set herself a goal. I reminded her that all she needed to pass Grade 7 was another ten percent. I promised her the modelling classes she wanted if she made the grade. I thought Jennifer had been coming around. Now she was dead.

We drove to Galt in the Volkswagen Beetle we'd taken to England and brought back on the ship. The service for Jennifer was in the cemetery chapel where my wife's funeral had been held eight years earlier. Even the minister was the same. My former mother-in-law, Helen Burrows, had chosen an elaborate pink and white coffin for Jennifer. While we were waiting for the service to begin she told me that Jennifer had been quite happy toward the end of her life. One weekend, she had gone swimming at Doris's cottage. Someone with a motorboat towed Patty and Jennifer around the lake on air mattresses. "Don't worry, Granny," she'd written. "Even though I went first as usual, I had a ball and it wasn't dangerous."

I staggered through a nightmare. I kept seeing Jennifer's last photograph. Her mussed-up curly hair. The tortoise-shell glasses comically aslant on her forehead. The goofy smile as she posed with some school friends, all of them in the white blouses and pleated tartan skirts of the school uniform. Jennifer had told me that she couldn't wait to drive back to BC with us. She'd written to Lynn that she'd saved all her old comic books for her. When I thought of letters like that I felt my heart would break.

To distract myself I looked around at the people in the room, most of them friends of Helen. My former father-in-law, Carl, sat in a wheelchair. His last unnecessary operation had left him paralyzed from the waist down. He glared at me until the lit end of the cigarette pinched between his fingers singed his fingertips. I remembered how deceitful and mean he had been when Mary died and I turned away from him.

A grave for Jennifer had been excavated next to her mother's grave, which lay in the Burrows family plot. Overwhelmed by sorrow and guilt I left Galt as soon as my daughter was buried.

Nearly twenty years passed before I visited the two graves. I found myself driving by Galt on a trip to a gallery in Ontario. I stopped at the cemetery, found the sexton and was directed to the graves. The area was fairly large yet I found Mary's and Jennifer's graves very easily. They lay near a small tree. Carl had inscribed Mary's gravestone with the epitaph *Beloved wife of Toni Onley*. My head swam as I read it and I sat down on the grass. I wept for a long time, stricken with grief. I could hardly stand up again. I should have cried like that years earlier but both deaths, occurring as they did with shocking suddenness, were for a long time at least partly unreal to me.

Following Jennifer's funeral, my former brother-in-law, Tom Burrows, and his new wife, Ida, joined us on the drive to Toronto, where they had an apartment and could put us up overnight before we drove on to Vancouver.

As we neared Toronto the traffic on the freeway slowed to a creep. Tom and Ida were ahead of us in their ancient Volvo. A huge De Soto with Idaho licence plates and a giant harmonica-shaped grill lumbered along behind us. In my rear-view mirror I saw a farmer and his wife, who appeared to be shouting abuse at him. He wasn't slowing down. *Meep-meep!* I honked my Volkswagen Beetle horn. *Meep-meep!* I rolled down the window to wave him off. But he slammed into my car, ramming the engine block into the back seat of the Beetle and bulldozing us into Tom's Volvo. My arm snapped back. Gloria's head whipped against the dashboard. Tom's car hit another, which struck a fourth car and on the collisions went, forward and backward in a chain reaction.

I staggered out of the car to assess the damage and see if help was coming. The smash-up stretched along the highway for some distance; dozens of cars were involved. A police siren howled. A cop stepped out of a cruiser. Gloria sat in the front seat trying not to move much. The cop squeezed into the driver's seat to take her name for his accident report. He looked at the rear engine that had been thrust into the back seat. He clicked his tongue against his teeth. "Boy, have you been creamed!"

The insurers wrote off the Beetle as scrap. We spent a couple of days in Toronto while Gloria had x-rays and we filed an insurance claim. Then we flew back to Vancouver and picked up Lynn.

Another lean period of my life began. We had no car but fortunately we had already rented a house in Kitsilano from some friends who were going to Africa for two years to teach. The house cost $200 a month but we had two apartments to rent out, one in the basement and one on the second floor, so the net rent was only $100. I had spent my Canada Council grant but Gloria had another teaching assistantship at UBC. Unfortunately, because of her neck injury she had to stop teaching less than halfway through the fall term. However, we received a small insurance settlement and lived off that for a while. Gloria also had a Canada Council grant to begin a Ph.D. programme. But the gallery scene was depressing. Alvin Balkind had sold the New Design Gallery two years earlier to take a salaried position as curator at the UBC Fine Arts Gallery, and the recent exhibition of my *Polar* series of collages at his old gallery had not sold well. Betty Marshall, the new director, told me that although it had been one of the best shows seen in Vancouver for a long time she was only able to sell one work, the smallest in the show.

Nationally the art market was also difficult. In Toronto the police busted Dorothy Cameron for *Eros '65*, her Valentine's Day exhibition that featured twenty-two different prints depicting the act of love. They charged her with eight counts of obscenity, one for each of the seven pictures that were supposed to have been obscene and one blanket charge covering the entire exhibition. The police offered to drop the charges if she took down the pictures but

Dorothy refused to bow to that sort of pressure. She fought them in court despite the cost and the threat of a two-year jail sentence. In the end they fined her $350 and she closed her gallery. She had subsidized it for the past two years, lost $25,000 and been nudged toward bankruptcy by the court case. Including my work, she had sold more than $250,000 worth of Canadian art over the six years of the gallery's existence. She had never asked herself, "Will it sell?" but always, "Is it worth showing?"

The events of the last few months had shaken my confidence. Becoming a full-time painter remained my one great ambition but, after years of scraping together a living, selling art didn't seem to be getting any easier. I'd already made so many personal sacrifices that I couldn't help wondering whether I should continue painting or try to get back into architecture. In England, I'd been corresponding with Jack Wise, who had painted with me in San Miguel de Allende and had recently immigrated to Canada as a farmer. He told me that he'd quit painting for good. Soon after Gloria and I returned to Vancouver we bought an old car and I went to visit Jack.

He and his wife, Jane, had moved to a remote part of the West Kootenays in BC. I drove down a logging road by the Arrow Lakes and found them living near a nudist colony. Buck naked, Jack kneeled on the roof of his adobe hut hammering down cedar shingles.

I honked my horn.

Jack stood up and waved, *"Mi amigo!"*

I climbed out of the car. "Christ, Jack! You're going to give me a castration complex."

He laughed and scrambled down a ladder from the roof. He had left a pair of pants on a sawhorse near the house and he put them on. Aside from the grey flecks in his beard he didn't appear much different. He wore his hair in a ponytail and was as lean as a rail.

Janie appeared and hugged me. Time had been harder on her. The ten years' difference between them had become more pronounced now that she was a woman in her mid-forties.

I shook Jack's hand. "So, you quit painting."

He gave a throaty chuckle. "After a year and a half of clearing land and building sheds I had a little time on my hands. I'm like the guy who announces to the world he's stopped smoking then sneaks off to the barn for a few puffs. I found myself doing a few drawings."

He led me into the house and showed me his paintings. Jack had become a very different person from the hard-drinking pistol-packing wild man I'd known in San Miguel. He showed me a series of perfect little miniatures bordered with a kind of abstract calligraphy in indigo and lighter blues, whose lines swirled in from the edges of the pictures to circle small red mandalas and tiny yellow Buddhas. They were personal fantasies based on archetypal Indian and Chinese images. I was surprised by the imagery and impressed by the exquisite detail of the paintings.

Ever since I had known him Jack had been interested in Eastern philosophy and he had recently begun studying meditation. As he showed his new work to me he described how it had come to him after he had given up painting. "It's kind of like that old notion that you have to give up something to get something. I'd totally given up on being an artist when all of a sudden the imagery started coming. It was like a cap had blown off an oil well. It just gushed out."

Up the hill from Jack and Janie stood the nudist colony of "Fort Freedman," named after the woman who owned the property, Jimmie Freedman. She invited me to have lunch there. Walking toward it, I noticed that Fort Freedman looked more like a kid's fort than a settlement and I had the first laugh I'd had in a long time. Scraps of plywood and two-by-fours nailed to tree trunks partially stockaded a cabin and some sheds so that colonists might walk around naked yet avoid the stares of curious passersby driving down the road. Inside Fort Freedman there were several sheds roofed with blue tarpaulins. I saw a few people washing in a stream-fed bathing pond that had been scooped out of the hill with a bulldozer.

The colonists had their meals in the largest log cabin. At the head of the table sat Jimmie Freedman, a small lady without a tooth in her head. Her naked breasts hung like empty purses as she ladled out a stew of roots and leaves from a carved wooden tureen. Seated by her was a bearded starved-looking young man, who seemed to be a combination of indentured servant, goatherd and bedfellow.

A black-eyed, wild-looking man with frizzy hair squeezed onto the bench beside me. I was alarmed by his appearance but he turned out to be a harmless dropout from nuclear physics at Harvard. The most freakish-looking people at the table had dropped out of several major universities.

I noticed that the logs in the cabin were stacked badly and not chinked; daylight shone through the spaces between them. There was no foundation or flooring in the cabin, either, just a dirt floor.

"When the snow flies around here," I warned, "you're going to freeze."

My remark was ignored by the colonists. Jimmie looked around the room at the rest of the group. "We know all about Canadian winters, don't we?" she said. "We've been cutting firewood. We'll be fine."

I shook my head. "It'll be pretty cold in here with a dirt floor and holes in the walls."

"You're such a worrier, Toni!" Jimmie giggled and the other colonists laughed at me.

I don't think any of them even had any winter clothes. Later I heard from Jack that after the first big snowfall they abandoned Fort Freedman and dispersed around the globe.

Jack left the Kootenays a few months later, in the early spring. He had rededicated himself to the sole-minded pursuit of art. He took a hundred dollars, loaded up their old truck with his belongings and a bundle of his drawings and paintings, and just left. He showed up in Vancouver. "Toni, I always wondered if I could be an artist," he told me. "Or if I could, whether I would have enough contacts or get-up-and-go or whatever it takes to make a living as one. I'm not worrying about that anymore." He rented a studio space in Kitsilano, a place where he could also live.

Later Janie called me from their homestead at the Arrow Lakes. She sounded absolutely desperate. "Where's Jack?" she asked.

"Hasn't he told you? He's moved to Vancouver," I said.

Apparently, he'd left some kind of farewell note. But he hadn't told her his plans and she hadn't heard from him since.

"He's taken off before," she said. "He'll be back."

But I knew that Jack had found himself a new girlfriend, a woman he thought could support him and help him sell his work. She was now helping him produce a show of batiks for the New Design Gallery.

"Janie, you're not going to like this." I paused, feeling uncomfortable at having to tell her but aware that she had a right to know. "Jack's taken up with someone else. You'd better forget him."

Devastated, Janie started crying. She hated me for telling her the news and hung up after I suggested she leave the Kootenays. I later heard that she eventually managed to get back to the States, although Jack had left her practically destitute.

My visit with Jack reminded me of my own commitment to art. More than a skill or an economic activity, it was my identity, the way I looked at the world. I realized that I could never change even if I wanted to, so I decided to continue building my career, however difficult it might be.

In Vancouver, Gloria, Lynn and I gradually pieced our lives together. Our rented house was in Kitsilano, the Greenwich Village of Vancouver, the low-rent district on the west side that lay between the highrise apartments of the West End and the exclusive West Point Grey homes near the university. Kitsilano had used book stores, second-hand clothing boutiques, and head shops with hash pipes and hookahs in the windows.

The New Design Gallery had closed with the sudden death of its director, Betty Marshall, and I had moved to the Bau-Xi Gallery, which had relocated to Kitsilano. There it had four exhibition spaces: a main one on the ground floor for temporary exhibitions and two print rooms and a gallery upstairs for the continuous display of work by gallery artists. In those days the art community in Vancouver was very small and studio space was cheap in Kitsilano, so artists like Audrey Doray and Brian Fisher had studios nearby. Roy Kiyooka lived in an apartment above the gallery. We all went to one another's exhibitions. Nobody did terribly well. The artists provided the wine and cheese for their opening nights. The exhibitions were as much about socializing and sharing ideas as selling paintings. It felt like belonging to a club.

My former brother-in-law, Tom Burrows, had decided to move to Vancouver and take pre-med courses at UBC. He and Ida rented the second-floor apartment in our house. A tugboat captain lived in the basement suite, and I used the rest of the basement as my studio. I guess I unwittingly became a role model for Tom because he soon switched from Science to Fine Arts and began creating his own sculpture, even exhibiting it.

That was the last thing his ailing father wanted to hear. Carl had had enough of artists in the family. He and Tom hated each other, so he assumed that his son had become an artist just to spite him. Shortly before he died he sent Tom a cassette tape in which he told him he was a shit and threatened to disinherit him. Tom called it "Krapp's Last Tape."

Some months later, when his father died, Tom and I talked about his prospects of an inheritance. "Do you think he cut me off?" asked Tom.

"I'll bet you ten dollars he hasn't left you a thing," I said.

For a moment Tom hesitated as if considering the odds. Then he laughed. "I don't think I'll take that bet."

Sure enough, his father hadn't left him a thing.

One of Tom's instructors in the UBC Fine Arts Department was an assistant professor, Iain Baxter. He was tall and boyish, with brown hair and long sideburns. Originally from Calgary, he had done a master's degree in education at the University of Idaho and another one in fine arts at the University of Washington. Although saying he was inspired by landscapes, he painted abstract, hard-edged geometric shapes on large canvases. He came to one of the shows of the minimalist work I was doing at the time and seemed really excited about it.

I began sketching outdoors with Iain on the beach at Spanish Banks near Kitsilano. Ever since I'd returned from England I felt guilty about my attraction to the landscape. Yet I felt compelled to draw ordinary things—the rocks, the driftwood on the beach, and the sea. I seemed to be throwing away years of effort and study and slipping back into the kind of watercolour painting I had done much earlier with John Nicholson. I had come so far in my pursuit of non-objective painting that it reassured me that someone as contemporary in outlook as Iain shared that interest.

The new drawings were not so much landscapes, however, as commentary on landscape, in which the forms of nature were rendered not in three dimensions but two-dimensionally. The green hills of the Isle of Man and the weathered brown fish boats in the harbours at Douglas and Ramsey that I had painted as a teenager had, through the intermediary process of abstraction, given way to scenes without any perspective. There were no foregrounds and backgrounds in these new abstract landscapes.

On one of our trips Iain showed me a book of reproductions of still-life paintings. Although composed entirely of glass and ceramic containers, these still lifes were like landscapes in the way the light fell on the objects and in the way the objects cast shadows. The bottles and ceramics had been used to portray light in a poetic painterly way. Iain had a tremendous eye and he knew exactly what I liked about each piece.

"Who is this artist?" I asked him.

"Giorgio Morandi," he replied.

Morandi—I'd heard about him before, an Italian futurist turned still-life painter, who lived in Bologna and painted the same kinds of objects over and over again. He never married and lived his entire life with his three sisters. In his studio he kept a collection of ceramic and glass containers. He'd spend a long time arranging a still life of pots and bottles until he had the relationship he wanted between light and form. Then he painted swiftly and directly, using subdued greens, umbers and shades of terra cotta.

Iain told me: "Toni, Bologna's full of medieval towers, and they say the bottles in Morandi's paintings look just like the city's towers."

When he told me that, it occurred to me that the opposite might also be true. If Morandi could paint a still life and create a landscape it was possible that landscape elements might be used to create a still life. The shapes I sketched with Iain slowly began to resemble familiar objects in the landscape like rocks and hills.

In *Chalk Field*, which I painted in 1965, I depicted a massive shape in the centre of the canvas and almost unconsciously added a horizon line. The line changed the relationships in the painting so that the massive shape now suggested a giant boulder on a beach, or even a mountain under heavy grey skies. I'd taken a step in my art that would have tremendous implications a few years later, for the time would come when I fully returned to painting the landscape. For the moment, however, aside from my sketching with Iain, I continued to paint abstractly and minimally, and worked in my studio.

Chalk Field, *acrylic on board, 20" x 25¾", 1965. Collection Vancouver Art Gallery*

Inspired by Morandi, Iain went in an entirely different direction. He extended the still-life tradition into plastics, which he regarded as the ceramics of the twentieth century. He searched garbage dumps for plastic milk jugs and bleach bottles that had been run over and flattened by bulldozers. He took them home, cleaned them off and arranged them into still-life compositions.

Then he got the idea of creating relief sculptures of them with a vacuum-form press. These presses come in all sizes because they are used for manufacturing everything from shrink wrapping to the moulding for neon signs. He talked Ted Scroggs, the owner of the Diamond Neon Products company, into letting him use their large vacuum-form press when the company was closed on the weekends. Then he brought in his still life and placed it on the base of the press. He laid a sheet of plastic over the composition, lowered the metal frame around the edges of the sheet to make sure no air escaped, and heated the plastic until it melted into a taffy-like consistency. He then turned on the vacuum and sucked out the air from

199

under the plastic. The heated plastic sheet flowed over his composition and took its shape. In 1965, Iain made forty to fifty of these original, witty still lifes and they were collected by galleries across the country.

His reputation grew steadily and in 1966 he joined Simon Fraser University in the new position of resident in the visual arts of the inter-disciplinary Communications department. One semester Iain was very busy preparing exhibitions but he only had to teach a single non-credit class that met for two hours each week over twelve weeks. He organized a happening that he called *An Attitude to Teaching* and he finished the entire class in a single twenty-four-hour period. Communicating with walkie-talkies, he and his fifteen students drove around Vancouver in three cars. He led them to a fashion show he was judging, several local galleries, a Japanese restaurant where they ate and analyzed Japanese aesthetics, then an all-night movie theatre and, finally, a coffee shop where they discussed the films they had just seen.

SFU had just opened and it encouraged experimentation but Iain's class was more like an exercise in sleep deprivation. After the class was written up in *Time* magazine, the university administration warned Iain that if he taught a class in a single day again, they might pay him for only a day's employment. The university president proposed a little conceptual piece of his own. He offered Iain an administrative job with a new title and a large pay raise. Iain had to resign from the teaching faculty in order to take it.

"Don't do it, Iain," I advised him. "If you have tenure, they can't fire you."

"The president's a good friend," he argued.

His "good friend" sacked him in 1971 after he finally joined the administration. Iain took his wife and kids and headed for Europe on an extended vacation.

As Iain Baxter, Jack Wise and I headed in separate artistic directions, Iain suggested swapping some art with Jack. Jack told me he was embarrassed because he couldn't think of a single Baxter piece he wanted to see more than once. His biggest complaint against Iain's art was that he'd made it by fabricating it in plastic. Naturally, Jack was outraged about Iain's *Bagged Place* installation at the UBC Fine Arts Gallery in 1966. The announcement for the show came in a plastic bag: "For Rent, Bagged Place—no students, no smokers, no drinkers, no pets, no children." Iain had encased a four-bedroom apartment and all the objects in it in plastic bags. He'd wrapped up everything from the double bed to the television set and the toaster. Even the toilet lay under a plastic sheet and he'd floated a ziplock bag in the bowl with a piece of his son's crap inside it. Iain maintained that working in plastic was just acknowledging a reality that we saw each day. He told Joan Lowndes in an interview in the *Province* in February 1967 that he loved plastic: "It's constantly alive," he said, "shining and new all the time, a fun-thing in a sad world."

"I came to Canada to preserve my integrity," Jack complained to me in a letter. "Any culture pushing plastic-bagged environments is just going to end up with bagged minds."

Jack and Iain couldn't have been further apart. Jack regarded painting as a sacred ceremonial act; in a letter he described to me how Rembrandt had painted while wearing his sword. On the other hand, Iain's strength lay in his fertile imagination and his invention of new art processes. Jack and the traditional approach he represented were being left behind. The future scared me a little. I could see that no matter how hard I might work, good painting, often created with great personal sacrifice, might fall out of favour.

The lines were drawn when the Toronto designer and critic Arnold Rockman came out to judge *Painting '66*, a show of BC artists at the Vancouver Art Gallery. He outraged the artistic community by splitting the $1,500 prize between three artists, one of whom was Iain Baxter, who had entered a "bagged landscape." This was a sealed vinyl bag of three horizontal compartments containing dark-blue water for the ocean, pine twigs and sand for the shore, and, as sky, light-blue-tinted water in which there floated a yellow plastic sun and a white plastic cloud. A month or so after the show the water grew hazy with algae. It was art with the shelf life of yoghurt. People were shocked that Rockman considered it to be not only an art work, but an important one. We were entering the age of Idea Art.

After the mid-eighties, the equivalent of Iain's bagged landscapes could be found on shopping bags as trendy decorations. In some of his innovations, Ian was a kind of avant-garde industrial designer in the field of plastic objects. He became primarily a conceptual artist and a graphic designer in two and three dimensions, rather than an artist in the traditional sense of the word. Many of his works were intended to be ephemeral and some of his later projects were not really visual art at all, but some of his plastic sculptures and his small landscape drawings are undeniably works of art and have stood the test of time. His ideas were always stimulating to me and contributed to my intellectual development, even though I considered some of his earlier work and most of his later work to be outside the realm of art.

Chapter 16

A Thirty-five-hour Wonder

When conceptual or idea art swept into Vancouver, my work underwent a profound change as well, but for a very different reason. It began with an experience that at first seemed completely unrelated to art—my first flight in a small airplane. In 1966, I taught a summer art course at Notre Dame University in Nelson, in southeastern BC. When asked to judge an exhibition one weekend at Anacortes on Fidalgo Island in Washington state, I declined because it was a twelve- to fourteen-hour drive each way and I couldn't get back in time for my Monday class. Then the organizer of the exhibition offered to take me there in a private airplane. I agreed to go, partly for the flight. I'd always wanted to learn to fly a small plane, though I'd never been up in one.

Friday afternoon the curator and his pilot friend landed in Nelson in a silver Beech Bonanza. I joined them and we took off and climbed over the West Kootenay mountains, flying west.

It was so effortless. I had so many questions: "Where could I learn to fly? What would it cost? How do you go about buying a plane?" He told me that the training wasn't too difficult and that owning and operating a small plane was not necessarily any more expensive than owning a luxury car.

After I juried the show, the pilot had me back in Nelson within two hours. I never got over the speed, convenience and excitement of flying.

I relegated flying to the back of my mind, however, because

Gloria was expecting a baby, and she, Lynn and I moved to Victoria in late August. I'd found a temporary position in the Fine Arts Department at the University of Victoria to replace a professor who had taken a year's sabbatical. My teaching and administrative duties were as light as if I were an artist-in-residence.

We moved into a rambling, slightly dilapidated house with a squirrel cage and a tulip tree. By coincidence it was located on West Saanich Road near the Victoria airport. On a sign beside the road near our house, the Royal Victoria Flying Club advertised flying lessons. Pickings must have been slim because the club instructors guaranteed you a pilot's licence for $500, no matter how long it took to teach you. I drove past that sign almost every day until the idea of taking the course grew into an obsession.

Gloria did not approve of my learning to fly. She worried that I might crash. My mother said, "If God had meant man to fly, he would not have given us trains." But I was stubborn. My life so far had been about a close relationship with the ground. That was about to change.

When the next cheque came from one of my shows, I signed up for the lessons and began training in a red Fleet 80 Canuck, a chunky little two-place airplane built in Ontario after the war. The plane was known as the workhorse of the Canadian Arctic. It had enough room in the cabin for two people as well as for cargo space. On floats it had once hauled a 1,200-pound moose out from a northern lake.

My teacher, Jack Shaw, had once been a trim flight jockey, humping supplies into wartime Burma with Chenault's Flying Tigers. Now he was a balding chain-smoker who kept opening the door of the aircraft and tossing out cigarette butts while we were flying. He never talked about the war or the friends he had lost except to mention the terrible conditions in China during the Second World War. He once told me that the air force had to post guards on the airstrip because the peasants would sneak onto it and run in front of aircraft taking off so that they would be killed and carried straight to a better afterlife.

Our talk was mostly about flying, especially about how to crash-land without killing yourself. Jack, like most old pilots, had a practical perspective on flying. One day we were on a long cross-country flight over the West Coast when Jack caught me looking down, mesmerized by the changing colours of the water. One small bay was a different colour, lighter than the rest of the ocean. It was an incredibly beautiful colour—a soft pale green. Jack leaned across me, looking down. "That's deeper than you think," he warned.

Jack taught me basic instrument flying and how to take off and land in the shortest possible distance. He also showed me how to recover from unusual positions. The Fleet 80 Canuck was a sturdy little plane, which could recover from almost anything if it had enough altitude.

Because he had flown in the war Jack had tricks to survive a crash that were not in the manual or would never be taught in flight training courses today. "There's a way to do a forced landing that you won't find in any book," he told me once, and he explained the manoeuvre. Then he tested me by snapping off the fuel-supply switch. "Pick your spot, Toni, we're going down."

The idea of the exercise was to find a way to cut your speed once close to the ground. The ratio was something like this: if you reduced your speed from 100 to fifty miles per hour, you increased your chance of survival by three hundred percent. "Well, there's two stout trees near the end of that short field," I told him. "They'll sheer the wings off, but we'll walk away." Jack opened the fuel cock and the engine came to life.

I soloed for the first time after only eight hours of instruction. On doing my pre-trip inspection, checking for loose objects, I looked behind the passenger seat and found hundreds of cigarette butts that Jack had thrown out while flying. Just like a cigarette butt tossed from the window of a car in motion, each butt had blown back inside and fallen behind the seat. I pointed out to him that we could have been engulfed in flames on any one of our flights. Jack's face blanched.

In less than three months I checked out as a pilot, scored high on my written exam and received my licence, becoming what more experienced pilots call a "thirty-five-hour-wonder." The point of this ironic description is that after such a short period of instruction all the new pilot has is a licence to learn, usually on aircraft more advanced than his old trainer.

The months I spent learning to fly slowly reinvolved me as an artist with the landscape. Sometimes while I waited for a lesson, I made pencil sketches in a small notebook that I carried.

I was returning to the landscape I had left far behind. Over the last ten years I had worked almost entirely in studios. In England I'd been so immersed in my windowless sub-basement that I'd actually contracted a fungus infection in my right ear. Now I drew outdoors all the time. Yet I was returning to my boyhood obsession with an entirely different eye, that of the abstract painter.

After learning to fly and to respond in a new way to the landscape, I was faced again with the challenge of parenthood. In mid-December Gloria went into labour and I took her to the hospital. It was a thirty-six-hour battle as she struggled to bring our child into the world. In the end, she had a Caesarean and the baby was born on December 17, 1966.

When I saw my son for the first time everything about him seemed miraculous, from his perfect tiny fingers and toes to his gnomelike little face. Even though I already had two children I felt overwhelmed when I saw him. Gloria humorously consented to call him James after my father because it was also the name of Henry James, the subject of her master's thesis.

Practising flying and teaching at the university took me away from home much of the time. I had been raised in a pre-liberated age when women looked after the family and the household, so when the skies beckoned I pretty much left Gloria to deal with Jamie and Lynn alone. Domestic concerns looked very small at five thousand feet. I remember reading a remark about Wordsworth hoping to write a poem and slipping out of Dove Cottage so that his sister and his wife wouldn't disturb him with "problems of a domestic nature."

Fortunately things worked out reasonably well. Jamie turned out to be an extremely good-natured baby who hardly ever cried. On the other hand the new addition to the family proved hard to accept for Lynn, now thirteen. Because I wasn't around that much, my daughter desperately needed a mother. I remember Gloria telling her, "I may not be your mother, Lynn, but I'm certainly your friend."

One night I received a call from the police. "Do you know where your daughter is?" the officer asked.

"She's upstairs in bed," I told him.

"Think again," he replied sarcastically. "Better yet, come to the station and pick her up."

Instead of going to bed, Lynn had gone out on the balcony, climbed down the tulip tree and run off with some of her new friends. They had smashed a few windows in the clubhouse at the nearby golf course and the police had caught her. The next day I had to take Lynn to juvenile court on a charge of vandalism. We muddled through the crisis. I might have been a negligent father but at least I could try to make it up to her and I hoped to get her to change her behaviour. However, because her mother had died when she was only two, seeing Gloria with Jamie seemed to be a constant reminder of what she had lost as well as an exacerbation of the survivor guilt she had felt after Jennifer's death. By the end of the school year she had became so resistant to any form of guidance that Gloria and I decided to send her to Strathcona Lodge, a boarding school at Shawnigan Lake.

After getting my pilot's licence, I could only get any flying in by renting a plane, something I couldn't afford to do very often. Then, in 1968, I had a fall show at the Mira Goddard Gallery in Montreal. After the FLQ bombings that spring and the general hostility toward English Canada, I expected to have a brick thrown through the gallery window. Instead, the show sold out and I found that I had earned enough money to buy a second-hand airplane.

Over Christmas, Gloria, Lynn, Jamie and I visited my parents in Summerland. After I announced my plans, my father, accustomed to surprises from me, mentioned that he knew someone selling an airplane.

At the airport, Dad's friend showed me a miserable little Air Coupe that seemed about ready to crumble apart. "My plane's a can of worms," the man admitted, "but there's a beauty on the other side of the airport—a green Champion SkyTrac. The owner's getting divorced. He'll probably let you have it for $5,000." I looked over the aircraft. It had a "tandem" cabin arrangement, with a seat for the pilot in the front and a seat for a passenger behind the pilot, and it seemed to be in good condition. I called the owner and bought it.

I hangared my new airplane at Delta Air Park, a short drive from Vancouver. Then I repainted the Champion SkyTrac in grey and yellow with blue-and-white tail feathers and a Greek delta sign. "What air force do you belong to?" joked one tower controller.

Ownership of a plane meant that I joined the brotherhood of pilots. These guys had fly-ins—fishing trips to lakes where they played poker together, and air shows that had everything from movies about flying to contests in which pilots competed in slalom, spot landing and flour-bombing events. For the flying fraternity there were membership pins, plaques and parties. I found these pilots to be the most outspoken of civil libertarians. They were always complaining bitterly about being overregulated by the Ministry of Transport. They believed that their safety was their personal concern, not the government's.

I enjoyed the company of my fellow pilots. But I wanted to use my airplane to get away from society into the wilderness where I could paint. The Champ's high wing made it slower-moving than other aircraft, with a top speed of only a hundred and twenty miles per hour; however, the wing enabled it to take to the air easily from almost any short airstrip, and thus to land in grassy meadows or even on sandy beaches as I grew more skilled.

Once I climbed into the sky at the edge of a storm cloud and noticed a rainbow. From the air it was not a bow but a giant bull's eye. As I flew toward it the bands of red, orange, yellow, green, blue and violet became more intense in colour as the circle of the rainbow became smaller and its dark centre grew darker. As I sailed through the centre of the rainbow the cockpit lit up with a blue light. I could hear the ozone sizzling. Then everything went black. I had entered a rain cloud. It was such an extraordinary experience that I ducked out of the cloud, found the rainbow again and passed through it once more. In and out of the rainbow I flew, 3,600 feet above Georgia Strait in my Champion SkyTrac. Before I knew it I was running out of gas. Fortunately I was not far from Delta Air Park and I glided down to safety. I've been chasing rainbows ever since.

As my confidence in my flying abilities grew, I carried passengers with me. I took Lynn up. She enjoyed it well enough but preferred the company of her teenage friends. When Jamie was older I took him and Gloria up occasionally, squeezing them both into the tandem seat behind mine. Although Gloria hated the takeoffs and landings, she found the flying pleasant enough. After we landed, I'd start painting and leave her and Jamie to go beachcombing.

By late 1968 I had established a routine of flying five or six times each month, often landing on Gulf Islands like Saltspring and Galiano. I carried tide tables as well as aeronautical charts. And before I took off I made sure I had camping gear in case I wanted to stay more than a day on the beach or field where I landed, or I had to wait for sudden bad weather to clear before I could return.

The two activities of flying and painting turned out to be complementary yet completely separate. As I flew I concentrated most of my attention on operating the aircraft; otherwise I risked falling out of the sky. My painting, on the other hand, became a kind of diary-keeping of my experiences of the lonely places I flew to, places that seemed untouched. I built myself a portable paintbox with a lid to hold my paper, paints and water tray. I'd sit down on a driftwood log or a rock and choose a view to paint—there were so many possibilities, each involving the sea, clouds, rocks, driftwood and the mountains.

On one occasion I started painting two large trees in a barren sandy landscape. Halfway through the image I decided it wasn't working so I turned the paper upside down to see what might emerge. As I continued painting, the trunks became two smoking kilns. I gave the painting to Jack Wise, my old friend from San Miguel, who wrote back in November 1972: "*Kilns* really knocks me out . . . a real painter's painting, deft, decisive, unhesitating refinement of the essentials, and to balance the logic, the rightness of the decision, a lush brush." It affected him a great deal. He described it as "alembic" and "alchemical" with "a warmth in colour, like blowing on a spark." I found this image of two kilns fascinating, later using it for an oil painting and a silkscreen print.

One of my favourite painting locations at that time was Vargas Island, uninhabited and just a few miles off Tofino on the west coast of Vancouver Island. Once the site of the oldest Native settlement in the area, it was only about a mile across by two miles in length. Long since abandoned by the Natives, its giant firs stripped away by logging, it was the kind of rocky barren landscape I preferred. For years I did more painting on Vargas Island than anywhere else in the

Camping at Ahous Bay, Vargas Island with fellow artist Richard Reid, 1968.

province. For example, *Shoreline*, 1971, was done at Ahous Bay, a broad stretch of hard sand beach on the west side of Vargas Island. The effects of light offered infinite possibilities—the white light in the mist, the variegated light shining through the dissolving and coalescing clouds off shore. The lagoon in the centre of the island filled and emptied with the tides. I never took much food with me because when the tide was out the table was laid—with clams, oysters, mussels and crabs.

Whenever I showed my new work I explained how I'd connected flying and painting. Reporters and art reviewers had a unique angle on me—"the flying painter." In 1972, in the *Vancouver Sun*, critic Joan Lowndes wrote "Onley, the Wonderful Man in His Flying Machine," a glowing review of my ten-year retrospective at the Bau-Xi Gallery. The hundred works exhibited ranged from my newest watercolours to the abstract expressionist canvas-on-canvas collage, *Joie des Enfants*, 1961, and some of the forty-two *Polar* canvases I'd done before travelling to England.

Now I began to work again with oil paints. For a long time I'd worked exclusively in acrylics because they dried quickly, suiting the speed of my decision-making. I used wooden panels with acrylic paint for the undercoat and basic shapes, then finished in oils. Oil kept its colour better and, unlike early forms of acrylic paint, didn't darken with age. A surface created in oil paint had a richer colour unlike the dry chalkiness of the early acrylics. Furthermore, oil dried more slowly so I could take my time painting. I could even wipe it off instead of repainting three or four times to get the effect I wanted in acrylic.

On my summer breaks from teaching I ventured farther afield. I flew to Penticton, visited my parents, did some watercolours, then went north to see my sister in Prince George. My flights grew longer: days, even weeks at a time. I crossed Canada in my Champion SkyTrac, delivering whole shows of unframed works on paper to galleries in Winnipeg, Toronto and Montreal, and returning for the openings. I visited Bob Murray in Georgian Bay, then explored the Badlands in the American Mid-West. In the spring of 1970, I actually travelled from Vancouver to San Miguel de Allende in Mexico. After I arrived someone stole my propeller right off my plane but I knew where to find it. A local woman bought stolen goods and resold them to their owners from her stall in the market. The routine was well established; if you were an old Mexican hand, you knew where to look.

On that trip south I found one of my weirdest landscapes—the San Carlos Tower. As I flew down the west coast of Mexico, just north of the seaport of Guaymas I spotted an abandoned black-top runway. A one-way strip, it extended from the shore to the rock face on a nearby hill. A derelict control tower stood nearby, flanked by blasted buildings, charred timbers and bomb craters. I made a low pass over the runway, half-expecting to draw ground fire, then landed to investigate this weirdly constructed airport.

Once on the ground, I recognized the movie site for *Catch-22*. I'd been fooled by the papier mâché buildings, the hand-painted charred timbers and the bomb craters that I now noticed had been filled with empty Schlitz beer cans. At the end of the runway I saw a stone windmill tower. Like most Hollywood exterior sets the tower was merely a facade. It had been built of two-by-fours, chicken wire and plaster, its surface carefully painted to look like stone. It had been split down one side by wind and rain.

This tower inspired several artworks the following year. In an oil-on-board piece, *San Carlos Tower with Black Cloud*, perhaps the most successful rendering of all, the tower and the mountains were accompanied by a strange black cloud. Later I made a limited edition serigraph print of the tower image, which appeared on the cover of the catalogue of my 1978 retrospective at the Vancouver Art Gallery.

Flying took me to unique landscapes and opened up new experiences to me. En route to Ontario in the summer of 1970, I climbed to the top of a thin sierra wave cloud hanging over a mountaintop in central BC. Once there, I shot off on a fast-moving west wind, reaching the city of Calgary hours earlier than the arrival time on my flight plan. I called up air traffic control to extend my flight plan to Medicine Hat, Alberta. But after I passed Calgary I saw the sun set behind the Rocky Mountains and realized that I'd never be able to reach Medicine Hat before nightfall. The airport there had no lights. Landing would be either dangerous or impossible.

The tailwind blew too strongly for me to turn back to Calgary, so I decided to land in a place identified on my map only as Grassy Lake, a two-silo whistle-stop. Fortunately I saw someone below my aircraft clearing a field with a small brushfire. I flew through the smoke so I could tell which direction the wind was blowing. By the time I touched down it was almost dark. It was like landing in a

San Carlos Tower with Black Cloud, *serigraph, 11¼" x 15¼", 1972. Exhibited in the Venice Beinnale, 1972.*

black hole. The plane coasted into a hollow, rolled up a little hill, then roller-coasted down the other side before it came to rest in the sandy loam. Miraculously, it didn't flip over.

Grassy Lake was nowhere in view, nor was there a lake on my map. I assumed that the lake must have disappeared many years ago. I heard the sounds of prairie birds nesting for the evening. The air was dry, fragrant with hay and wild flowers, entirely different from the salty air of the coast. In the darkness I heard voices. Then I saw flashlights. About seventy-five people—most of the village, it seemed—approached my aircraft, thinking I had crashed. I introduced myself and an old-timer remarked, "We haven't had a plane here since a barnstormer came in 1935. He landed his biplane in this very field. I remember it from when I was a kid."

The villagers practically carried me on their shoulders to a dilapidated turn-of-the-century hotel with a bar. Everybody wanted to buy me a drink. Hours later, I staggered upstairs to my room and dropped onto the bed. The mattress felt like iron. The plain white sheets were so worn out from washing that my toes went through them.

My reception had been so enthusiastic that I wondered whether I'd be allowed to leave Grassy Lake the following day. The next morning, I rose at five o'clock and sneaked out to my airplane. I taxied out to a gravel road. The road was long and straight, with no telephone wires, and I easily took off from it. That was the kind of adventure flying opened up for me.

Chapter 17

Robert Rauschenberg's Dog

I was at UBC at a time when old barriers had fallen and all manner of new ideas and practices rushed into Vancouver. It was the late '60s and early '70s, when social experiment and the search for utopia were in full swing. Hanging out in the warmest, most relaxed city in Canada came easily then. In trying to eliminate poverty the Liberal government pumped money into unemployment insurance and funded a cornucopia of citizen-participation projects. The era saw an explosion of kitschy crafts like tie-dying and candlemaking. People wore mood rings, meditated on lava lamps, and stuck candles into wicker-basketed Ruffino bottles. They hung fluorescent posters under black lights and throbbing strobes; they crashed in friends' pads, got busted and freaked out. The artistic lifestyle developed its own conventions and there was even a certain pressure to conform to them.

In the Fine Arts Department, a delightful cast of characters embodied the freewheeling atmosphere of the art world. Among the artist-professors who were my colleagues was Glenn Lewis, who taught ceramics, collage, photography, sculpture and video film-making. When I walked into his class one day, Glenn was nowhere in sight. A scruffy black-and-white dog sat on a chair at the front of the studio. A few students were talking at the work tables nearby.

"What's going on?" I asked.

A student pointed to the chair. "This is Robert Rauschenberg's dog. You know Rauschenberg, the famous artist? Glenn told us his dog was going to teach the class today."

I went looking for Glenn. He wasn't in his office or anywhere else in the Fine Arts building. I later found out that the dog *had* belonged to Rauschenberg. It had been a puppy from his dog, Laika, given to a printmaker who worked for him, who, in turn, had given it to Glenn. To be fair to Glenn, in retrospect I think he may have been testing the students to see how much they would put up with. The "anything goes" attitude of the time did provoke a certain amount of irony among art teachers.

My appointment at UBC came about through my attendance at a conference held by the Fine Arts Department in the spring of 1967. It was near the end of my one-year contract at the University of Victoria. With a family to support, I was looking for work, and Bert Binning, the department chair, offered me a lecturer's position.

In his late fifties, balding, with wire-frame glasses and a grey flannel suit, Binning looked and acted like a business executive. In fact he was the mover and shaker who had created the department in 1955 by convincing the UBC administration that the visual arts represented a legitimate field of academic inquiry. He was a painter himself, well known for his whimsical abstract seascapes in which fishing piers and rigged seiners became pleasing line drawings.

Binning put his arm on my shoulder. "How about it, Toni, we could use someone like you in the department."

"I'd love to do it," I replied. "But I'm an artist, not an academic."

"So am I—at heart." Binning grinned. "We need a practising artist to develop new courses like printmaking in the Studio Arts Program. You're just the man."

I accepted and we shook hands on the deal. "When you finish in Victoria, Toni," Binning said, "you come on over."

That fall I began teaching, and Gloria and I bought a house in the Dunbar district of Vancouver, at Twenty-eighth Avenue and Collingwood. I had four sections of Fine Arts 100: Principles of Design, a total of eighty students majoring in architecture and art history. I set them exercises in selecting and combining shapes, just as I had done in collage, then I showed them how to work two-dimensionally in several media.

I also got them to think about three-dimensional art forms because the basis of both sculpture and architecture is space and volume. But rather than teaching them to sculpt in clay or stone, I worked with "found art" sculpture projects. To create their projects, they salvaged metal objects such as a battered oil drum, a wrecked automobile radiator and a rusty iron bedstead on casters. I hired a welder to fasten their sculptures together and we planned to place the pieces around the campus.

Three of my students climbed the chain-link fence at a cannery to hunt for scrap. They encountered an obstacle they'll never forget.

In the middle of the night, I answered a phone call from the police.

"This sounds like a wild story," said a police officer, "but we're holding three guys at the station who claim they were doing an assignment for your class."

I recognized the names immediately. "They're my students, all right, and they were only after junk."

The police agreed to release them with a warning.

I taught another studio course in historical techniques. The students called it Fakes Anonymous because we copied historical paintings using the materials and the techniques the artists had used. The idea was to give the art history students a better understanding of how medium can influence style. However, there was only so much we could do. I complained to Binning that the students would never truly understand Dürer or Rembrandt unless they had the chance to do some etchings.

He shook his head. "We don't have the money to buy an etching press, Toni."

I had been creating etchings since my trip to London in 1965. I offered him a small press I was no longer using on condition that I taught etching in the course.

The interest generated by the studio arts classes led the department to expand the program. Soon we were offering a bachelor's degree in studio arts. It puzzled me at first that my best students seemed to come from art history rather than the studio arts program. When I left the Fine Arts building in the evening, the lights in the classrooms were still blazing because the art history students were working late. That was the kind of fire in the belly that young artists needed. Eventually I realized that the difference between the two groups of students was that the art history students had to make sacrifices to find painting or sculpting time.

Students from the studio arts program seemed preoccupied with the economic survival of the young artist. I remember one class where we discussed the issue for the entire period. We came up with a list of well-paid trades like plumbing or TV repair that would not be completely exhausting yet would provide enough financial security to allow them to make art in their spare time.

"One percent of the people studying art become artists," I told them. "Even fewer make a living at it, so don't give up a good day job. Don't think you're not an artist just because you're not making a living at art. You could be driving a cab. You could be waiting on tables. You could be doing anything. If someone asks, you can say 'I'm an artist.' That'll sustain you."

"You made it," commented one of my students. "You're an artist now."

I agreed, but pointed out, "I don't make a complete living by selling art. I'm also a university teacher. I've only made it this far because I'm so stubborn that I can't imagine doing anything else."

While I taught at UBC, Binning and I got along superbly. I respected him very much. Some artists teach for financial security, but Binning taught because he genuinely believed in art education and the role of art in society. Not until the last years of his life did he relinquish some administrative and social responsibilities and start painting in earnest, moving into tight, hard-edged, colourful abstracts.

On the weekends, I'd load up my Champ SkyTrac with navigational charts, tide tables and camping equipment, then fly to beaches up and down the coast. I took Binning up in my plane once. In spite of his heart condition, he wanted to see the coastline and the ocean from the air. "I can't go above five thousand feet, Toni," he instructed me, tapping his chest. "Doctor's orders."

The art community in Vancouver reached a critical mass during those years. Travel across the country had never been cheaper and the city's mild, snow-free winters drew tens of thousands of eastern Canadians. As the Vietnam War dragged on many young Americans fled to Vancouver too. At the time people believed that a public

Point Grey, *1971, etching, 4" x 4¾".*

aware of art might be more critical of hypocrisy and social injustice. On the negative side, an honest expression of feeling seemed more important than technique and formal training. Accordingly, the number of professional and semi-professional artists in Vancouver grew from forty or fifty to about 300.

Fuelling the cultural ferment was the tweedy-looking Oxford graduate and ex-history professor, Tony Emery, who had employed me in Victoria and who had now become the director of the Vancouver Art Gallery. Emery, who produced more shows and events than any director has since, was a well-educated Brit with horn-rimmed glasses and a bushy, grizzled beard. Notwithstanding his classical education, he hawked art exhibits like a regular P.T. Barnum, even mounting shows at the racetrack and the baseball stadium.

His best idea was the Special Event series that attracted people who worked downtown and who were looking for something interesting to do during their lunch hour. The Vancouver Art Gallery

Silent Path, 1971, etching, 3¾" x 3".

brought them in with poetry readings, dance performances and music recitals. Earle Birney, John Robert Columbo and Andreas Schroeder all read their poems. New York theatre director Richard Schechner came. Even filmmaker Jean-Luc Godard put in an appearance.

One of the most notorious art events held during that period was the *Piano Destruction Concerto* by a New York performance artist, Ralph Ortiz. He came to Vancouver on a Canada Council grant to destroy a piano. An earnest audience arrived to be greeted by a lime green upright piano standing in the centre of the main gallery. At the appointed hour Ortiz strode toward it brandishing an axe. With a tremendous crash, he brought the axe down on the piano. It burst open, showering the audience with broken keys, splinters of wood and spatters of blood from the plastic bags he had hung inside it. White mice scurried out of the wreckage and ran underfoot, causing part of the audience to stampede. Several people were heard to ask loudly, "This is art?"

Although the Vancouver Art Gallery set new records for membership and attendance in 1971, the Board of Directors tried to discourage Emery from organizing such events. They represented the private collectors in the city, the black-tie crowd that had traditionally supported the gallery and its exhibitions as a way of enhancing the value of their private collections. Emery resigned on principle. He concluded that art was not more widely appreciated because of a lack of art education and so he left Vancouver to teach art to schoolchildren in the West Kootenays.

During this period of frantic experiment in the arts, I discovered silkscreen printing. It had begun as a technology to replace hand-lettered signs at the turn of the century. After Op artist Andy Warhol screened prints of red and white Campbell's soup cans in the early 1960s, it emerged as a major twentieth-century art form. Fine art silkscreen printing was termed serigraphy to distinguish it from commercial applications.

My involvement began accidentally in 1968 when Simon Fraser University commissioned a suite of prints from me and twelve other

Sketch for my first serigraph, 1968. Collection of the Tate Britian.

Vancouver artists to commemorate Canada's centennial. Initially, we were supposed to make lithographs with Bob Bigelow, a master lithographer from the prestigious Gemini GEL workshop in Los Angeles. Bob was a skinny long-haired fellow with a Fu Manchu moustache and a thin intense face. I still remember how shocked he was when he discovered upon his arrival that SFU had no lithography press.

To do any printing at all, he was obliged to build a silkscreen press, a relatively simple apparatus consisting of a piece of silk stretched over a wooden frame hinged to a baseboard. Onto the silk, you attached paper, wax or photosensitive stencils to block off certain shapes. Once you lowered the frame, you used a rubber squeegee to push the printing ink through the silk around the stencils onto the paper. More colours and shapes could be added to the print, one at a time. Each time you added a new colour, you had to change the stencil to protect the areas already printed.

I cut out a stencil with several shapes suggesting earth, rocks and cloud formations. Bigelow printed each part of the stencil in a different colour of silkscreen ink. Gradually, a thickly inked abstract landscape emerged. But I found the opacity and flatness of the colours frustrating. I wanted the same transparency as in a watercolour, where a thin wash of colour over white paper can create the effect of light. I decided to try to invent a transparent ink, since none existed at that time.

I got Bigelow to mix a little colour with some varnish, and I cut out a triangle from part of the stencil. He pulled a proof, and a triangle of transparent colour with the white paper showing through it magically appeared! This transparent figure suggested all the possibilities of watercolour. It meant that I could probably overlap colours to produce subtle effects new to silkscreen.

I later explored these possibilities with a young printmaker, Bill Bonnieman, a big man with aviator-style glasses, a straggly beard and a mound of woolly shoulder-length hair. He saw the world in terms of printmaking. "It's all just ink on paper," he mused. "I make a print—that's ink on paper. When I'm through, you give me a cheque—ink on paper." He puffed on the cigarette butt dangling from his lips. "Then I take a bus to the bank and get some money— ink on paper. I walk to Behnsen's to buy supplies—more ink and paper."

I had met Bill in 1963 when we both rented studio space in the same building on Granville Street near Dunsmuir. To lower a large painting from the third floor, one of Bill's studio mates sawed off part of the railing around the landing in the stairwell, then replaced it to conceal the damage from our vigilant landlord. But he forgot to either secure the railing or tell Bill about it. When Bill heard me downstairs he leaned over the railing to take a look and fell down one storey. Fortunately he was not seriously injured.

"I came from up there." He pointed to the third floor landing. "I don't think anybody's got a grip on this crazy thing called 'art'."

Bill and I printed in the basement of my house. I'd make a pencil drawing, rough out a colour scheme for the print, mix the colours of the inks, then cut out a paper stencil like a jigsaw puzzle. Bill would place part of the stencil on the silk, then start screening. As the colours and shapes appeared on the prints, I improvised new shapes and colours, overlapping and interlocking them, moving from lighter to darker ones.

Ever inventive, Bill contributed two great ideas to the process. The first was a method of achieving a greater tonal complexity in the prints. He put transparent extender on one end of his squeegee and a colour I'd mixed on the other, then manipulated the squeegee on the silk to create a smooth gradation of the colour. We referred to this effect as a "blend." Next, Bill figured out how to print blends running in two different directions. He told me he'd dreamed it. He rigged up a counterweight for the silkscreen press so that he could quickly turn the hinged frame, enabling him to open it from right and left as well as from top and bottom. This meant he could squeegee a blend in one direction, turn the frame, add a new stencil and colour, and squeegee in another direction. By overlapping the two blends, he could create a further blend and an almost infinite number of different colours.

People who bought the prints would ask afterward, "How did you do that? What colours were you printing?"

There was no easy answer to this because we worked intuitively. We'd just improvise after the second or third stencil. Editions of twenty prints hung drying on lines I'd strung across the room outside of the printing area. The process of creating blends was tricky and sometimes did not produce a good result. Occasionally we'd develop an image through several successive printings, then mess up on the final colour and ruin the entire edition. We both took such failures philosophically because the nature of the process made them unavoidable.

In our first year we produced eight different portfolios of prints. As my watercolours became more recognizable as landscapes, the subjects in my prints changed as well. For example, the dominant form in *Vargas Island*, 1969, suggests a rock pile faceted by sunlight on a beach. In its January 3, 1969, issue, *Time* featured a reproduction of *White Stone*, 1968, as typical of the abstract landscape imagery of my prints and described me as "one of the few leading Canadian artists whose work still contains references to landscape."

The new prints proved very popular because younger collectors with modest budgets could acquire them. In the early 1970s my watercolours and oils commanded prices of $500 to $3,000, while a similar image with the same palette of blues and greens and umbers printed onto a textured paper would cost only $40 to $100.

Gloria started handling most of the correspondence with galleries, and the Onley household became a cottage industry. Bill not only enjoyed working with me but also found that the technical skills he developed led to printmaking jobs with other artists in Vancouver. Printmaking was an exciting creative activity that was financially beneficial for both of us. We went on to produce 314 editions over a twenty-one-year period.

As my print sales began to lift off, I felt increasingly remote from my colleagues in the UBC Fine Arts Department. Their concerns seemed to have nothing to do with the practical world of a working artist. There was Lionel Thomas, who was fascinated by the idea of space travel, UFOs and extra-terrestrials. He'd turn on his stereo and blast his students with the theme music from *2001: A Space Odyssey*. We called his classroom "Mission Control."

There was Glenn Toppings, the only artist I ever met who actually died of self-neglect. I often saw him at gallery openings, casually attired in a black leather jacket and a dress shirt open at the neck. A gentle, likeable man, he'd run his fingers through his red beard as he studied each of the pieces on display. Glenn was active with other artists in negotiating royalties whenever public galleries exhibited their work. He simply never looked after himself. He chain-smoked and, as a sculptor, worked intensively with fibreglass and paint. He often slept in his studio amid the toxic fumes of curing fibreglass without even opening a window. At the age of forty-two he was found dead in his studio one morning. The entire Vancouver art community turned out at his memorial service, and Gloria intensified her campaign to get better ventilation for the silkscreen production area that would be set up in my studio from time to time.

And then there was Herb Gilbert, whose views were diametrically opposed to mine, and with whom I shared an office. Herb's tenured position as a Fine Arts professor made it possible for him to agitate for environmental conservation, nuclear disarmament and world peace, all in the name of art education. I was all for these causes, but not as studio projects.

We split the first-year studio arts students between us. One year Herb spent most of his studio art supply fees on rolls and rolls of coloured ribbons.

That infuriated me. The entire budget should not be spent on one project. "What are you doing, Herb?" I asked.

"We're going to festoon the trees on campus."

"That's a kindergarten project!" I retorted.

He sighed and patiently corrected me. "It's an environmental consciousness-raising project, Toni."

Herb had been a pretty fair painter once. He'd won an Emily Carr scholarship and, like me, had spent time in San Miguel de Allende and sold his work to the Vancouver Art Gallery. Then he created happenings, and soon developed an expanded notion of art that included organizing demonstrations. In 1971, when the US tested a nuclear bomb in Amchitka, Alaska, he assigned a protest march to his students. They had to wear sackcloth, pour ashes on their heads and wail in front of the US Consulate in Vancouver.

When Herb finally got his sabbatical, he made himself a Druid costume, donned a Viking helmet and painted himself a passport: *Herb Gilbert, Citizen of the World.* He attempted unsuccessfully to use this unique document to cross the Yugoslavian border. He somehow gained access to a World Peace Conference in Britain and wound up on the cover of a British tabloid. When he returned to Vancouver he

At UBC with fellow professor Herbert Gilbert, 1968.

showed me a photograph of his intervention. He had climbed onto the stage in his Druid's robe and held up a globe of the world before the assembly.

When Binning stepped down as the chairman of the department in 1968, a new generation of artists started teaching in the studio arts program. For the most part, they rejected the idea of trying to sell their work through private galleries. They argued that turning art into a commodity compromised their ideals. That didn't stop them from applying for every sort of government funding, however, and so began the grand era of art grantsmanship.

Among the new part-time instructors was my former in-law Tom Burrows, who had dropped out of pre-med classes to become a sculptor. He built himself a shack on stilts in the squatters' community on the Maplewood mud flats in North Vancouver and lived rent-free until the municipality bulldozed the shacks. Then he got a sculpture commission from the Surrey Taxation Office by submitting as a maquette a little wooden abacus he had bought in Chinatown and proposing to have it fabricated in steel on a vastly larger scale. The giant steel abacus seemed to be an austere northern echo of Claes Oldenburg's giant oilcloth hamburger. Vancouver was growing its own pop art, getting more like New York every day.

We developed a master of fine arts degree, patterned after the one at the Slade School of Art at the University College of London. For the seven or eight students in the program, the two years of studio work was supposed to be the equivalent of the first stage of an artist's career. Instead of spending the summer working when the university was not in session, MFA students were supposed to develop a major project. The new program coincided with a widespread fascination with conceptual art. Some students proclaimed the death of painting and stalked the corridors, making jerky pictures with video cameras. One graduate student handed in a project that consisted of a charcoal sketch detailing a plan to wrap Mount Seymour in cellophane. Another designed a performance piece in which he created his own degree and commencement exercise. He invited the president of UBC, who was far from amused.

It was difficult to assess this work. At that time there was a strong anti-elitist bias among most of the instructors in the creative arts that resulted in creative writing and studio arts courses being marked on a pass/fail system, even though the rest of the university used a grading system. The acting head of the department went along with this. I became one of the last to grade students in studio classes. I felt it was unfair to the good students to pass someone just for showing up. I also reasoned that everybody had a right to know where they stood. Many students needed to show good grades to get into another university programme, and a pass/fail mark did not work for them.

Bert Binning had spent the best years of his creative life trying to lick the Fine Arts department into shape. As far as he was concerned, the main purpose of the studio art courses was not so much to train artists as to provide a better education for students in art history and architecture. He was a dedicated teacher, much loved by his students and impatient with those he felt were distracting the school from its objectives. He also left a body of work that represents a significant contribution to the visual arts of this part of Canada.

I was personally disappointed with the direction the department took after Binning retired, but I soon came to realize that this new

direction was, more than anything else, a kind of involuntary align-
ment with the larger art world outside of Vancouver, where painting
in the traditional sense was temporarily overshadowed by the trendy
new forms of conceptual art, pop art and multi-media art. For artists
like me, it was something to be humoured rather than opposed.

Chapter 18

The Northwest Passage

Teaching a summer art course in 1972 in St. Andrews, New Brunswick, initiated a chain of events that took me to the Arctic. Rather than travel that month, my wife Gloria had stayed in Vancouver with our son Jamie. As a result I was staying by myself in the guest cottage of the Walkers, a prominent Liberal family in New Brunswick.

One afternoon, Willa Walker, the president of the local chapter of the Liberal party auxiliary committee, rushed over. A very tweedy-looking lady with a pronounced British accent, she exclaimed, "Toni, you'll never guess who's coming to dinner—Pierre Elliot Trudeau."

Wearing a striped T-shirt, levis and sandals, the fifty-three-year-old prime minister arrived late that afternoon. He and his family had been vacationing on Campobello Island. A tremendously energetic man, Trudeau seemed bigger and taller than his stature of five-foot-nine. After the Walkers introduced us, he lifted his two-year-old son, Justin, up onto his shoulders and ran around the house, stamping the ground and neighing like a horse. His wife Margaret looked very bored.

Trudeau had heard of me from his younger brother Charles, an architect in Montreal, who had bought some of my paintings and on two occasions had had me over as a house guest, even giving me a room that had a carved wooden figure of Saint Anthony in a niche over the bed. Trudeau, who loved talking about ideas and new experiences, passed Justin to Margaret and asked me to join him on a walk before dinner. We wandered down a path to the St. Croix River, which ran through a grove of trees at the back of the Walkers' property.

"How did you get here, Toni?" he asked.

"I flew in my Champion SkyTrac. It's a single-engine two-seater plane."

He looked very surprised. "You flew from Vancouver?—Clear across Canada?"

When Trudeau mentioned that he'd taken a few flying lessons himself, I reached into my trouser pocket for my wallet. "I've got a picture of the plane right here."

Two brawny RCMP security guards in Hawaiian shirts, plaid Bermuda shorts and RCMP boots were following us. One of them lunged at me, obviously thinking I might be going for a gun.

I raised my hands and waved the wallet.

With a grunt, the guard turned away. It was embarrassing but he wasn't allowed to take any chances.

Trudeau gave one of his classic Gallic shrugs. "You see that?" He chuckled mischievously. "You see what I put up with?"

At the river we skipped stones together and talked about painting. Trudeau commented that an abstract collage from my *Polar* series that his brother owned reminded him of the austere beauty of the Arctic. Later, Richard Gwyn was to mention in his biography of Trudeau, *The Northern Magus*, that "the muted abstract but disciplined landscapes of Toni Onley are among his favourites."

I explained that I had never been up north but thought the Arctic represented our last escape from the problems of overpopulation and pollution. In a crowded world, Canada could claim thousands of miles of unoccupied territory.

"Of course, it's the last frontier," he said with growing enthusiasm. "There are places in the Arctic that still aren't mapped." Of all our prime ministers, Trudeau was the greatest outdoorsman, a skier, surfer, scuba diver and canoeist. In one of the few personal essays he ever wrote, "Exhaustion and Fulfilment: The Ascetic in a Canoe," 1944, he said, probably of himself, "I know a man whose school could never teach him patriotism, but who acquired that virtue when he felt the vastness of his land." Trudeau believed the Arctic played an important role in our national identity, even though few Canadians had ever seen it.

I had looked into flying north. "There hasn't been a Canadian painter in the Arctic for thirty-five years, not since Jackson, Harris and Varley, " I observed. "I'd love to paint there some day."

"Would you?" Trudeau looked thoughtful for a moment. He had a passionate interest in the Arctic. In 1970, he had passed the Arctic Waters Pollution Prevention Act. "Why don't you leave it with me, Toni."

The following January, I wrote a letter to remind him of our conversation and sent him a serigraph print, *Ice Flow*. He promised to look into a trip for me and his office subsequently mailed a list of commercial air carriers operating out of Frobisher Bay, Baffin Island. The ticket prices all proved too high for my budget and I couldn't imagine how I could get out from Frobisher into the Arctic landscape, so I postponed the trip. Then I received a letter from Trudeau, dated April 10, 1974.

"My Dear Onley," he wrote. "Am I not right in believing that travel to Baffin Island by sea would in fact be a far preferable option for you in that it would enable you to sketch northern and Arctic scenes on the way there and back as well?"

He offered me a place on the Canadian Coast Guard Service ship, the CCGS *Louis St. Laurent*, one of the world's largest icebreakers. A $30-million, 13,000-tonne vessel for clearing ice from the shipping lanes in the eastern Arctic, it would also be taking scientific and navigational measurements and evacuating a number of polar scientists from Arctic bases.

The Canadian Coast Guard sent me an itinerary and a supply list. Their Arctic-bound ships usually carried officials from the Department of Mines and Natural Resources, radio technicians to put up navigation beacons, and polar explorers. Yet they had also transported members of the Group of Seven to the Arctic: Jackson in 1927, Jackson and Lawren Harris in 1930 and Fred Varley in 1938.

I called the Coast Guard for some last-minute advice. "Don't forget to bring a dinner jacket," they informed me. "A dinner jacket?" I asked. Just as in the British naval tradition, one dressed for dinner at the captain's table and toasted the Queen.

The trip started late because we were caught in a dock strike in Montreal. The *St. Laurent* might have spent the summer behind a picket line if not for our commander, Captain Fournier, a dark, heavy-set, determined man. After waiting until three o'clock in the morning when the strikers had all fallen asleep, he had one of the boilers fired up, then ordered the bosun and a few of the men to cast off the ship's mooring lines. As the *St. Laurent* glided away from the pier, I was awakened by the noise and shouting from the pickets on the dock, who were throwing beer bottles that smashed harmlessly against the side of the ship.

Many people think of the High Arctic as a godforsaken wilderness. I temporarily shared that dismal view as we sailed out of the St. Lawrence, first to Dartmouth on the Atlantic coast, then north through the Strait of Belle Isle and along the coast of Quebec and Labrador. I thought I might be travelling into a kind of cold hell, dark and flat and miserable. But as we travelled north the summer days lengthened until they contained nearly twenty hours of light. Although we were on a very large ship, the scale of that landscape dwarfed us. As the ship sailed alongside Baffin Island, the fifth-largest island in the world, I saw the longest unnamed mountain chain in the world, the colossal rugged mountains that formed the spine of the island.

I sat painting in the ship's enclosed crow's nest about 100 feet above the water. I had my drawing board jammed against the window in front of me with my watercolour paints beside me and a heater at my feet keeping me warm and drying my watercolours as I painted them. Subtle colours were revealed to me as I studied the sea ice. I found that if I looked to the south side of the ship, I saw greenish-blue colours, while on the north side, the ice shaded toward rose. The colours kept shifting with passing cloud shadows. I looked, painted, then looked again. I drifted into a state of rapture.

I imagined seeing the landscape as a painter might have 200 years ago on a British naval expedition to find the Northwest Passage, perhaps a junior officer with a degree from Woolwich Naval Academy commissioned to paint the Arctic hinterland and take notes on the landscape and sparse vegetation for the benefit of the Royal Society and the botanists at Kew Gardens. Among the nineteenth-century British explorers, I recalled some very accomplished watercolourists like George Back, Robert Hood and Samuel Cresswell. Perhaps my imaginary officer would have returned to

England and produced a book of watercolours, picturesque views of the Canadian Arctic accompanied by descriptions of the Eskimo, as the Inuit were formerly known, their earlier name derived from a North American aboriginal word for "eaters of raw flesh." This was the kind of painting done by John Weber, who accompanied Captain Cook to Vancouver Island, Alaska and Hawaii. Long before photography, these illustrations and books provided the world with its first views of the Arctic.

When we passed through Navy Board Inlet between the north end of Baffin Island and Bylot Island, the passage grew so narrow that I felt sure I could have thrown a rock across it. The sea in the inlet seemed so calm that it felt as if we'd stopped moving. A low fog rolled in and the *St. Laurent* sailed entirely by radar. The captain rang me on the telephone. "What's it like up there?"

My perch was high above the fog. "Bright sunshine! It's beautiful. Come on up," I suggested, smiling to myself at the thought of the captain struggling up the ladder in the hollow mast to the crow's nest. Fournier was too rotund to fit inside the mast, not that he would try.

A few days later as we headed into an area north of Baffin Island, the captain dispatched the helicopter to reconnoitre the sea ice. The older, heavier pans of multi-year ice, which had a faint green colour, were harder for the ship to break, and when we hit very large chunks of ice, the ship reverberated like a temple gong. Sometimes when we passed large pans of ice the crew would siphon off the water on top of them. When the ice melted in the sun, the salt separated from the sea water and sank down into the ice, leaving pools of fresh water suitable for drinking.

Every year, more than 50,000 icebergs calve from glaciers in Greenland and are swept by the wind and tides into Baffin Bay and Davis Strait, where they slowly melt. Some loomed 300 feet tall, bleeping on the ship's radar screen. By daylight they looked like floating apartment blocks. At night, borne on the black water, they glowed a spectral green. Whenever we passed a really big iceberg, a few crew members would come up on deck to watch.

I remember a night later in the voyage when two or three of them, men from Nova Scotia and Newfoundland, leaned against the railing of the ship and watched a huge iceberg pass. One of them said, "Remember in '62 when we were in Baffin Bay and we came up on this big SOB? Must have been all of thirty miles long, it fair chilled the air." Then they carried on talking about wonderful bergs long since gone.

Maurice Haycock, a retired Arctic geologist, now a painter and historian, had joined the trip at Pond Inlet. Captain Fournier and everyone who served in the Arctic knew Haycock, who had worked there since 1926. Now he contacted passing ships by radio and hitchhiked around the Arctic with his oil paints and ham radio.

Haycock had that ruddy outdoor look of a man of the north. He resembled A.Y. Jackson, who had befriended him and taught him how to paint. Because Haycock and I got along so well together, I offered him a watercolour that he liked, teasing him, "I want to commemorate our relationship, Maurice."

"Oh, Toni, I can't accept without reciprocating," he replied. "I'll take it on one condition: that I give you a painting."

He never painted on the spot as I did, so I had to wait about a year. Then a heavy carefully wrapped parcel arrived in the mail. It was Maurice Haycock's Arctic painting, executed with a rough scumbling brushstroke and a thick, crusty impasto. He painted like A.Y. Jackson, too. It was of the Queen Charlotte Monument, a free-standing rock off Coburg Island, the same rock I had painted for him.

On Haycock's suggestion the helicopter pilot flew the captain, the ship's doctor, the chief engineer and Maurice and myself to Beechey Island, the site of the 1845 winter camp of the tragic Franklin expedition. We explored the remains of the camp on a long gravel and shale beach beneath high, forbidding cliffs. In 1846, the sea ice trapped Franklin's ships, the *Erebus* and the *Terror*, off King William Island. The following spring most of the men abandoned the trapped ships and fled southward toward the mainland. They disappeared into the frozen wastes where they may have been reduced to cannibalism before dying. Sir John and twenty-three of his men were left behind to die on board the ship.

The campsite on Beechey Island was littered with discarded tins, barrel staves and lumps of Welsh coal. Less than a mile west of the campsite, we found the graves of three of Franklin's men. Because the Arctic permafrost made it impossible to dig graves Franklin's party had heaped stones over the bodies and erected painted wooden

At the Franklin cenotaph on Beechey Island, 1974. Photograph by Maurice Haycock.

markers. Looking at the one that memorialized the young Petty Officer John Torrington, I imagined that his body might have been so well preserved by the cold that his face would still be recognizable. Later, when his body was exhumed by a scientific expedition this proved to be true.

I am predisposed to like solitary places but Beechey Island seemed eerie and unsettling. "You'd think their ghosts would be hovering around," I said to Haycock, "guarding the Franklin mystery."

A few days later on the voyage, we sailed to Thule, Greenland, to begin the evacuation of the research stations of the North Water Project, a three-year international project to investigate the North Water phenomenon—a very large open area of the sea which never freezes—and its effect on the Arctic environment. Then the ship sailed north between Ellesmere Island and Greenland, through the narrow passage between Cape Alexander and Cape Isabella, headlands that some call the Northern Pillars of Hercules. There we hit a barrier of multi-year ice, hundreds of years old, some of it as thick as nine feet.

The captain rammed the ship into a weaker part of the ridge, reversed the engines, backed away and ran at it again. At times, he forced the ship on top of the ice, our propeller screws churning the air, until the weight of the vessel broke through. During the ramming and lurching that night, I felt certain the ship would be holed and readied myself to flee to the lifeboats.

The following night, at midnight, a flare was sighted from the Cape Herschel research station on Ellesmere Island, and the captain ran our vessel onto the ice about four miles from Pim Island. That evening, as usual, I ate with the captain and his officers. Their routine was to discuss their sailing orders after dinner. I listened quietly. Then the captain took out a bottle of scotch.

When he filled my glass, he asked, "Toni, you go between decks, what's the scuttlebutt?" He turned to his officers and remarked, "I've never known a crew that didn't have some beef or other."

I took a drink of whisky. I suggested diplomatically that he do something for his inside crew who, unlike the deckhands, never got to go off the ship. "Captain, I've been ashore several times on this trip. I know some of the men would like to go, too. They're in the Arctic for three months and they never get ashore at all."

"Shore leave, is that what they want?" He topped up the whisky in my glass. "Very well, we're going to be near Pim Island for a few days. We'll send them ashore tomorrow."

Pim Island lies between Greenland and Ellesmere Island at a latitude of seventy-eight degrees. It was as far north as we would travel on the voyage. Fritz Muller, the forty-eight-year-old Swiss Canadian who directed the North Water Project and had joined the ship at Thule, told me he had found a site on Pim Island suitable for a research station, but it was strewn with bones and skulls plundered by foxes and polar bears from some nearby graves. He had established a research station on Ellesmere Island instead.

At six o'clock the next morning, the bosun's whistle sounded over the ship's intercom. "Now hear this. All those wishing to go ashore, assemble on the flight deck at 0700 hours."

When I got there it looked as if all the engineers, cooks and stewards who were off their shift had crowded onto the deck. Not being deckhands, not one of them had proper winter clothing, not even mittens, let alone fur-lined boots. Some of the men just wore nylon windbreakers, which were all they needed on the ship, just for running from one hatch to another. I saw the head cook wearing his floppy white chef's hat.

One of the men, his teeth chattering as he stood on the deck, explained, "We'll just take a quick look at the island. Then we'll come right back."

However, the ship had only one helicopter. It took poor old Blackie, our Trinidadian Canadian pilot about four hours to ferry everybody to the island and back to the *St. Laurent*. Desperately, he sweated over each flight. If anything went wrong with the chopper some of the crew might be stranded on the island without shelter. Blackie, due to retire after the voyage, shook his head when I saw him between flights. "Man, I can't believe this."

The last men returning from Pim Island were on the verge of suffering from frostbite. I watched nervously as they climbed from the chopper, stamped their feet, and shoved their hands into their pockets or warmed them under their arms.

"Anyhow, we got there," said one man. "Now at least we can say we've really been to the Arctic."

I turned away, sorry that I'd ever mentioned the idea of shore leave to the captain.

At supper that night, Captain Fournier had an unusually large appetite. He poured himself a large glass of port and grinned at me. "Toni, I think that's the last we'll hear about shore leave."

At Cape Herschel, the *St. Laurent* evacuated four scientists, their belongings and their supplies. It took until mid-afternoon to transport them to the ship. Next, the ship stopped at Coburg Island to pick up the three polar scientists stationed there.

The weather closed in, grounding the helicopter on the ship and marooning several people on Coburg Island, including me because I'd gone out for a look at it. Fortunately the hut, the sleeping bags and some food and fuel hadn't been moved to the ship so we had enough supplies to wait for the weather to break.

I rose early the next morning and went for a walk. The clouds hung very low to the ground: we were socked in, but I could see for miles in either direction along the beach. Giant blocks of ice, each as large as a house, floated in the bay or had been thrust upon the shore of the island. Under the strange ambient light filtering through the clouds, the ice blocks glowed brilliant aquamarine, as if lit up from inside. The scene reminded me of the Blue Grotto on the island of Capri in Italy where the sunlight streaming through the water at the entrance illuminates the cave. On Coburg Island, the snow on top of the icebergs had melted, and the water percolating through the ice left narrow channels through which light entered to make the icebergs glow like the finest Venetian glass.

The wind at my back died down. There were no insects or birds; except for the sound of my own breath, I stood in a silent world. I headed for a bluff that I estimated to be about a fifteen-minute walk away. Visibility in the Arctic was much better than in the city, so I underestimated the distance. I walked for several miles until I grew worried and turned back. The wind had been creeping up behind me and now it almost sliced me in two. By the time I got back to the camp I felt half dead.

"Where have you been, Toni?" asked Fritz Muller. When I told him what I had been walking toward, he exploded, "That's ten miles away!"

Others in the group expressed concerns for my safety as well. Polar bears roamed the island. "It's bloody dangerous to go walking out there," said another man. "Take a gun with you next time."

The clouds lifted and the helicopter flew us back to the ship, which, dangerously low on fuel, had burned thirty tons each day they waited for the weather to clear.

It was now well into winter, a season of storms in Baffin Bay. On September 27, after dropping the scientists off at Thule, Greenland, we ran into a ferocious sea with forty-foot waves. Yet on the bridge, the captain looked at home in the high seas. I heard him singing a French Canadian ditty. He smiled when he saw me and rubbed his hands together. "Ah, this is what I like, some real sailing."

The ship rocked through a forty-five-degree angle. The sea was so rough that the cook skipped the evening meal and made us sandwiches instead. That night the ship was buffeted by sixty-mile-per-hour winds. I was pitched back and forth in my cabin, trying in vain to keep my belongings from crashing about, and got little sleep. The next day as we headed into Lancaster Sound it was impossible to paint. When the *St. Laurent* finally reached Resolute Bay on Cornwallis Island, I left the ship and flew to Montreal. From there, I went back to Vancouver, where to the consternation of the university administration, I was late for my first semester of classes.

The eastern Arctic had been the most extraordinary landscape I had ever seen. It provided the simplicity of line and shape that I sought in my work. I had to get back, yet I could hardly ask for another trip on a government icebreaker so soon after making the last one. I mulled over the idea of flying there. I had thought of it even before I sailed to the Arctic. I had written to the Canadian Owners and Pilots Association and purchased maps of the route. However, it was clearly too dangerous to cross Hudson Bay in a small plane that could not land on water. To fly over vast reaches of ice-clogged sea was to put eternity beneath my wheels, but with a different kind of plane I would have a chance of surviving.

In the meantime, my art sales had been growing quickly. In the spring of 1975, I sold my Champion SkyTrac and bought a Lake Buccaneer flying boat. Unlike a float plane, it had retractable wheels and a sturdy hull that was designed to land on water. Any far northern route in the eastern Arctic lay over water, or at least within sight of water, so if I had engine trouble, I could land and radio for help.

A new opportunity to visit the Arctic came that summer through Wally Brennan, a master printer I'd met at the Nova Scotia College of Art and Design in Halifax. I arranged to assist him in teaching lithography to the Inuit artists of Cape Dorset, Baffin Island. Toronto artist James Houston had already established printmaking at Cape Dorset back in 1957 to assist the community to become economically self-sufficient as they abandoned their nomadic hunting lifestyle. As a result the Inuit in Cape Dorset were almost entirely devoted to making prints and carving in stone and ivory. The year I headed north, the per capita income in Cape Dorset had reached about $20,000, making it one of the wealthiest places in North America. Now the West Baffin Eskimo Co-operative had hired Wally to teach them an additional printmaking technique.

Flying to Baffin Island would have been a much shorter trip if I could have followed my original plan to fly up the east shore of Hudson Bay and across the great stepping stones of Salisbury and Nottingham islands. No one on that route had fuel to spare for me, however, so I hopped across the prairies to Ontario where I stopped for a week's visit with Robert Murray at Pointe au Baril in Georgian Bay. From there I flew north to Montreal, then to Fort Chimo where the treeline ended, and on to Baffin Island, a distance of almost 1,200 miles.

In Andrew Gordon Bay, I hit bad weather. The cloud ceiling dropped to 800 feet and kept falling. I had to find Cape Dorset by dead reckoning. The airport's automatic direction finder, a low-frequency radio beacon, had broken down, so the dial on my instrument panel just showed a dead needle. I figured that the first promontory I flew over would be the Cape Dorset Peninsula, and I stayed close enough to the land so that I wouldn't miss it and fly out to sea. I had told Cape Dorset my estimated arrival time and they had been trying to fix their ADF. Suddenly the ADF beeped over my headset and the needle on the dial sprang to life. I was right on course and I followed the signal to the airstrip. The crosswinds were gusting at fifty miles per hour, but I made a safe landing.

Because I was the first plane to get in that week, two RCMP, one of them Inuit, drove up in a jeep. The sergeant asked, "Did you bring up any booze?"

Guessing that Cape Dorset was a "dry settlement" where bringing in liquor was against the rules, I answered, "God, no! I didn't bring up anything like that."

The Inuit constable cursed me. "You silly bugger, you came all the way from Vancouver and you didn't bring any booze."

I learned I'd made a major miscalculation. Booze was practically a currency up north. In Cape Dorset, a bottle of whisky sold for as much as $300. The two officers wouldn't talk to me for a week afterward. When I saw them talking to some people on the street, they pointed me out as "That stupid guy who didn't bring any scotch."

I found Cape Dorset very much in transition. Its 800 inhabitants had just got television. They were drinking 700,000 Cokes a year, an astonishing amount considering how few people lived there, and they all seemed to chain-smoke.

Though Wally and I could talk a streak, the artists in the workshop spoke Inuktitut; therefore, he and I demonstrated lithography by showing how a master printer worked with an artist, while an interpreter translated the most important concepts. With a special grease pencil, I drew right onto a piece of Bavarian limestone. Then Wally etched the stone with diluted acid to raise the drawing lines slightly and make the blank areas attract water. After that, we sponged the stone, whereupon the parts not covered by the crayon became wet, while the greasy drawing repelled the water and remained dry. We then applied an oily ink with a roller; it adhered only to the drawing, being repelled by the wet parts of the stone. Then we placed a sheet of paper on the stone and ran the paper and stone through a press, repeating this for each print in the edition.

The Cape Dorset co-operative had experimented with bone, wood, sealskin and linoleum printmaking. With lithography, the Inuit artists could draw right on the stone and make a large number of prints from a single drawing.

The most gifted artists seemed to be the older men and women like Kenojuak Ashevak, known for her playful owls, and Pudlo Pudlat, an ancient-looking man who seemed to have a lot of children and grandchildren. These artists had the strongest memories of the Inuit traditions and of hunting.

One of the artists in the workshop asked me to join a seal hunt after we'd finished our work. Four of us headed up to Pudla Inlet in a Montreal canoe, a long green, canvas-and-wood canoe with an outboard motor. We spotted some seals in the water, and the men blasted away with their rifles. Someone managed to harpoon a few of the seals before they sank and we hauled them aboard. One of the men cut out a seal eye and offered me the delicacy. I popped it into my mouth. It tasted not unlike a raw, salty egg but with a harder, chewier texture. I managed to get it down and grin as if I enjoyed it.

One morning in August, I woke up and found Cape Dorset deserted. The Arctic char were running and all the Inuit had gone fishing at Tassikjakjuak, about ten miles northwest of the settlement. I arrived in my plane to find dozens of green Montreal canoes pulled up on the riverbank beside canvas tents.

Everybody seemed at ease in the way people generally relax while camping. The men trapped the fish in an ancient stone weir, then caught them by hand and tossed them onto the riverbank. The women cleaned the fish and hung them to dry for winter food. Everyone shared the catch.

Thinking I'd practise my fly-fishing on the run of Arctic char, I took my fly rod out of my plane, stepped into the river, and started casting. All the Inuit stared at me as if I'd gone mad. "What can he be doing?" someone asked in Inuktitut. A young Inuit man in gumboots waded into the river and pulled an Arctic char from between my legs as if to say, "This is how you catch a fish." Everyone laughed. Fishing was no sport for the Inuit but a harvest that would get them through the long winter.

I learned more about the ways of the Inuit. I never met one of them who carried a compass or map, yet they always knew where they were. They could read signs in the sky: colours on the undersides of clouds that were reflections of the colours of what lay below. A dark patch or streak underneath a white or pale grey cloud is called a "water blink." It is a reflection of the blue-black colour of open water some distance away, and an Inuit hunter might go in that direction to look for seals. The reflection of the colour of a land area, perhaps a pale ochre, is a "land blink"; of an area of ice, an "ice blink." The reflected colours are infinitely subtle and nearly invisible to most non-Inuit observers.

Toward the end of my stay I flew into a bay to paint some water-colours. When I returned to the shore, the fast-moving tide had gone out and my plane was nowhere in sight. Frantically I hurried down the rocky beach. I thought that the plane must have been holed and sunk. The Inuit who had been fishing nearby gathered around me. "Where's my airplane?" I asked desperately. "My air-plane!" They all started laughing. Some of them rolled on the ground, gasping with mirth. Then they canoed me around a point of land into a bay of deeper water and showed me the airplane. They had been worried about the ebbing tide so they pulled up my anchor and towed the plane into a better location. That really touched me because they had helped me without being asked. Survival in the Arctic means looking out for one another.

By mid-August the first frost had arrived and the brilliant Arctic flowers were dying as the days grew shorter. It was time for me to leave Cape Dorset while the good weather held. My Inuit interpreter had named my plane the *Nauyauyaq*, which means young seagull. And like a sea bird, I was flying south for the winter. As I took off, I dipped my wings in farewell to the small crowd of well-wishers who had come to see me off at the airstrip.

It would be eleven years before I returned to the Arctic. I and the Quebec poet Claude Péloquin had done three books of paintings and poems together, and now we wanted to do a book about the Far North. The federal government was concerned with maintaining sovereignty in the Arctic, and agreed that our project could be seen as a manifestation of Canadian cultural sovereignty. We were offered passage on the CCGS *Des Groseilliers*, a new red-hulled Coast Guard icebreaker. At 6,000 tons, it was much smaller than the *Louis St. Laurent*. It had a 3,000-horsepower engine and a crew of sixty, both men and women, a sign of the changing times. It was a Class 3 ice-breaker, which meant it could cut through ice up to three feet thick.

In the lithography workshop at Cape Dorset's West Baffin Eskimo Co-op with master printer Wallace Brennan.

We left in May 1986 on a voyage to Lancaster Sound, the eastern entrance to the fabled Northwest Passage. The *Des Groseilliers* was breaking through the winter ice earlier than had ever been attempted, thereby adding six weeks to the short ten-week shipping season in the Arctic.

I had less time than on the *Louis St. Laurent*, so I knew I had to maximize it by finding a good place to paint. In this case it was the bridge, a restricted area, so I had to gain the captain's confidence to work there. Luckily I sailed with Captain Guimont, a man of warmth and humour who was well liked by his officers and crew. He welcomed me onto the bridge and called upon the ship's carpenter to make me a larger drawing board that could be wedged under one of the windows to make a suitable work surface. I taped my watercolour paper onto the board, set my watercolours nearby and was able to paint there in comfort for the entire voyage.

Because the *Des Groseilliers* was attached to the port of Quebec and cleared ice from the St. Lawrence River as well as the Arctic Ocean, her crew came from Quebec, too. Even the sign over my bunk directing me to my lifeboat station was written in French. I joked with the captain about whether or not an anglophone like myself would be saved if the ship sank.

The whole Labrador coast was iced in at that time of the year, so Captain Guimont took the eastern lead up the west coast of Greenland, which is ice-free early. About sixty nautical miles south-west of Disko Island, we encountered a large number of icebergs. I described their appearance in my Arctic diary: "At 0730 hours we sail into a forest of large icebergs. Clouds race across the sea, casting shadows over the floes. Colours are constantly moving and changing. The reflection of ice on the low clouds makes an eerie, pale yellow light. Icebergs shaped like giant sculptures change their forms as we glide past them. Stark white when the sun strikes them, they turn translucent cobalt blue or emerald green when a cloud shadow creeps across them. Then they dissolve like ghosts into a snow shower only to reappear, now differently shaped, continuing their slow journey to the North Atlantic."

With so much to paint and nearly twenty-four hours of daylight, I could hardly sleep or even eat. One day, painting between eight in the morning and nine o'clock in the evening, I completed fourteen watercolours—the most I had ever done in a single day. After dinner, I dropped onto my bunk in exhaustion. One morning a puzzled deckhand asked, "What on earth are you painting?" I replied, "The stillness and the exact gradations of radiant light."

Through the icebergs, we headed north into Baffin Bay toward the ice pack. We had open water along the Greenland coast, then we had to break our way northwest through the ice for 600 nautical miles to Lancaster Sound and Admiralty Inlet.

When the ship reached a particularly big ridge of old hardened sea ice, I watched Captain Guimont as he scanned the ice, looking for any weaknesses in the ridge, then directed the ship to start breaking the ridge at a particular spot.

Péloquin was such a passionate character that he couldn't keep quiet. "Why don't you steer that way?" He pointed to another ridge. "It doesn't look very big there."

No one else on the bridge uttered a word. They were shocked at Péloquin's remarks. The captain, who had thirty years of experience in icebreakers, turned red. "Claude's going to get himself thrown into the chain locker," I muttered to myself. "I just know it."

But Captain Guimont simply told Péloquin. "I'm captain of this ship. It goes where I tell it to go." After a few minutes of battering, the ship cracked the ice ridge and broke through it. The tension on the bridge dissipated. Captain Guimont grinned and seized Péloquin in a bear hug.

Disko Island off the coast of Greenland was now fifty miles east of the ship. My Arctic diary records my fascination on that day with the colours of sky and sea. "For a time today I stop painting and simply watch the veil of colours playing over the sky and ice with soft pink Disko Island looming out of the white sea ice. This is what Turner calls 'the dewy light on which the eye dwells so completely enthralled, when it seeks for its liberty.' He continues, '[I] think it a sacrilege to pierce the mystic shell of colour in search of form.' The sky is pale cerulean blue rising into a dusty raw umber on which pearl grey clouds edged in lamp black and ultramarine blue drift silently, creating cobalt violet shadows over the ice. Distant ice becomes a soft pale ochre. This is a mystic world, receiving and emitting rays of light, floating on a blue-black sea. We in our little shell-like ship are locked into the ice, and drift with the changing scene, pirouetting ever so slowly, as if to the time of a celestial clock. In the space of twenty-four hours I see and paint 360°. The sun swings in a giant arc to the south of our position, like a pendulum."

Captain Guimont often looked at my work. After I'd been painting for some time, I gave a little exhibition in the officers' mess. "What a pity the crew can't see this, Toni," remarked the captain, a popular commander because he always thought of his crew. "Why don't we get everybody who's not on duty tonight to come to the officers' mess? You can show your watercolours and talk about them, and Claude can read some of his poetry."

The *Des Groseilliers* had a big officers' mess, so about twenty officers and crew trooped into it. Because it was still daylight, we could look out at the seascape.

"It's all white!" one crew member exclaimed. "I don't know where you're seeing all these colours."

Others in the audience agreed. I pointed to the port side. "Come out onto the deck here and tell me the colour of the ice." We all went outside and looked at the ice.

Someone shouted, "It's white—"

"No, look closer," I replied.

"I guess it has sort of a bluish tinge to it," he conceded. "The shadows are doing it."

"That's right," I said. "Now, come to the other side of the ship and tell me the colour there."

"Holy Moses!" cried one man. "It's pink!"

That got the crew going. They had been looking at the Arctic without really seeing it. Next, I wanted them to see it with my eyes.

"If you really want to see the colours, look at the landscape upside down," I said. I bent over at the waist and looked out from under my arm to show them.

This occasioned general laughter but a few crew members imitated my posture. I encouraged the rest of the crew to try it. "If you really want to see the colours you've got to do it." There was more laughter, but shouts of agreement soon followed. "Now you can see it." I said. "Because you're not used to looking at the landscape upside down, the colours that escape the eye now stick out like the bone on your ankle."

When I greeted the captain on the bridge the following day, he seemed annoyed with me. He beckoned me aside. "I'd like to see you in my cabin, Toni."

"Now I'll have to face the music," I thought to myself. I followed him into the room.

"Sit down and shut the door," ordered the captain. "The crew hasn't been the same since you gave that talk on perception." Then he grinned. "They've been going around with their heads up their asses."

Part of the *Des Groseilliers'* mission was to assist the freighter MV *Arctic*, a Class 4 commercial icebreaker, in the trial run of her new fittings. With a hardened hull and a new bow, the freighter was strong enough for the thick ice, but it was so long it sometimes got stuck turning among the pans of ice in Baffin Bay. At times it could only move a quarter of a mile in two hours, trailing far behind us. At top speed, the *Des Groseilliers* cut its way through the ice at about six knots. It was fitted with a bow knife that acted like a glass cutter, splitting the thick ice pans as far as a mile ahead.

As we broke through the ice we took one hell of a pounding, but I carried on painting. My Arctic diary records my determination: "Between the ice ridges I have developed enough sea (or ice) legs to stand at my drawing board and do some very loose watercolours of the delicate pale shadows in the trapped icebergs and ice ridges—the pale cobalt-blue tones on the large expansive pans of ice, the sharp whites on the sides of vertical ridges, and the deep thalo green shadows in the recesses between the blocks of ice."

We were headed to the most northerly mine in the world, Nanisivik on Baffin Island, to help the MV *Arctic* pick up a symbolic ton of zinc ore. It turned out to be a very bad idea because travelling too early in the spring threatened the fragile Arctic environment. I remember watching chunks of ice go scudding out from under the boat. The Arctic kittiwakes dived for food in the ship's wake. At first I thought they were looking for food thrown from the galley, but then I realized they were heading for the dung-coloured algae that grew on the underside of the ice. The algae was the bottom of the chain of life in the Arctic. All kinds of fish fed on the algae and birds and seals fed on the fish. Polar bears and killer whales fed on the seals, so a single oil spill could threaten a whole ecosystem.

In Admiralty Inlet, several parties of Inuit hunters camped on the ice were angered by the ship passing nearby so early in the year. The captain invited a delegation aboard. Clad in fur parkas and polar bearskin pants, the marks of true hunters, the Inuit complained that animals could hear the ship from more than seventy miles away, so their game had been frightened off.

Meanwhile, we'd noticed that a group of narwhals was following the ship through the ice. The narwhal is a rare Arctic whale that has a beautiful dark mottled skin and a long, twisted ivory tusk, reminiscent of a unicorn's horn. I warned the captain, "We're making a false lead into the inlet for the narwhals. When it freezes over, they'll be trapped under the ice and suffocate."

In the spring of 1915 at Disko Bay in Greenland, a thousand narwhals had been trapped in a savssat, a sheet of ice that forms across the mouth of a fjord and expands toward its head. The Inuit chopped holes in the ice for the whales to breathe but the water froze almost as fast as they could cut openings. Amazingly, the whales, even different species of whales, took turns coming to the holes to breathe. In the end, however, the bay froze over and all the whales died.

The captain's face clouded. He could see the whales from the bridge. The *Des Groseilliers* was supposed to rendezvous with the MV *Arctic* in Admiralty Inlet and, if necessary, assist it in reaching Nanisivik and the zinc mine at the head of the inlet. The MV *Arctic* was stuck in the ice about a mile west of us.

He stopped the ship, saying, "There's nothing in my orders saying I have to take this ship into Nanisivik." Without the engines running, everything went very quiet.

The false lead in the ice froze over as the icebreaker turned back toward Lancaster Sound. For a time, the narwhals were safe. As for Claude and I, the captain arranged for the helicopter to fly us to Nanisivik where we caught a plane south to Montreal.

The North has remained with me in many ways. I understand and appreciate Inuit culture and I realize how important it is to conserve the Arctic environment and wildlife. The watercolours I brought back have inspired some of my best oil paintings, while the intensity of my first experiences there in 1974 set in motion a profound change in my life. I kept a detailed account of my excursions and in 1989 Douglas & McIntyre published my journals as *Onley's Arctic: Diaries and Paintings of the High Arctic*. The book has over a hundred reproductions of my Arctic drawings, paintings and prints, as well as photographs and a map showing the routes I followed.

Chapter 19

The Million-Dollar Sale

When I returned from the Arctic in 1974, I was due for promotion to full professor, but that would have meant an even greater involvement in university life. I handed a letter of resignation I had written on board the icebreaker to George Knox, head of the Fine Arts Department.

Knox, who had been a wartime British naval officer before he became a world-class authority on the eighteenth-century Venetian painter Tiepolo, asked me into his office. He was as disdainful of the excesses of contemporary art as I was, and he didn't want me to leave him alone on the sinking ship of traditional art. "What's this I hear about your quitting the department, Toni?" he asked. "We need you here. I'm giving you a year's leave of absence to think it over."

I hesitated, then replied, "Fine, if that's the way you want it, George. I'll take a year off, but I'm still going to quit."

In 1975, I resigned from the university again. I telephoned him, "Did you get my letter?"

"I tore it up," he grumbled.

"I've got a copy," I said. "I'm not coming back."

After ten years at UBC, my resignation shocked my friends and family. When my father heard the news, he couldn't believe I had done anything that rash. After all, he reasoned, I only came to campus three days each week. With Christmas and statutory holidays, I had five months off. "Toni," he admonished, "it's a living for dead men!"

"No," I replied, "it's a lot of work and responsibility that takes time away from my art. I don't need the salary any more, I need the time. Besides, as a teacher of technical skills in a time of conceptual art, I am no longer needed."

Financially, the decision came easily. My landscape paintings were reaching a growing audience because they had a wide appeal. One critic described my work as haunting because a view of nature without people and buildings gave the viewer a feeling that the land existed for him alone. However, commercial success took some planning and management. I painted my watercolours on eleven-inch by fifteen-inch paper, so that they were easily mailed to art galleries across the country, where they were matted and framed. I spent almost a month each year making serigraph prints, popular among young professionals who could afford to spend $100 on art. I also sold reproductions, prints and postcards of my watercolours, the latter printed on oversized cards so they'd be displayed in museum shops separately from the standard rack-sized cards. Furthermore, I had become a West Coast celebrity, interviewed on radio and featured in several TV documentaries.

As early as 1970, I had supplemented my salary as a UBC professor with a larger income from art gallery sales. By 1975, my sales had increased so much that if I had still been drawing a university salary, it would have scarcely paid my taxes. But when I telephoned my mother to tell her the good news, she hectored: "That's all very well, Toni, but your father and I want to know when you're going to get a job."

In 1978, the Vancouver Art Gallery held a thirty-year retrospective of my work. With 341 pieces, it was the largest one-man show they had ever had. That year, I sold even more art. By 1979 my sales had reached the point where I was beginning to feel I could buy anything I wanted. Around 1980 I acquired a BMW to replace my old Mazda station wagon.

Although most artists are forced to give a dealer exclusive access to their work, I insisted on using a dealer in every city where there was interest and on the right to sell paintings from my home. During the 1970s, I had about thirty dealers across Canada and a handful in the US. Tracking that inventory and keeping my dealers honest proved enormously challenging.

One notorious dealer tried to trick me with an empty account book, complaining, "Toni, there haven't been many sales this month." I had run into a few buyers and I knew he was lying. The next time I came by to see him no one was in the office, so I looked through his desk. He had a second account book showing the sales he had covered up. I immediately pulled my work from his gallery and insisted that he settle my account.

Another dealer kept selling out his artists' shows. The red sale stickers went up as soon as a show opened. I discovered that he was buying up his artists' paintings in order to boost their value. Meanwhile he put off paying them by telling them he was keeping a running account. When he actually did sell something, he kept the money in term deposits for months, pocketing the interest.

Whenever I confronted dealers like these, they'd try to placate me by telling me the cheque was in the mail, or even denying the sales outright: "You must be mistaken, we don't have those paintings." That's why good records were essential. Eventually, I hit on the idea of business reply forms. I'd send each dealer a list of the etchings, serigraphs, watercolours and oil paintings I had shipped to him. The form had two copies and included a reply section so that we both had a one-page record and the dealer could easily confirm arrival of the inventory. However, we still had to write or telephone many dealers to check up on my sales. Even with these precautions, some dealers continued to steal from me, or they went bankrupt and their creditors seized my paintings even though I still owned them. Galleries also had fires and thefts and sometimes they had no insurance.

In the vast majority of retail businesses, inventory has to be purchased, but art is always given to dealers on consignment. For beginning artists, the rationale is that the dealer does not know whether he can sell the work. For established artists, the rationale is that the artist controls the prices. But when an artist has reached the point of selling very well at good prices, the dealers expect to keep to the same arrangement. Ultimately, I began to insist that some galleries purchase my work at a dealer's discount.

I have painted a dark picture of some of the dozens of commercial galleries I have dealt with since 1958, but I hasten to balance this by adding that many of my dealers were efficient and honest. I owe a great deal of gratitude to them. I have good memories of Alvin

Gloria and James, Silver River, BC, 1975.

Balkind and Betty Marshall of the New Design Gallery of long ago in Vancouver; of Dorothy Cameron and Doris Pascal in Toronto; of the Thomas Gallery under Dr. Ted Thomas and Mary Beamish in Winnipeg; of the Bau-Xi Gallery and the Heffel Gallery under Ken Heffel in Vancouver—to name just a few of the galleries and dealers from my past. Recently I have had good relationships with the Winchester Gallery in Victoria and the Ballard-Lederer Gallery in Vancouver.

Unfortunately, during this same period of so much success, my domestic life spiraled out of control. The very qualities Gloria and I had initially admired in one another drove us apart. Her intellect and logic, enormously helpful to me in managing my business affairs, on the personal level seemed to make her too restrained and cautious for a risk-taker like me. She had been unhappy for a long time about my flying and my artist's self-centredness, which often led me to ignore her, our son Jamie and my daughter Lynn. She also felt that supporting me in various ways took all her time and made it difficult, if not impossible, to achieve anything of her own. When these feelings became strong enough, we separated. When I moved out in the fall of 1975, she remained in the house with our son to carry on an art publishing business we had established together, and in 1981 opened a small art gallery on Granville Island.

While we were growing apart I had a series of affairs, culminating in a firecracker relationship with a slim, sharp-tongued blonde—I'll call her Laurie—who was a performance artist and poet. Among my mistakes in that relationship was to advise her on a multi-media piece combining her poetry with a view of the stars. She had planned to punch some black paper full of holes and hang it from the ceiling in the hall of the Western Front gallery. I urged her to take the performance to the planetarium where they could project any sky she wanted. Although she did that, she was furious at me for "taking over" and I had to promise not to attend.

Events came to a head at Opal Beach, Oregon. While Laurie was reading in our motel room, I sat painting on a large rock out in the bay. Suddenly an orca breached near me. He was so close that I heard the rushing sound of his breath as he sucked air in through his blowhole. To my amazement, he lingered by the rock, watching me with his big beady eye. I had heard of people having these amazing encounters with whales, and fearing that I'd scare him away, I tried to avoid looking directly at him.

"Hi, there," I said. "Don't spray any water on my painting, please."

For the next hour or two while I painted, he stayed nearby. When I walked back along the beach the whale followed just beyond the surf. I climbed the embankment to our motel, a 1940s-style white clapboard building that looked as if it came from an Edward Hopper painting. Then I looked back and saw the whale still in the bay. The whole scene was extraordinary.

When I reached the room, I told Laurie what had happened. She slammed her book shut. "Toni, you're so full of shit," she snapped. "You come up with these stories all the time."

"He's right out there!" I protested.

We had a pair of binoculars with us. I passed them to her and she looked out the window.

"God! There is a whale out there—I can see it blowing!" She set the binoculars down. "But there's no way it followed you."

We had another argument during which she repeatedly tried to destroy my experience, and I finally went to bed exhausted. Poor Laurie could hardly sleep and she got up again around twelve. To clear her head, she took my Mazda out for a drive. The road from the motel cut inland for a mile or two and passed some large sand dunes. She climbed up one of them and sat in the moonlight, mulling over our relationship. When she returned to the car she realized that she had dropped the car keys in the sand.

Forced to walk back to the motel, she arrived about three o'clock in the morning. In tears, she burst into the motel room and shook me awake. "Toni, I hate to tell you this. I've lost the keys to your car and had to leave it down the road."

Groggily I turned over in bed, "Don't worry, Laurie, we'll sort it out in the morning."

The next day I asked the motel owner to drive us to the car. We looked around the dunes. I asked Laurie to show me where she'd walked.

"It's no good," she said impatiently. "It's like finding a needle in a haystack. We should break into the car and hot-wire it."

Laurie hadn't noticed that she had left footprints in the sand. I followed them up the side of a nearby dune. Then I found the impression she had made when she sat down. "Which pocket were the keys in?" I asked.

"The right one! Toni, this is not going to work."

I put my hand in the impression on the sand left by her right buttock. I felt around in the sand a little bit and found the keys.

"How did you do that?" she asked.

I jangled the keys in my hand. "Look, you don't believe anything I tell you. You told me I was full of shit about the whale. Now I don't want to talk about it."

After that we broke up for good. Laurie decided to take a job in the US. Before her departure she took a boat cruise to Alaska. About two days out, as she was leaning against the railing of the ship and staring at the mountains and the fjords of the inside passage, another woman joined her. "Isn't it gorgeous," she commented. "It reminds me of a Toni Onley painting." When Laurie returned to Vancouver, she telephoned me. "Toni, I hate your guts, but I have to tell you this before I leave for New York." She repeated the woman's remark.

I laughed. "What did you do when she said that?"

"I threw her overboard," she replied.

When Gloria and I finally separated, I moved onto a two-storey hippie houseboat in Coal Harbour, in downtown Vancouver near the Bayshore Inn. Built on a weathered West Coast barge and covered with cedar shakes, my new home had a toilet and shower, a tiny kitchen and a living room with cabinets and a bunk bed where I slept. On the second floor, there was a balcony and a tiny bedroom. I converted that room into a studio with a painting wall where I could nail up canvases for oil paintings and work away at them.

At the time, which was about 1976, I cultivated a certain rough look. I grew my hair, thinning on top, until it fell almost to my shoulders, long and curly at the back and sides of my head. I had a moustache and a beard, and a wardrobe that consisted solely of jeans and a Levi's jacket. I felt I had rebelled from any conventional middle-class aspirations. I had quit my job at UBC, become a full-time painter and separated from my wife. After my relationship with Laurie came crashing down, I turned inward and concentrated on my art.

Back in 1965, I had started to use Chinese goat-hair brushes. In Chinatown I bought a *fude*, a long bamboo-handled goat-hair calligraphy brush, and *sumi*, a carbon-based ink made from the soot of burnt vegetable oils bonded with animal gelatin and produced in China and Japan according to age-old formulas. Accustomed to the stiff sable brushes employed in British watercolours, I found the soft, pliable, larger brush propelled me toward a new technique and a new approach to painting. A stroke, as in watercolour, could never be redone. If the brush was too wet, then the *sumi* ink spread too far. The unexpected blurs and white areas where the brush eluded the paper added a vitality and spontaneity to each painting.

To help me create greater texture with my brushstrokes, and rich-looking washes through the gradations of ink, an artist friend, Chin Chêk Lum, gave me some bolts of thick, very absorbent handmade paper that he had brought out with him when he fled China ahead of the revolution. I am still using this paper, long after Chin Chêk's death.

I began painting landscapes with wide horizontal lines and overlapping monolithic shapes that spread and blurred on the paper, untitled works that suggested boulders sitting on a broad beach. I would charge my brush with ink, meditate briefly and then plunge in. Because I painted with black ink instead of colours, I had to reduce the complexity of light and shadow to simple brushstrokes and flat washed tones. Light, medium and dark ink were the only "colours" I had to convey the image.

I learned of an eccentric Chinese monk, Pata-shan-Jên, a poet and drunkard who created a thousand paintings for each year of his eighty-five-year life. Like other Chinese painters, he sought to depict his images by the barest minimum of brushstrokes. Sometimes the unpainted parts of his paper suggest the sky or the distance between one mountain and another one, farther away. If he left a winding space between two mountains, the white space was a river. He used what is now referred to as a "boneless" or "lineless" approach where each shape and colour bleeds into another, so that his images of fish, flowers, trees and rocks appear to be engaged in conversation with each other.

One of the British watercolour painters I most admired, the eighteenth-century artist Alexander Cozens, had tried using this lineless technique. Although British watercolourists also relied on the swift and skilful delineation of shapes and the gradation of colour washes to suggest the effect of light on colour, their approach evolved from concepts such as perspective and realism. Cozens proved something of an exception. In his 1784 book, *A New Method of Assisting the Invention in Drawing Original Compositions of Landscape*, he advised painters to take as large a paintbrush as they could handle, dip it into ink and water, and make blots and washes to create new and more spontaneous forms in their paintings.

In my landscapes I tried to synthesize these Eastern and Western aesthetics. The only other Canadian landscape artist I knew who had moved in this direction, if ever so briefly, was Fred Varley of the Group of Seven. From Vancouver he wrote to a friend in Halifax, "BC is heaven. It trembles within me and pains me with wonder as when a child I first awakened to the song of the earth at home." He added, "I often feel that only the Chinese of the eleventh and twelfth centuries ever interpreted the spirit of such a country." While renting a studio in Lynn Valley in 1934, he tried painting "The Dumpling," as he nicknamed Lynn Peak, in a mixture of Western and Chinese styles, omitting outline and perspective.

In my case, I had been trained in the British watercolour tradition of the use of outlines and detail, but once I began to use the Chinese brush, I sought the spontaneity of the Oriental aesthetic. It was also a further development of my experience as an abstract expressionist painter because it was a direct response to the materials—the brush, paint and paper. The Japanese called it "the way of the brush." As Kuo Jo-hsu wrote in Sung dynasty times:

> The brush must be nimble, move swiftly in a continuous and connecting manner, so that the flow of life is not interrupted as the thoughts precede the brush. But the brush is also in the thoughts and when the picture is finished, all the thoughts are there and the image corresponds completely to the spirit. When the painter is inwardly serene, when his spirit is at ease and his thoughts calm, the mind is not exhausted and the brush not restrained.

In the western tradition, there is a discontinuity between conception and execution that the eastern tradition seeks to eliminate. We have all heard of the artist who dreamed that he was looking at a great painting, then woke up and started to execute it. That is an extreme case of the western approach to art. To use the oriental approach, instead of following a plan I tried to let the work emerge from the process. I created many *sumi* ink landscapes in my studio and the exercise helped me not only to refine my brush technique for my watercolours painted out of doors, but to develop a Zen approach to landscape painting generally. The different types and sizes of Chinese brushes I now use to create my watercolour landscapes are described in detail in my 1999 book, *Toni Onley's British Columbia: A Tribute*.

Meanwhile my personal life continued to feel empty and incomplete. Then in the fall of 1976, Susannah Blunt, a painter friend living in a houseboat next to mine, arranged for me to meet Yukiko Kageyama, a young Japanese woman employed as a nanny by two of Susannah's friends. About medium height, Yukiko had a striking oval-shaped face with a high forehead and jet-black hair that she often pinned back. Initially, I felt reluctant about making any commitments, especially because of the big difference in our ages. She was twenty-eight and I was turning forty-eight. Yet we were attracted to each other, and her Japanese appearance and culture made her the most exotic woman I had ever dated. Her first impressions of Vancouver were delightful. She told me it seemed like a big park to her, that the city even scared her a little because the streets looked so empty compared to those of a Japanese city.

Yukiko had been raised in Itami, a small town near Osaka. After high school, she had drifted for a time through a number of jobs, working for the Sumitomo insurance company, then later as a dental hygienist. Because young women were expected to marry, bear children and leave the workforce, it was a fairly typical pattern. Women were never given much responsibility or serious opportunities in the workplace. Accordingly, Yukiko's father had tried to match her with the son of the local Shinto *bonze*, or priest. As religion is often conducted along commercial lines in Japan, this son would inherit his father's temple. Because Shinto priests preside over everything from marriage vows to student prayers to pass the university entrance exams, Yukiko would have been set for life. She had her own ideas, however, and began studying English with the idea that she would leave Japan and live overseas for a year.

When I knew her better and her English had improved, she explained, "I didn't fit into Japanese society—a husband and two kids—and I wanted to speak better English. My teacher, who was from Berkeley, said, 'It's a good idea for you to go abroad'." Her teacher met Susannah's friends while they were travelling on a train with their baby daughter during a study tour in Japan. Yukiko's teacher arranged for her to work with them, and she applied for a Canadian visa.

"I thought I could speak English well enough to get by in Canada when I left Japan," she told me. "But on the airplane to Vancouver, I asked for orange juice and they couldn't understand me."

At first Yukiko simply awakened my sympathy because she seemed so adrift in a new culture. As she was only paid room and board and a very small salary, she had little money to do anything, so I took it on myself to show her the city. It was the role I most often took in my relationships with women, that of guide and protector. Not all women were happy with this. But where Gloria would have been annoyed, Yukiko was pleased.

As our feelings for one another developed, Yukiko became my first true meeting with the Orient. Her culture seemed so different, even in dress. Sometimes I wondered how many Western clothes she owned. She often did housework in a *yukata*, a cotton kimono. One time when her employers were away on a trip, she organized a dinner party where she wore a beautiful kimono, served Japanese food and seated me beside her, almost ignoring everyone else at the table. It was as if she were arranging our marriage.

Our relationship, particularly later when we travelled together, amplified the new direction in my work toward an Oriental view of painting, the approach suggested by Japanese calligraphy and Zen philosophy of improvisation or "the song of the brush." The natural rhythm and spontaneity of Zen-influenced art in Japan appealed to my sense of what I was doing while painting watercolours. The Japanese style of painting had evolved after Buddhism had spread to Japan from China. To chronicle their moments of enlightenment amid nature, Zen monks used brushwork that was quick, expressive, economical and powerful, with small areas of wash. Such an approach seemed to be an appropriate progression from my early experiences with abstract expressionism in Mexico and the landscape painting I did after I could fly to remote wildernesses. These intuitions were further reinforced when Yukiko and I studied *shodo*, Japanese calligraphy, together. I could never replicate our teacher's brushstrokes until it came to me that I should also think of the negative spaces, those parts of the paper that were untouched by the brush. I couldn't read the Japanese *kanji*, of course, but I didn't need to understand the words to appreciate the effects of the brush.

Then in the spring of 1977, I had an emergency call from Yukiko. She telephoned me about a burning smell in the couple's house. She was alone with the baby, and I quickly drove over. The house, an older one in Kitsilano, had a chimney fire. I rang the fire department and they put a hose down the chimney. Unfortunately, in dousing the fire they left an awful mess in the living room. When Yukiko's employers returned home they were furious.

"You shouldn't be giving us hell," I exploded. "You should be thanking me. That fire could have burned down the house and killed Yukiko and your daughter."

The conflict between Yukiko and her employers grew. In May she quit her job and moved onto my houseboat. Officially, in order to satisfy her visa requirements, she became my son's nanny for the occasions when he stayed with me. The summer and fall of 1977 that we spent together marked one of the happiest times of my life. Because my work sold so well, I had no financial worries. I painted all the time and I'd fallen in love. The inconvenience of two people crowded onto a small houseboat never troubled me. Nor did the breakdown of my kerosene heater in the winter when I had to strip it and lay it out in pieces on the kitchen counter to try to fix the carburetor. Even after rain water leaked through the roof of the houseboat and dripped onto our bed and we had to hang sheet plastic from the ceiling, I wouldn't have traded places with anyone else in the world. Finally, Yukiko and I were forced to abandon our home when the city council of Vancouver passed a bylaw that evicted all the houseboats from Coal Harbour.

We rented a penthouse on nearby Haro Street in the West End and I listed my houseboat for sale at $28,000. The shortage of moorage space in Vancouver made it difficult to sell, however, so instead of $28,000, I settled for $18,000 from a lady who offered to make time payments. She only made one. She ripped out the two murals I had painted on the boat and peddled them. Then her next two cheques bounced. Before I could reclaim the houseboat, she had resold it and gone underground. I flew over the houseboats moored in Richmond, spotted mine and landed to reclaim it.

A young man answered the door and I explained the situation to him. "This is my houseboat. I haven't been paid for it yet."

He looked devastated. He had just invested his entire savings in the houseboat. "It's all the money I've got," he stammered.

I felt sorry for him. "Forget it," I told him, "the houseboat's yours now. I've had a lot of happiness on it and my whole life's changed as a result. I hope you're as lucky."

I eventually tracked down the woman who had swindled me. She had already spent the cash, so she offered me some land in

Hawaii instead. Like a fool, I accepted. She was long gone by the time I learned that my new property lay under a lava flow.

The next few years were even better for me. After Gloria and I were divorced in 1979, Yukiko and I were married in a small civil ceremony at the city registration office. My son Jamie, then thirteen, served as a witness, and my daughter Lynn as the ringbearer. In 1980 we bought a $250,000 house with an indoor swimming pool on Musqueam lands off Southwest Marine Drive and began to live in the kind of luxury that I had never dreamed possible.

Challenges still came my way, of course, including meeting Yukiko's family in Japan. When we went to Osaka in 1978 before we got married, her father, a lensmaker at Minolta Camera, and all her male relations were very cool to the idea of a foreigner joining their family. "You might as well have told them you were marrying a gorilla," I said to Yukiko after I had met them. "I'm a Western guy with a beard who's over twenty years older than you."

However, Yukiko's mother and her maternal grandparents liked me. They could see that I loved Yukiko and could support her very comfortably, that she could likely return for visits and that I would try to make her happy. I remember sitting on the tatami in her grandfather's living room one evening and drinking sake with him. We could not carry on a conversation, but we laughed together and he kept refilling my glass and asking Yukiko's grandmother to take pictures of us together. Grandmother, who held the family's purse strings, assured me that the rest of the family would not give me any trouble.

Meanwhile the sales of my work kept increasing in Canada. Several factors operated, among them an extremely high rate of inflation. Speculators flipped land, houses and apartment buildings for large profits over a matter of months. Some of the investors looking to exploit other commodities began to buy up art, particularly the work of artists who had died and whose art was therefore limited in supply. Sotheby's, the international auction house specializing in fine art, sold a Fred Varley canvas for $170,000. In June, Granville Street art dealer Kenneth Heffel paid a record $240,000 for an early Lawren Harris.

Japan, 1978.

Contemporary art got a boost as well from the Trudeau government, which encouraged the development of Canadian art through the 1975 Cultural Property Export and Import Act that granted substantial tax concessions on purchases from living Canadian artists. An investor could deduct the fair market value of the art up to 100 percent of taxable income over five years when the work was donated to an accredited institution. Ironically, this happened soon after a whole generation of young Canadian artists had rejected the idea of art as a commodity to be bought and sold. To make their anti-commodity statements, many artists were working in forms such as happenings, performance art and video. None of this new art was collectible. Consequently paintings, etchings, prints and other unique art objects, especially work done in the 1950s and 1960s, skyrocketed in value.

In addition, major Canadian corporations expanding their operations out west began investing in Canadian art. Not only did it serve as excellent public relations, but it proved to be a good investment. CIL Paint, Shell Oil of Canada, and the TD Bank were among the many companies that purchased my work.

Besides helping Canadian artists, these developments aided Canadian public art galleries, too, because most of their collections came as gifts from corporations and wealthy benefactors. If corporate and private investors donated art to a public gallery, they were entitled to tax breaks and the goodwill of the community, whereas if they sold it on the open market, they had to pay a capital gains tax. The tax advantage of donating Canadian art became a powerful incentive to buy it.

Early in 1980 Robert Davidson, the thirty-three-year-old owner of the Move Gallery in Gastown, offered to find a buyer for all my as yet unsold art work. His knowing grin, black curly hair and pointed beard gave him a slightly Mephistophelean air. He was very confident. "All your work, Toni. Just estimate the value and I'll find a buyer to invest in it."

At first, I was stunned. "Is there anything about my soul in this?"

I was skeptical, but expressed some interest. Davidson came to my studio and photographed every piece I had. He put together six albums of photographs, then took them to potential buyers on an all-or-nothing deal to corner the market on Toni Onleys.

Davidson was assisted in this enterprise by Sam Houston, a twenty-five-year-old Halifax art broker who was born on Baffin Island and spoke fluent Inuktitut. He was the son of James Houston, who had set up the printmaking co-operative among the Inuit that I had visited in the Arctic, and he had been successfully selling collections of Inuit art. Sam introduced Davidson to a multi-millionaire realtor in the Fraser Valley to whom he had already sold a substantial amount of Inuit art. "Toni's Million Dollar Sale," as the newspapers called it, went through on August 1, 1980. The buyer wanted his name kept secret, so in the press that followed, we referred to him as the "Fraser Valley Phantom."

This sale—actually $929,000—proved the largest sum ever paid to a living Canadian artist. To gather the pieces, a Loomis security truck pulled up to the Bau-Xi Gallery and loaded the fifty-six paintings I had with them. The rest of the work was collected from my studio and everything was locked up in a warehouse in Yaletown in downtown Vancouver. Altogether the collection included 1,287 pieces, with individual prices that ranged from $100 for a small etching to $7,000 for an oil painting. My prints, of which I had thousands, were represented in the collection by one print from each edition.

Under the initial terms of the deal, I was not allowed to put new work on the market for two years. However, I had prior commitments for three shows and we subsequently agreed that I could sell work out of these scheduled exhibitions. I had been selling my watercolours for $650 each. I informed my galleries that I wanted to double my prices. All the dealers warned me that the new prices would impede my sales. I figured that wouldn't be such a bad thing because I didn't need the money.

Despite the warnings, the sale triggered a run on my work. I had a September show at the Bau-Xi Gallery of forty watercolours and fifteen oils based on my travels on the West Coast. No reservations were taken on any of the pictures until the show opened. Buyers, other artists and members of the press crowded into the gallery on Monday night. I entered, wearing a three-piece suit, with Yukiko on my arm in a kimono, and the CBC camera crew asked us to re-enter the gallery so they could film my arrival. Within a half hour, a third of the watercolours were gone.

"I guess you're going to retire now, Toni," commented one reporter.

"Artists never retire. My best work's ahead of me," I replied. "For years, I've struggled to survive and to find the time to paint. Those days are over."

To celebrate my million-dollar sale, I bought a Rolls-Royce Silver Shadow II and was subsequently photographed with it for the cover of an issue of the *Financial Post*, which featured an article on my unprecedented financial success. The further publicity resulting from my purchase of the Rolls triggered feelings of jealousy and anger in many artists. In the entire country, there were very few who didn't teach art or were not relying on Canada Council grants. If you included craftspeople doing macramé and tie-dyed shirts, BC alone had 3,500 full-time artists in a population of about three million. Their meagre incomes classified most as highly skilled members of the working poor.

Some people claimed I had sold out. But why shouldn't a painter live as well as a lawyer or a banker or a company president? American artists like Robert Rauschenberg or Frank Stella easily earn as much as a million dollars every year. And what of the multi-million-dollar salaries we pay to sports figures in Canada? Talking about money and art seems vulgar to some people. Yet for better or worse, money also generates enormous public interest.

In a 1986 article in *Saturday Night*, "Why Does the Press Savage Success?" Conrad Black commented that English Canadians, unlike Americans, "are suspicious and hostile towards success . . . [because they] regard achievements, other than by professional athletes and geriatrics, as somehow un-Canadian." I had my share of attacks in the press for daring to be a financially successful living Canadian artist, but I also had my defenders. In the *Vancouver Sun* of August 8, 1980, Christopher Dafoe urged the public to applaud my large sale. Comparing my situation with that of David Milne, the now highly regarded Canadian artist who worked and died in extreme poverty, he concluded, "It is somehow satisfying to see a good artist reaping part of his reward while he is still alive to enjoy it."

The biggest dealer in Vancouver got in on the sale as well. For about $400,000 the Heffel Gallery bought 165 paintings from the Fraser Valley Phantom, including some of my *Polar* series, the collages that had become famous after the Tate Gallery acquired one in 1963. Within a year, the Phantom had resold half of his collection for as much as he had paid for the entire collection. Then he sold the other half of the collection for about $500,000 to an investment syndicate consisting of a North Shore businessman, a lawyer and an investor. Later, one of the members of the syndicate had his part of the collection stolen from a warehouse in Richmond. Those paintings have yet to surface.

In 1983, because of my high visibility in the arts community and my past association with Prime Minister Trudeau, I received an invitation to dine with Queen Elizabeth II. The invitation read:

> The Master of the Household is commanded by Her
> Majesty to invite Mr. and Mrs. Toni Onley to a Dinner
> to be given by the Queen and the Duke of Edinburgh
> on board H.M.Yacht Britannia at Vancouver.

I showed the gold-embossed invitation to Yukiko. Tired of public appearances, she turned away. "They only want to see you. I don't want to go."

"Yukiko, don't do this to me," I pleaded. "What am I supposed to do, go alone? This is the Queen of Canada. It's a royal command!"

"I haven't got anything to wear," she pouted.

"Why don't you wear your kimono from Matsuyama," I suggested. When we had visited Japan in 1978, we had bought a hand-painted kimono created by a famous Japanese artist, one of the country's "living treasures." At this, Yukiko gave in and I accepted the invitation.

On the night of the event, I drove our Rolls-Royce to the harbour where the yacht *Britannia* lay berthed. The brightly lit ship was 412 feet long, the size of a football field. The several hundred onlookers on the dock cheered as Prime Minister Trudeau and his three sons arrived with a motorcade of RCMP cars. Not to be upstaged in his own province, Premier Bill Bennett appeared in a second limousine five minutes later.

Yukiko and I strolled up the gangplank and joined the guests on the deck of the ship where an admiral, with a red leather-bound brass telescope tucked under his arm, greeted us. In the lounge, the royals waited to receive the line of guests. The Queen, surprisingly small, wore a simple navy gown and a silver tiara set with diamonds. By her side was an RAF group captain, who was also her personal pilot. He bent over to the Queen as Yukiko and I approached and whispered our names.

"Your Majesty, Mr. and Mrs. Toni Onley."

The Queen tipped her head slightly in my direction and offered a white-gloved hand. In my excitement, I squeezed it a little. Her arm immediately stiffened. Protocol limited one to a light touch of the royal appendage.

Bored, scowling a little, Prince Philip avoided shaking hands with anyone by clasping his arms behind his back. Extraordinary, I thought, he's not really a tall man. In photographs, he just appears to be tall because he's so thin and because he's taller than the Queen.

The Queen studied Yukiko. She had her long black hair pinned up in a traditional Japanese style and wore her black and white Matsuyama kimono painted with ocean waves and the richly embroidered red-and-gold *obi* or sash that her father had given her. Yukiko bowed deeply. The Queen then spoke to her about the kimono and of life in Japan.

When Yukiko joined me in the lounge, her face was lit up with pleasure. She whispered, "The Queen's not threatening or anything like that. She's just like somebody you could meet anywhere. She's lovely!"

In the dining room, Yukiko and I joined the other guests at a horseshoe arrangement of chairs and tables. The Queen sat at the head of the table. We dined on twenty-two-carat-gold-edged Spode Copeland china. The cuisine was French, a delicate *filet de grenobloise* with *pommes fondantes* and a marvellous *supreme de dindoneau smitaine*, and for vegetables, *petit pois a la menthe* and *carottes au beurre*.

Afterward, I had the briefest of opportunities to speak to the Queen. It was an occasion for small talk. During our meal, a bagpiper in a navy-and-scarlet tartan kilt had walked around behind the guests, playing a Scottish air. When he reached the Queen, she flicked her wrist and he disappeared.

"Your Majesty," I observed, "the piper only played half of the program on the menu."

"I don't like the pipes," she remarked.

I smiled. I suppose she must be tired of hearing them, I thought. At Balmoral Castle, the royal family is awakened every morning by a bagpiper, a tradition initiated by Queen Victoria.

In the lounge afterward, I got into a conversation with the Queen's doctor. To my surprise, he had seen my book of watercolour reproductions, *A Silent Thunder*, and he asked for some tips on watercolour painting, which was his hobby. The Queen's household staff doubled as a ceremonial guard, and they were going to perform a military tattoo on the dock by the ship. An announcement was made to ask everyone to assemble on the upper deck to watch it. The Queen remained in the lounge, as she would walk out to the main deck with Trudeau and his sons and her train of ladies-in-waiting.

"I'd better go," I told the doctor.

"You can stay here," he replied.

The Queen came over. "Mr. Onley, would you and your wife join us on the main deck?"

At 10:30 p.m., Yukiko and I walked out with the Queen. The twenty-six-member Royal Marine band marched down the gang-plank. They wore navy uniforms with white pith helmets, and their silver and brass instruments gleamed as they played *Beat the Retreat*. Flashes from cameras on the dock went off. The crowd cheered and applauded when the Queen appeared on the main deck. I stood behind her. In my tuxedo, with my beard and balding head, I must have resembled Edward VI. It amused me to think that the spectators may have wondered, "Who is that man with the Queen?"

Chapter 20

A Burning Question

The news of my million-dollar sale seemed to have appeared in one too many papers and magazines. For the June 1981 issue of the *Financial Post*, I posed on the hood of my Rolls-Royce. The magazine cover read: "The Onley Way to Riches." In September 1983, two Revenue Canada officials came to my house on a field audit.

We sat in my dining room. The senior official, the elder of the two auditors, was a lean greying man in his late fifties. Shakespeare's description of Cassius in *Julius Caesar* sprang to my mind. Apparently, his expertise lay in assigning values to art and heirlooms. He asked, "Do you like flying?"

"Of course, I do," I replied.

He smiled as if something had pleased him. "So, operating your plane is not entirely a business expense, is it, Mr. Onley?"

"What do you mean?" I asked.

"By your own admission, you fly your plane for pleasure." He rubbed his hands together in anticipation. "Don't you see, that means you're deriving a personal, taxable benefit from it."

"No, I use the plane to go painting."

He ignored me. For him, taxation functioned within the pleasure and pain principle. If you did something you liked, then it couldn't be work. If he classified my flying as a hobby, the department would be able to challenge my last three tax returns. He closed his notebook. "Let's take a look at the contents of your studio, shall we?"

As we walked downstairs to my studio on the ground floor, the second auditor bantered with me. A roly-poly Chinese Canadian in his early thirties, he was probably an MBA. A number-cruncher, he carried a sophisticated-looking calculator. He tried to inject a little bonhomie into the undertaking. Half-jokingly he asked how much I'd charge to give his daughter painting lessons. Then he dropped a bombshell:

"Mr. Onley, the department will need a complete inventory of your work. The tax department is reclassifying you as a manufacturer. For unsold works, you will not be allowed to deduct the production costs as an expense. This means you must keep an inventory record and pay tax on the cost of producing every artwork until it is actually sold, at which point you can claim the expense."

"That's crazy, it'll put me on the breadline," I objected. "Do you know how much work I have in my studio?" I led them to the storage room. There were stacks of paintings. Over a year I could easily paint a hundred watercolours and twenty-five oils. Like other artists, I usually sold only a fraction of my work. In fact, some of the work was experimental and would never be sold—in business terms, a research and development effort. Now Revenue Canada wanted to tax me on the production costs of all my unsold works, going back for years. My production costs, including the cost of owning and operating my airplane, were huge. I could receive a bill for half a million dollars. There was no way I could pay it.

I didn't know the larger issue at the time. I was one of four hundred Canadian artists undergoing an audit that year. Most were painters and writers who taught for a living and deducted expenses for studio rentals, travel, and writing and art supplies. They found themselves declared "hobbyists." The tax deductions they had claimed in the past were denied. In the case of actors in repertory theatre companies and classical musicians who had been claiming expenses as freelancers, Revenue Canada recategorized them all as salaried employees. Actors who might be in a company for only part of a year suddenly found they had lost all their deductions and were taxed as full-time employees. The ninety-nine musicians in the Toronto Symphony who were guaranteed forty-eight weeks of work were only paid for 19.5 hours per week, so they were classified as part-time workers ineligible for travelling expenses or a depreciation allowance on their instruments—some of which cost tens of thousands of dollars.

Suddenly all these artists and performers owed several million dollars of back taxes with compounded interest. Ironically, those unable to pay forfeited their Canada Council arts grants. One government department supported them and the other seized their grant money.

That year, Revenue Canada had reinterpreted the tax legislation in order to generate more government revenue. Expenses for the Trudeau administration had spiralled out of control during the inflationary 1970s and early 1980s. By 1983, the Canadian government had a record $28-billion deficit for the year, over seven percent greater than the entire gross domestic product. Meanwhile the accumulated government debt rocketed to $128 billion. In the scramble for money, the government sought new revenue. Most of the country's taxes were paid by salaried workers, so Revenue Canada utilized a new computer program to identify self-employed taxpayers and recategorize them, whenever possible, as salaried workers. Some of them happened to be artists and that was how investigations like the one into my work began.

The auditors outlined the new rules for me. From then on, if I wanted to write off expenses like operating my plane, or travelling on a commercial jetliner to paint in Japan, I'd have to sell the paintings I made on these trips before I could make any deductions. If I made a second painting or a print based on the same image, I'd have to recalculate my original deduction. The record-keeping required was mind-boggling.

"Wow! You've got a lot of work here," said the younger auditor as he stared at the paintings stacked under my desks. "This must represent a lot of unrecovered production costs you've been incorrectly writing off as expenses."

"No one sells all their work," I retorted. "How am I supposed to be able to pay taxes on the cost of creating all this unsold work?"

"You can do what manufacturers do, Mr. Onley," he answered. "They have a year-end sale, declare their profits and losses, then move into next year's product line."

I groaned in disbelief. I couldn't get through to these guys at all. "The art world doesn't work that way," I told them. "I can't have a year-end sale. Everybody would wait for the 'fire sale.' It would destroy my prices." I looked from the blank face of one auditor to the other. "Very well, if I'm a manufacturer, what do other manufacturers—people who make things out of iron or steel—do at the end of the year?"

"This line of discussion isn't getting us anywhere." The older auditor waved his hand dismissively. "Steel manufacturers melt unsaleable products down. The metal's recycled into new products."

"What if I burnt my work? Then it wouldn't exist. There'd be no inventory, so no tax to pay on unsold paintings."

The two auditors turned to each other in alarm. The younger man tittered, "You wouldn't burn all your art, would you?"

Defiantly I replied, "You leave me no choice."

He pulled out a cabinet drawer where I stored watercolours. "You're not serious. You'd rather sell me a watercolour for five bucks than burn it?"

"No! I'd burn it first." I just about slammed the drawer shut on his hand. "How can I ask $1,600 for a watercolour in January and let it go for five dollars in the fall? The only way I can get out of this mess is to burn all my paintings."

The younger auditor chuckled. He had decided my threat was a little joke. The older man smiled patronizingly. They didn't believe I'd burn my work. They left my home shortly afterward, planning to return later in the month to finish the re-assessment.

They hadn't reckoned that I was serious about destroying my paintings. As sickened as I felt about destroying all that good work, I simply couldn't afford to pay taxes on it. I tried to console myself that I was young enough to create many more paintings. Then I agonized about choosing the art to destroy. I decided to start with about a thousand serigraph prints. Each print had a value of $250 at the time.

The more I thought about destroying my work, the angrier I became. I decided to make a public bonfire. I wrote a letter of complaint to several ministers in the government. I told people I knew that I was going to burn my work publicly on Wreck Beach, which was near my studio. As I spoke to other artists, I learned that my taxation problem was more common than I would ever have imagined. Several other people had just been put into a similar position. The story of the government's new tax grab began to break in the newspapers. I contacted the media, telling them I planned to burn a thousand of my prints.

Some people doubted that I'd go through with it so I promised a reporter at Vancouver's BCTV that I'd burn a print on camera. When he came over with a TV crew, I picked out one of my favourite landscapes and led them into my backyard. I took a lighter and set the print on fire.

I felt miserable watching it twist in the flames. Then it blackened and turned to ashes. I could almost taste them.

"Why are you doing this?" asked the reporter.

"It's cheaper than going to court with Revenue Canada. Even if I win, I have to cover my expenses," I explained, adding, "and it's their court." Special federal courts and federally appointed judges decide tax law. Then I delivered my ultimatum. "Thursday, October 11, I'm going to burn all my prints, bag the ashes and mail them to Ottawa."

Vancouver TV stations broadcast the footage that day. It was picked up by their affiliates and flashed across the country. The newscast of me burning my print in protest of the government's taxation policies went national. It had an immediate impact.

Shortly afterward, the Canadian Conference for the Arts asked Prime Minister Trudeau to intervene in the dispute between artists and Revenue Canada. They pleaded with Revenue Minister Pierre Bussieres to declare a moratorium on applying this new taxation policy to artists.

Questions were raised in the House of Commons. During Question Period John Fraser, the Progressive Conservative Member of Parliament, asked the Liberal Minister for Communications, Francis Fox, if he was going to stop me from burning my work.

"He's doing this as a consequence of a long period of harassment by tax officials," commented Fraser. "I would ask the minister whether he has done anything to intervene and save this Canadian art, or if he intends to sit there while the art burns."

Fox replied that he had brought the issue to the attention of the Minister of National Revenue. Fraser countered that Fox hadn't given much of an answer for a minister whose responsibilities included the advancement of Canadian art.

Just before the date I'd set, Jack Webster asked me to appear on his BCTV talk show. While I sat in the dressing room, one of my auditors telephoned me:

"It doesn't matter if you burn your paintings or not," he snarled. "We're going to tax you on the production costs anyway."

The call threw me off balance. I appeared on the program sick with dread that I might burn the prints and still be assessed. Webster hammered me. "Are you, Mr. Onley, or are you not—a millionaire?" The implication was that if I were rich, then I must be evading taxes. I failed to make the point that it was not only my case that was at issue but also the government's lack of a consistent policy toward the arts. Canadian institutions such as the CBC, the Canada Council, the Art Bank and public galleries encouraged artists, while Canadian tax policies threatened them by this new interpretation of the tax laws.

When I returned home I received a telephone call from Joe Clark. Back in June, he'd lost the leadership of the Progressive Conservative Party. He hoped to raise the taxation issue at the next sitting of the House of Commons. He wanted to put the leadership issue behind him and put his best foot forward. Clark urged me to hold off on burning my work. Later, he called back, promising to table a private member's motion to establish an all-party-committee on the taxation of Canadian artists.

The day of my protest, about a hundred people gathered at Wreck Beach. Other artists, like painter Jack Shadbolt and the writer George Woodcock, came to express their support. Even my old colleague from the Fine Arts Department, Herb Gilbert, put in an appearance in his Druid robe and horned Viking helmet. He carried a "Ban the Bomb" sign.

I shook my head. "You're at the wrong assembly, Herb." He looked surprised. Any assembly was the right one for him.

Camera crews and reporters from the major daily newspapers crowded around me. "There'll be no bonfire today," I told them. I'd written to the minister of communications on September 20, protesting Revenue Canada's actions. Armed with Clark's offer and a last-minute telegram from the minister, I held a press conference instead. In the end, I guess Fox didn't want me to appear on the national news burning a million dollars worth of art, because he'd wired me that morning: "I will be meeting shortly with my colleague, the Minister of National Revenue and will present, to the best of my ability, the concerns of Canadian artists. I would hope that this evidence of the seriousness with which your grievance is being treated constitutes proof of our good faith and will prompt you to reconsider, at least for the present, further action."

It looked like the government was prepared to act, so there was no need for me to burn my work yet. A few journalists complained afterward that I'd chickened out. But at that point, I didn't need to do anything more. I had won the first round by drawing national attention to the issue. I could always burn my prints later. Besides, what artist would destroy his work if he felt there was any reasonable alternative?

Joe Clark did get his private member's bill before the House of Commons. That November 2 speech was his first after losing the party leadership. As he stood, members on the government and opposition sides of the House rattled their desks and applauded.

"As Toni Onley, one of Canada's foremost artists, has demonstrated by his threat to burn one million dollars worth of his art, Revenue Canada has placed artists in an intolerable situation," Clark said. "It is inconceivable that our taxation system would provide an incentive for artists to destroy their works of art and a penalty if they do not."

He moved that the House of Commons convene an all-party committee to discuss the issue. It passed unanimously.

Back in Vancouver, however, I still received calls from my auditors. "When this thing is all over," I told my senior auditor, "you'll have a set of rules for dealing with artists. Right now, you're dealing with them either as manufacturers or as business people with no reasonable expectation of profit."

"How can we define an artist," he grumbled. "Every second person's got a mother or an aunt who paints. Anyone could be an artist and start deducting expenses for their car or house."

I pointed out, "The UN has a good definition of an artist—basically, someone who is recognized by his peers as an artist or has a degree in Fine Arts, who has a track record of selling his work, is collected by museums, and who makes part or all of his living from his art. That definition has already been accepted in France, Denmark, Sweden and the United States."

Clark's committee sat about three months. The bound report came out in favour of many things that Canadian artists had recommended. Then Revenue Canada, which had stalled for months, made concessions. In March 1984, the minister agreed that artists might deduct travel expenses related to the production of art works in the same year. As well, musicians could deduct the cost of their lessons, and the minister made the profitability rule more flexible. Finally, he conceded that re-assessments of artists would only go back for two years instead of four.

By then, all hell had broken loose over taxation in Canada. Back in BC, I was complaining, "Wait a minute, don't forget the artists!" We almost had a taxpayer revolt, particularly over the issue of quotas for tax auditors. A journalist had uncovered a damning memo in Toronto. For each working hour, auditors in the section dealing with commission sales reps and unincorporated businesses had to recover $700 in taxes above what the taxpayers had declared. The implications of this were horrendous. Ultimately, Canadian artists were almost left off the national agenda. New taxation legislation was not introduced into the House of Commons. A deputy minister of revenue resigned. The minister withdrew the financial quotas that he had set for tax auditors. Finally, the Liberal government fell in the following election.

However, the auditors at Revenue Canada were career civil servants. They hadn't forgotten about me. I wriggled on their hook for a long time. I've been required to keep a diary of my travel expenses and to date each painting; otherwise, my deductions could be denied.

In addition, Revenue Canada rearranged the timing of one of my sales in 1981 and of a major purchase I claimed in 1982. I had sold the paintings from my book *A Silent Thunder* for $100,000 to Canarim Investments. They purchased the work in December 1981. I wasn't paid until January 1982, so I listed it as a 1982 sale, calculating it for income tax on the cash accrual basis I had used for years. Revenue Canada pushed that sale back into 1981, one of my best years. My income tax for 1981 shot from the twenty-two-percent corporate rate to the forty-seven-percent corporate rate. The interest rates were eighteen percent that year and were compounded over the intervening years to 1983. Next, the tax department moved one of my major expenses forward. This was the $60,000 purchase of my Wilga ski plane in 1981. The plane was produced in Poland, so although I paid for it in 1981, it wasn't delivered to me until 1982. By moving the sale backward and my purchase forward and then adding compounded interest, Revenue Canada was able to bill me for $62,000 in unpaid taxes!

At least I drew some satisfaction from triggering a tax protest. For once, Canadian artists garnered tremendous national coverage and received some measure of relief. In the end, the tax issue touched everybody in the country who had ever been in business for himself. The experience left me permanently disillusioned with the tax system, although the experience of fighting Revenue Canada gave me a new faith in democracy.

I owe a great deal of thanks to Arthur Drache, the renowned Canadian tax lawyer, who contacted me when the news of my proposed art bonfire first appeared in the press and on TV. His office was in Ottawa, so he was in a great position to help. He told me that I was "either very stupid or brilliant," that my case was going to make new tax law and that he would like to represent me pro bono. Without Arthur, artists, writers and musicians would not be described in tax law today. Arthur later wrote a book on the subject, *Taxation and the Arts: A Practical Guide*, which he dedicated "to Toni Onley, who started the battle and continues the struggle."

I won my main battle with Revenue Canada, because now visual artists are able to elect under the Income Tax Act to value their inventory at nil. This means that they can deduct all their costs of creating art in a particular year from their sales income for that year, an arrangement which not only makes sense because artists are not simply manufacturers, but which permits them to survive financially while they create their art.

Chapter 21

The Maharajah's Palace

In the winter of 1982–1983, I travelled to India with George Woodcock to collaborate on a book about George's return to India many years after his original visit. It all started at the Hyatt Regency hotel in Vancouver with a fundraiser for CIVA, the Canada India Village Aid society, which George and his wife Inge had co-founded.

I approached George as he ordered a whisky at the bar. At seventy, he was white-haired and partially bald above a broad forehead. He was easy to spot with his horn-rimmed glasses, tweed jacket and black tie. George considered himself an anarchist and the black tie was his version of the anarchist's flag. Douglas (now George) Fetherling's biography of George was called *The Gentle Anarchist*. As Fetherling pointed out, George's book, *Anarchism: A History of Libertarian Ideas and Movements*, can be found in every bibliography on the subject and continues to be reprinted by Penguin.

Over the years I had admired him as Canada's "Man of Letters." George had emigrated from England in 1949, a year later than I had. We both came over on the *Aquitania*, George from London where, as the editor of the literary magazine *Now*, he had published George Orwell and Sir Herbert Read. By the time I met him, he had written over forty books and hundreds of articles on politics, travel, biography, literature and poetry, and had founded the critical journal *Canadian Literature*.

I had tried to introduce myself to George once before. "I'm Toni Onley, the painter," I had said.

George never made small talk. "Indeed you are," he had replied in a particularly plummy British accent. The conversation had ended there and I hadn't dared speak to him since.

However, I had been invited to the CIVA dinner by some mutual friends and I could see empty tables everywhere in the room. "The seats are only a quarter full," I said to George. "How is CIVA going to do financially?"

"We'll be lucky if we make our expenses tonight," he said.

"George, why are you fundraising this way? You're a world-class writer," I said.

Nearby stood George's wife, Inge, short and solidly built, a force unto herself. She turned on me.

"It was Patwant's idea, not mine. I like the kind of event that builds grassroots support—like book sales in church halls."

George, who knew better than to argue with Inge, slipped back to the bar, leaving me to confront her. Among George's associates, Inge had a reputation as "the tiger at the gates." Anyone who wanted anything to do with George went through Inge.

I explained my fundraising idea. "George is one of Canada's most important writers and he's an old India hand. I have a pretty fair reputation as a painter. I was going to suggest that he and I go to India and write a book about it. We'll sell the book and my paintings and make some real money."

Inge considered the idea for a moment. "I'll ask him. CIVA needs all the help it can get."

George telephoned the following day. "Toni, it's a bloody good idea! How soon can we get started?"

We developed a plan for a three-week trip. The Woodcocks had started CIVA in 1981 to assist their old friend Patwant Singh, an Indian writer and editor, to set up a rural hospital outside of Delhi. Initially, Patwant had asked the Woodcocks to form a "Friends of Kabliji Hospital" society, but they wanted to do more for India than that. Our forthcoming trip would provide an opportunity to find other organizations worthy of CIVA's assistance. The central theme of the book would be a comparison of contemporary India with the country he had described in 1964 in *The Faces of India: A Travel Narrative* and in 1967 in *Kerala, A Portrait of the Malabar Coast.*

"We'll make all our own arrangements and travel by the luck of the road," said George. "We won't be tourists. The trip will be determined by unplanned encounters, the small places to which chance leads us."

In December 1982, Inge, George, Yukiko and I left for India. We were joined for the first part of the trip by the chairman of CIVA, Tony Phillips, a UBC psychology professor, and his wife, Margo Palmer. As soon as we landed in India, our problems began. At the Delhi airport, George, Inge and I breezed through immigration. Canadians didn't need visas to enter the country. However, Yukiko, still travelling on a Japanese passport, did need one. The immigration officer denied her entry and threatened to send her back to Japan.

I argued with the Sikh official. He insisted that Yukiko would have to leave.

I went for George. Like a pukka sahib, he confronted the officer "She is a guest of Mrs. Gandhi. If you put Mrs. Onley onto the next plane from India, questions will be asked."

A Major Gill appeared and identified himself as an aide to Indira Gandhi. The supervisor's face blanched. He quickly stamped Yukiko's passport. With relief, she hurried past the counter.

We drove about fifty miles from Delhi to Ghamroj and Patwant Singh's country home. As the editor of *Design*, an architectural magazine, he had used his knowledge to convert an abandoned farmhouse into a villa for weekend and summer retreats. It had a high-ceilinged reception room for parties, and several guest bedrooms.

Patwant had met the Woodcocks on their first visit to India in 1961. At the time, he was something of a playboy, and when the Woodcocks started the Tibetan Refugee Aid Society for Tibetans fleeing Chinese rule, he had been rather sceptical about the project. In 1978, however, he almost died of a heart attack and the experience profoundly changed him. He suddenly needed to have a purpose in life. He found it one afternoon while travelling to his house in Ghamroj. He had noticed some villagers by the road waving for help. He ordered his driver to stop the car and he found a woman in a litter, dying in childbirth. Patwant drove her to a military hospital in Delhi where some of his friends were able to save her and the baby. Shocked at the abysmal state of rural health care so close to

Delhi, Patwant decided to build a hospital at nearby Kabliji village. He remembered the Woodcocks' earlier charity and contacted them for help. That was when George and Inge were inspired to found CIVA. They had seen on their visits the poor health of the resettled Tibetans and their lack of education.

A bearded Sikh in his fifties, Patwant wore a starched black turban, a grey Saville Row suit and black Guccis. He was very dignified, with a crisp, almost military bearing. In a pronounced British public school accent, he spoke of the hospital's accomplishments. "We have twenty beds in the general ward, and twenty in the eye care and cataract ward. Kabliji Hospital did 1,500 operations last year and provided aftercare, too."

The hospital consisted of a few well-designed but modest one-storey pavilions constructed of stone blocks. It lay on the edge of a barren field near stunted stalks of corn and sugar cane. I watched an Indian farmer in a white ankle-length cotton dhoti behind an ox, harrowing the earth with a wooden plow, a scene unchanged for 2,000 years.

George was walking a little slowly, the years telling on that seasoned India traveller. I drew his attention to the farmer with his primitive plow. "Where do you start, George? The problems in India seem overwhelming."

George smiled. "Do you know what Ghandi said? 'One step is enough for me.' We have to do whatever is possible, however small the scale. Maybe one small initiative, reasonably well implemented, like a stone thrown into a still pond, will send ripples outward through Indian society." Then he chuckled, "Actually, Gandhi filched that 'one step' quotation from Cardinal Newman."

Painting Amber Fort over Masta Lake, Jaipur, India, 1982.

If anyone would know that, it

had to be George, I thought. In 1971, he had written a biography, *Mohandas Gandhi*. He hoped that CIVA could provide a practical example of Gandhi's belief and George's anarchist conviction that India should be organized at the village level, emphasizing individual initiative and responsibility instead of relying on state economic and military power.

At the hospital entrance, the nurses clasped their hands in the traditional Indian greeting, *namaskar*. Then they garlanded our necks with bright yellow marigolds and dusted our foreheads with sacred red powder.

Seeing the women, I realized that in addition to its medical benefits, Kabliji Hospital had improved the status of women in the community. Forced to marry at puberty in this part of India, the village women were kept in purdah and rarely seen. Their work at the hospital enabled them to move into the community again. They even earned a little money and with that economic power gained greater independence from their husbands and their husbands' families.

The women led us through the clean, white-washed hospital rooms. The patients had clean bedding, many of them receiving medical attention for the first time in their lives. The men and women in the hospital thanked us with such a deep and genuine sense of gratitude that I felt close to tears.

Unfortunately, the hospital doctors were retired Sikh military men, recruited by Patwant. They treated the other staff members as if they were little better than servants. It grated against George's sense of equality, not to mention CIVA's goals of individual empowerment. He asked Patwant if he was going to train any paramedics in the neighbouring villages.

"I don't want any of those fellows flapping their dirty dhotis around my place!" Patwant replied. His attitude changed later, but during that visit he showed the typical contempt of the professional Indian for the uneducated village labourer.

From Delhi, we planned to drive toward the border with Pakistan, to the state of Rajasthan, the most barren and sparsely populated in India, and then fly south to coastal Kerala, a lush area of lagoons and beaches. From there, we would fly to the holy sites at Orissa on the Bay of Bengal on the northeastern coast of India. Then we would travel to Darjeeling in the far north and visit the Tibetan

Some young admirers, Jaisalmer, India, December 1982. Photograph by Yukiko Onley.

settlement the Woodcocks had helped to build, which was now run by the Dalai Lama's sister-in-law. In all, we hoped to reach twenty different Indian cities across the subcontinent.

For the drive to Rajasthan, we hired a Sikh, Surgit Singh, a shifty, rather heavy-set driver *wallah*, who had learned his English in the army and had been recommended to us by one of Patwant's acquaintances in Delhi. Surgit promised to find us a second English-speaking driver and to rent us two brand new, air-conditioned Ambassadors, the chunky Indian car modelled on the 1959 British Morris Oxford. Instead, he showed up with two ancient vehicles that must have been at least twenty years older than he had promised. Their air conditioning had long since broken down and they lurched down the road like wheeled tin lunch boxes.

Surgit proved nearly homicidal behind the wheel. Climbing a hill behind a truck on a narrow two-lane highway in Rajasthan, he thumped the car horn to signal the truck driver to pull over and let us pass. When the driver refused, Surgit swore under his breath and leaned on the horn. Finally, at the top of the hill, he cut in front of the truck, slammed on the brakes and jumped out of the car. The truck screeched to a stop.

"What's he doing?" I said. "We're going to get killed if he doesn't get the car off the road."

Surgit charged over to the truck, yanked open the door and punched out the driver. Then he returned to our car and drove us away.

We were so shocked that none of us knew what to say to him. George cleared his throat. "Mr. Singh, we engaged you as a driver. We cannot allow this kind of behaviour. Brute force is not the way to solve problems."

Surgit snapped, "Babu, this is India. I know India."

Our party—George, Inge, Yukiko, the Phillipses and me—alternated between Surgit's car and a second driven by Ranjit, a tall, skinny, clean-shaven Sikh with a wispy moustache and a snaggle-toothed grin. He had to be directed by vigorous finger pointing because he could barely understand English. "No problem, sahib," he grinned, whenever we tried to tell him anything.

On one occasion, the radiator in Ranjit's car broke loose from the chassis and the fan beat against the radiator. Ranjit pulled over the car and opened the hood. He then tied the radiator back into place with a piece of his shirt tail. "No problem, sahib." When that effort failed, we helped him wedge the radiator into place with a rock so we could limp into the nearest village for repairs.

The sun scorched us as we drove through the blistered cinnamon-coloured land of Rajasthan. In the towns, farmers in bright pink and blue turbans, their skin blackened by the sun, haggled in the marketplace. Along the roadside, Rajasthani women in red and orange saris carried baskets of small stones balanced on brass pans on their heads. The stones would be dumped into potholes in the road.

Despite the heat, George sported the same jacket and black tie that he had worn to the CIVA dinner months earlier. I shook my head.

"I don't think anyone is going to take offence if you take off your jacket and tie, George. You'd be a lot more comfortable."

He rested his pencil, then he loosened his tie. "I'll think about it."

I finally convinced him to take off his jacket and tie. At the next stop, I folded them and put them in the back of the car where they were out of his reach.

George Woodcock, Jaisalmer, 1982.

As top-heavy trucks rattled past us toward Jaipur, George concentrated on recording the scene in a small exercise book. Rusting sooty buses rocked down the opposite lane to Delhi, passengers riding on the rooftops clutching the luggage racks as the buses lumbered along.

George had a dense narrative style that reflected his boyhood reading of nineteenth-century British naturalists like Thomas Huxley and Charles Darwin, and Edwardian explorers such as Aspley Cherry-Garrard, who wrote an epic account of a terrible

Antarctic journey. Initially, George thought of becoming a naturalist or explorer himself, then realized that he was fascinated more by the prose than by the science. Travelling through the Rajasthan desert, George noted in his journal how the monotony of the vista made the few visual interruptions—a kite picking over a bullock's skeleton, a gazelle staring at us then leaping away—stand out in dramatic contrast.

I noticed the strange way he held his pencil. Instead of holding it between his thumb and index finger as most people do, he placed it between his thumb and middle finger. His index finger stuck straight out. He then manipulated his thumb and middle finger like a pair of tweezers with the pencil clenched between them. Whenever our car drove over a bump, his hand bounced off the paper. He would place it back on the paper and jot down another word. Then we'd hit the next bump. He never gave up writing.

George described his note-taking as a kind of personal shorthand. When he and Inge retired to their room each night, he sat down and read over his notes. A single word or phrase triggered whole associations of ideas that he then recorded at length. A whole chapter would eventually emerge from a few words. He'd bang out a first draft on his battered Olivetti typewriter and fill in the broken letters by hand.

"I never do more than two drafts of anything," George told me. "The rest is monkeying around." As a watercolour painter, I could identify with this approach.

The city of Jaisalmer impressed me more than any other place in Rajasthan. Shortly after we checked into our hotel, I asked Ranjit to take Yukiko and me to a hilltop outside the city. It was an arid spot near a cemetery with rock ledges that overlooked the city's western wall. I took out my paintbox and taped a sheet of watercolour paper onto the lid. Then I sat down on a crumbling stone slab, balanced the paintbox on my lap and began painting.

Even at the end of my first week in India, I had trouble adjusting my palette from the cool light of the West Coast to the blinding hot light of the desert. The sky above Rajasthan was a pure, intense blue, as if enamelled, unlike the cloud-strewn lighter blue to which I was accustomed. The city of Jaisalmer, much of it yellow sandstone, turned a fabulous golden colour in the late afternoon light.

Yukiko was painting a watercolour as well. I had started teaching her painting a few years earlier and she had brought her paintbox and a camera to India. Suddenly she noticed something peculiar about the ground around us. "Why are there all these ashes?" she asked.

When we had arrived at the hilltop, we had found ourselves in a cemetery of the city's nobility, filled with crumbling *chhatris*, or memorials, each consisting of a dome and four columns over an upright stone slab with the face of the dead man on it.

Yukiko was looking at a pile of ashes near us. I finished my painting and walked over. I plucked out a charred bone. "A body's been burned here," I exclaimed. "We're sitting on a cremation site!"

Feeling a little ghoulish, but with our painting done, we left the area and drove back to our hotel.

Our last destination in Rajasthan was the city of Jodhpur where the riding breeches known as jodhpurs originated. There, in the sprawling Chittar Palace where we spent the night, I met my first Indian maharajah. His name was Jodhpur, for according to custom, the maharajah was named after his city. Like other Indian nobles who had been stripped of their property and wealth by Indira Gandhi's government, all Jodhpur had left was his palace, so he had built a suite in it for his family, and turned the rest of the building into a hotel. On the terrace, the prince had placed a restaurant and beer garden with speakers that boomed out rock music.

We met the maharajah through a letter of introduction George had brought from some Indian contacts. Jodhpur's manservant knocked on the Woodcocks' door, then on the door to our room. In the hushed tones of official protocol, he announced, "His Highness would like you to join him for drinks tonight. Her Royal Highness sends her greeting." Just as if we were meeting Queen Elizabeth and Prince Philip, we were obliged to address the maharajah and the maharani as "your royal highness" on our first meeting. Afterward, we would be allowed to address them as "sir" and "ma'am."

We followed the servant down a dimly lit hall in the Chittar Palace. The construction of the palace started in 1928 and finished in 1943, a few years before the end of the British Raj, so it reflected

Lake Palace, Udaipur, India, Christmas, 1982.

the conceits of the Indian princes of that era. The palace had scalloped archways and a dome like London's St. Paul's Cathedral, but now it was falling into disrepair. The ceiling had cracked. Moth-eaten tiger skins adorned the walls, accompanied by nineteenth-century photographs of princes on shooting parties with large numbers of slaughtered tigers lying at their feet.

Finally we were led into a large room in the royal quarters and greeted by the maharajah and the maharani. Jodhpur, a handsome, fine-featured man in a white V-necked cardigan sweater and brown loafers, looked as if he had just stepped from the pages of *Gentleman's Quarterly*. When George asked him about a public trust fund the maharajah had established to keep some of the family money from the hands of the central Indian government, Jodhpur explained that it could be used for projects benefiting people in his former realm.

George, who had been seeking assistance for CIVA, told him of our work at Kabliji Hospital. He suggested that a similar project could be started in Jodhpur. He explained it in terms of Gandhi's idea of village self-sufficiency.

289

"Ah, Mohandas Gandhi," sighed Jodhpur, "a great man and a world soul."

"I daresay a great deal can be accomplished in the villages by clean water, a small dispensary and just one trained nurse," said George.

"Alas, if I only had the power, but various official matters prevent me from acting as I truly wish," replied Jodhpur in his impeccable British accent. "If you only knew my difficulties as a maharajah in India now." He excused himself from supporting any charities but promised to get in touch with us if the situation ever changed.

We were joined by an officious professor from Oxford, Jodhpur's old alma mater. The conversation turned to the negotiations between Britain and China over the future of the colony of Hong Kong. Discussions were at a very early stage then, and I had a keen interest in the conversation.

However, I had been seated to the left of the beautiful maharani, a lithe young woman dressed in the traditional Rajasthani gold-threaded shawl and a long skirt inlaid with tiny mirrors. Gold bracelets dangled from her wrists, and she wore a necklace of gems and a single diamond stud in her right nostril. I could hardly take my eyes from her. As I held my glass of scotch, I cocked one ear toward the professor, the maharajah and the Woodcocks and lent the other ear to the maharani.

She apologized for the neglected state of the palace garden. We had all noticed the shabby remnants of an English-style country garden. Among the broken marble fountains, thin screeching peacocks foraged over patches of brown lawn and dead shrubbery.

"You should have seen the palace in the days of Grandfather Maharajah Umaid Singh," she said, "but you can't get good help nowadays."

It happened that I had been reading about Umaid Singh, the despot who had built the current palace, one of two palaces in which he had lived. He had lopped off the hands of masons whose workmanship did not meet his high standards. If he could insert a razor blade between two blocks of pink granite, the culprit lost his hand on the spot. I couldn't let her remark pass without comment.

"I read about your grandfather and his masons," I said.

The maharani immediately changed the subject. "How cold does it get in Canada?" she asked. "Does it snow all year round?"

I made a fatal mistake. I told her I had been to the Arctic and had lived with the Inuit on Baffin Island.

She clapped her hands in delight. "Don't say another thing. We must get the little princes."

She led me off into a parlour in their suite and sat me down on a stuffed leather stool that had been fashioned from an elephant's foot. Then she went to get her children. In marched a husky ruddy-faced English nanny in an apron with four fat little princes waddling behind her. She pulled out four more stuffed elephant feet and sat them down beside me. The nanny and the maharani disappeared, leaving me to regale the boys with tales of the Inuit who fished through holes in the ice and ate raw seal, and I entirely missed the conversation about the future of Hong Kong.

All the members of our party got along very well in India. George and I were creating a book that was going to improve the lives of a few hundred villagers in India, and a keen sense of this mission sustained us through many difficulties. In Jaisalmer, Tony Phillips chased a terrier-sized rat out of the room he shared with Margo. When we complained to the manager, who was of the Jain religion and therefore venerated all forms of life, he seemed upset that the rat had been frightened. Tony had to barricade the space under the door to keep the rat from returning. For her part, Yukiko never once complained, even though she was accustomed to staying at the best hotels. She quietly downed the hottest curries, although she greatly preferred the subtleties of Japanese cuisine, the delicate flavour of soba noodles, shrimp and vegetable tempuras.

"Yukiko, you're a real brick," remarked George.

Blushing, she demurred, "It's really nothing." I think she spent most of the trip in awe of George because he was such a famous writer.

We encountered many obstacles and Inge's determination was a valuable asset. On one occasion, George and I were standing in line at a crowded airline ticketing office, trying to buy the last seats to Kerala in southern India. An army colonel entered the office, walked to the head of the line and took our seats. In India, officers are allowed to do that.

George turned to me, "I think it's time to get Inge."

Inge was puffing on a cigarette outside the building. I told her what had happened.

"I'll see about that!" She stubbed out her cigarette and stormed into the building. She marched to the counter. "Bring me the manager!" she shouted.

Indians seem very English to me in at least one respect. They hate public disturbances. There must have been about a hundred people in the room. Everyone stopped talking. A harried-looking official opened his door and ushered us into his office. He told Inge there was nothing he could do.

"How dare you!" she sputtered with rage. "This is simply not on!"

He shrank before her, drawing his head and shoulders toward his body. He spoke into the telephone, then hurtled out of the office and down the corridor. Tickets were found. I suppose some other passengers got bumped from their seats.

As we journeyed south into the more populated regions of India, it became harder to work on our book. George and Inge told me that they obtained some privacy by telling people they were meditating. To clear some personal space, when crowds gathered around me and vendors pressed trinkets on me as I painted, I simply said I was meditating. Someone in the crowd always understood and translated for me.

At the tip of the Indian subcontinent, Kanyakumari, I amazed George with the lengths I went to in order to paint. The site was sacred, and religious pilgrims and beggars thronged the streets. Near a temple dedicated to the Hindu god Shiva, a teenaged mother who was begging from me pinched her baby to make him cry. I retreated down a street jammed with people, where megaphones blasted music from one side of the street to the other. Gobs of spittle dotted the pavement. Rotting food and refuse filled the gutters.

Leaving George, Inge and Yukiko behind, I fled to the rocks where the land came to a point forming a breakwater between the Bay of Bengal and the Arabian Sea. The spot was sacred to Parvati, the wife of the god Shiva, the destroyer and reproducer of life. At the Kumari bathing *ghat*, men and women were praying and immersing themselves in the heaving turquoise sea. From a jetty nearby, a rickety passenger ferry, belching black, oily diesel smoke, carried hundreds of pilgrims to the Vivekananda Memorial, an island where an Indian swami had launched his religious crusade in 1892.

George found me sitting on some rocks near the jetty and painting the island. There were no toilets for the thousands of pilgrims waiting to board the ferry, so ordure lay on the rocks all around me. I looked up from my painting. I couldn't think of anything to say to him except, "Look at the size of these turds."

He nodded, wrinkling his nose at the stench. "Such small people and such big droppings. It must be their vegetarian diet. Can you imagine the elephants?"

George watched me paint for a while, then he grew restless. "I don't suppose you'll be too much longer, will you, Toni?" We were in a wretched spot and I rushed the painting. It was not one of my most successful watercolours of India.

Over the journey, George and I realized how much we held in common. Both of us had been raised in England and emigrated to Canada with our parents. In George's case, his parents had emigrated to Canada before he was born, but when their farm failed, they returned to England with George. He had grown up in Shropshire in

Yukiko and sacred cow, India, 1982.

such impoverished circumstances that his parents never celebrated his birthday.

"I think I became a writer because my father died young. He was scarcely forty, and he was a gifted musician. I have always felt compelled to complete that life artistically," George said.

"My father was worried I was going to cut off my ear and live off the family," I told him.

"Your father is still alive?" he asked.

"Very much so. He and my mother live in Penticton. He's something of an artist, too—an actor, and a great storyteller."

George smiled. "I'd like to meet him sometime."

I tried to imagine George and my father. There was maybe ten years between them. No, that meeting would never work out, I told myself.

Both George and I were self-taught and neither of us had gone to university. George thought of himself as a wordsmith, a craftsman of the language who could turn his hand to journalism, criticism or travel writing. He saw me as equally gifted, a visual artist who had done everything from industrial design to drafting.

"I think creativity comes from psychic wounds," said George. "My wounds came from the discipline of the English school system and the brutal way in which school spirit was promoted. The intellectual was viewed as a sort of weakling."

"Maybe you're right, I had a pretty miserable education. I went to a Catholic school run on the model of the Spanish Inquisition."

Our book became a true union of talents. While George wrote his travel diary to describe the changed political and sociological aspects of India, I prepared my record—watercolours of the places we had seen. I never place people in my pictures, so I left it to George to populate the book with India's 700 million people. Before coming to India, I thought I'd paint the natural landscape as I did in Canada. However, in an ancient over-populated country such as India, the landscape was seldom free of signs of habitation, so the most prominent features were often architectural, such as the fortresses and city walls in Rajasthan that were built by the warring Rajput princes hundreds of years earlier. Thinking of the architecture that kept appearing in my landscape, I proposed calling the book *The Walls of India*.

"India is a country full of invisible walls on the symbolic level," said George.

"It's more like a continent with countries in it," I said.

"Exactly," George agreed. "There are walls of language, walls of caste, walls of religion, and a high wall between the rich and the poor. There's the title of our book—*The Walls of India.*"

The last place we visited was Darjeeling in the foothills of the Himalayas in northern India. When we drove up into the city it was snowing and miserably cold. The Woodcocks remembered an English-style hotel from their last visit and directed the taxi driver. The hotel stood on a hilltop above the city. The hotel porters hauled our luggage up a path from the road and we followed them up the hill. In exhaustion, George dropped onto a bench at the top of the path. He was feeling his age. I took out the flask of McDowell's whisky I carried and handed it to him.

Then we climbed the rest of the way up the hill and checked into the hotel. The place had sharply declined since the Woodcocks had stayed there years earlier. We nearly froze to death that night under the thin blankets.

When Yukiko and I met the Woodcocks for breakfast the following morning, we noticed that George had caught a nasty cold. He was drinking a little whisky for his cough.

"It's miserable here, just look at poor George," said Inge. "I think we should go to Delhi."

George nodded, "It's time we left India."

"We just got here," I argued. "What about seeing the Himalayas? I was hoping to paint Mount Kanchenjunga." It rose high above Darjeeling. At 28,209 feet, it is the third-highest mountain on earth, only 819 feet shorter than Mount Everest.

"Seeing Mount Kanchenjunga is a matter of luck," said George. "One can stay in Darjeeling for a week and never see it."

"Before you make up your minds, let Yukiko and I take the car into town to see if we can find a better hotel."

I told the driver to take us to the Everest Oberon Hotel, one of the best hotels on Observatory Hill in Darjeeling. Though the hotel was an ugly grey limestone edifice, the view from it would be spectacular, if the clouds ever lifted. However, when I asked at the desk about rooms, the clerk informed me the hotel was closed for renovations.

I asked for the manager and explained our predicament. "I'm a painter. We have a very famous Canadian writer with us. I know your hotel is closed but we would really appreciate it if you could fix up two rooms for us."

The manager listened carefully. He took a ring of keys from the desk and led me to a wing of the hotel that was not being renovated. He showed me two marvellous wood-panelled rooms with stone fireplaces that would be lit in the evenings. He also promised to find me a Sherpa guide to take me to Tiger Hill to paint Mount Kanchenjunga.

When the Woodcocks saw the hotel they decided to stay. It had everything they had missed at the first hotel, even some of the older staff. To George's delight, the hotel chef even knew how to make crêpes Suzette and *pomfret amandine*.

The next morning Yukiko and I were awakened by a Sikh lighting a fire in our fireplace.

"Bed tea, sahib?" he asked.

Then it dawned on me. They served breakfast in bed. He carried in a tray with a pot of tea and eggs, toast and jam.

When he opened the heavy drapes to our room, the light was fantastic. The clouds had parted and I could see the Himalayas. Mount Kanchenjunga glittered like a blue diamond. The guide the hotel manager had found picked me up in his car, and I left George, Inge and Yukiko to go exploring.

The guide took me to the market to buy some Tibetan winter clothes, then we drove to Tiger Hill, about a thousand feet higher than Darjeeling. I had an unobstructed view of the mountain and of the Himalayas, even of Mount Everest. Frost lay upon the ground at Tiger Hill. My guide gathered some sticks and made a fire behind me to give me a little warmth and to dry off my watercolours. For the next few days I rose early, at four or five in the morning, and worked for a few hours. For that brief period, the clouds dissipated and the blue and white mountains appeared.

While I painted, the others visited the Tibetan Refugee Self-Help Centre that the Woodcocks had helped fund. Located near Western

Lebong Road, on the lower slopes of Darjeeling, the centre was about a ninety-minute walk from the centre of the town.

Dark green tea bushes filled terrace after terrace. The centre operated much like a co-operative, with about 400 workers and their families living there. In one building, Tibetan men carved and painted decorations on tables and wooden chests, or created ceremonial pottery. Tibetan women in their *chupas*, ankle-length cloaks, carded wool, then spun it on wooden treadle machines. They dyed the yarn, then wove it into cloth bags, belts and carpets.

George, Inge and Yukiko met Mrs. Gyalo Thondup, the Dalai Lama's sister-in-law, a jolly plump lady who had married the Dalai Lama's elder brother. She showed the Woodcocks all that had been accomplished since the centre had been established in 1959. She kept thanking them for their help.

"Please, no fussing," said Inge, who hated lengthy expressions of gratitude. "We did no more than we could."

"You have to see His Holiness the Dalai Lama," she said. "He would be disappointed if you didn't see him when you get back to Delhi."

Characteristically, George felt embarrassed by the attention. Later at the hotel, he told me that he and Inge had been among the first Westerners to visit the Dalai Lama, and His Holiness had never forgotten the help they gave him. Other people had never kept their promises.

"I'd like to meet the Dalai Lama," I said.

"I've met him," remarked Inge.

George shrugged.

That was as close as Yukiko and I got to meeting the Dalai Lama.

In the meantime, the trip to Darjeeling had yielded another benefit. The Woodcocks found a potential CIVA project in Darjeeling. A French Canadian priest was starting a school to educate the young village women in the area. He seemed to be a very practical man and the Woodcocks planned to present his proposal to the CIVA board. We left Darjeeling shortly afterward, my paintings done, and the Woodcocks satisfied with the work accomplished by their first Indian project.

In January we returned to Vancouver where George took a few

months to finish writing *The Walls of India* and to negotiate a publishing contract with the Toronto publishers, Lester & Orpen Dennys. The book was expensive because it included twenty-five colour reproductions of my paintings. Initially we were supposed to receive funding from the Canadian International Development Agency, but none came. The publishers went ahead anyway.

I had done about fifty watercolours of India, including the ones we had used in the book. The Vancouver Art Gallery allowed us to display them, and we sold about twenty at $1,600 each. CIDA matched the funds we had raised three to one, so that we obtained $128,000. Later CIDA also matched all our book royalties.

We used the money to continue funding the Kabliji Hospital with an emphasis on education. Our next project was to ask twenty-five villages to nominate one woman each to be trained as a health-care worker and paramedic at the Kabliji Hospital. These women were to spend four years at the hospital and then become barefoot doctors in their communities. We reasoned that if we trained people, then they would train others, and our money would be better spent than on buildings and equipment. Our decision turned out to be the correct one because of the ensuing political unrest in India. Our hospital came very close to being destroyed.

As a moderate Sikh of some influence, Patwant was soon caught between the Indian government and Sikh extremists fighting for an independent homeland. He was on a hit list and was even attacked as he walked his Dalmatians in the Lodhi Gardens in Delhi. A man leaped out from some bushes and pointed a revolver at him. With his cane, Patwant knocked the gun out of the man's hand.

In 1984, a contingent of Sikhs who were fighting for an independent homeland in the Punjab were in the Golden Temple at Amritsar. Indira Gandhi cleared them out of the temple with a military assault on June 3, 1984, in which many Sikhs were killed. In reprisal, her Sikh guards assassinated her on October 31.

In the three days of violent anti-Sikh riots that swept Delhi and northern India after Gandhi's death, a mob burned Patwant's summer house to the ground. The rioters destroyed his wonderful art collection and looted anything of practical value, including his appliances. When he registered an official complaint at the local police station, he found his refrigerator there.

Sher Shan Gate, *Purana Qila, Delhi, watercolour.*

"That's mine!" he exclaimed.

"Prove it," replied the police chief.

Another mob marched on the Kabliji Hospital. Fortunately, it was the weekend so the Sikh doctors were in Delhi. The women at the hospital formed a human chain around the buildings. The mob would not harm them so the hospital was saved.

News of the fighting in India disheartened us, but we were also proud of the nurses who had saved the hospital. We remained involved with Kabliji Hospital and we initiated contacts with other non-governmental organizations in India such as Seva Mandir, which operated from Udaipur in Rajasthan and helped tribal people to select their own development goals.

I became a CIVA board member after my trip to India and helped organize other fundraising projects. My home could hold about sixty people so I organized exclusive catered dinner parties. I would create hand-painted invitations, each with a miniature Indian landscape for the ticket buyers. I would also donate a silkscreen print as a door prize. In addition, I'd offer paintings for sale and we'd make more money from that. We sometimes raised as much as $11,000 in a single evening. With the CIDA funding formula tripling the donations, we sometimes made over $30,000. People dressed in black tie and running shoes and we had a lot of fun. After dinner, I'd go to my studio downstairs and finish a large oil while wearing a paint-splattered tux. Guests, wine glasses in hand, would drift in and watch. At the end of the evening one of the sixty guests would win the painting in a raffle.

Inge never felt comfortable with these exclusive dinner parties, even though they raised a lot of money for CIVA. She never attended any of them and George wouldn't defy her beliefs by coming alone. Still, we maintained a cordial relationship.

She asked me once, "Are we still friends, Toni?"

"Don't worry, Inge," I told her. "What we're doing is far more important than our odd spat. As far as I'm concerned, you and George are like family."

After our trip to India, George and Inge got into the habit of coming to my house. The Woodcocks lived fairly close to us and Inge would drive. George enjoyed talking about art because it was so different from writing.

George had had a serious heart attack in his fifties and now his health had begun to fail. Eventually his legs were affected so he had to walk with a cane. One day he telephoned me, "Toni, I can't come to your place any more because I can't make the stairs."

I told him he did not have to climb any stairs because we could visit in the studio at ground level instead of the living room higher up. I asked Inge to drive into the garage where there was a door into the studio. George was happy with this arrangement and came over quite a few times. He sat in my easy chair facing a wall of art books with a glass of whisky in his hand and we talked and looked at my recent paintings. I would sometimes ask a few of his closest friends over and we would have a little party for him. He loved that.

George was the sort of Englishman who never really expressed much emotion. However, in the last few years, those barriers broke down. Usually, when I went to his house, he would meet me at the door and politely shake my hand. On one visit he said, "Come on,

George Woodcock at his typewriter. Photograph by Yukiko Onley.

Toni, give me a manly hug." We embraced and I felt quite touched. George had a few long spells in the hospital and knew that he might die soon. Nevertheless, toward the end of his life he took on a number of new writing projects. He explained to me that old people sometimes have an immoderate inclination to acquire or create, as if enacting a ritual to ensure a long life. If they are writers, they start more books than they can ever hope to finish.

First he wrote a poetry sequence, then he tried fiction writing again, a medium he had abandoned in 1950 on his way to Canada, when he had thrown the manuscript of a novel overboard. Now he reworked the concept of a discarded film script into a novel, and planned another novel about a naturalist travelling in South America. Then he started a new translation of Marcel Proust's *In Search of Time Lost*, all 3,400 pages of it. He described this ambitious work as "perhaps the most hubristic survival act of all." That he should live long enough to complete it seemed improbable to him, yet he still wanted to do it.

I remember his impatience. "I've got to get going, Toni," he said. "My work is not going to be accomplished posthumously."

"It's okay, George," I replied. "I know, you've got work to do."

Since he was too frail to attend his eighty-second birthday party, a speech he had written was read to about a thousand of his friends—writers, artists and publishers. The city council declared him "a freeman of the city of Vancouver." As an anarchist, it was the only government honour he ever accepted, probably because it gave him the right to fire a cannon once a year within the city limits.

Inge telephoned on Tuesday, January 15, 1995. George hadn't been able to walk up the stairs in their home, so she'd had his study and his couch moved to the ground floor. That morning, George had been typing at his desk. He called out to her. "Inge, help me to the couch. I feel a little tired." She helped him to the couch where he suffered a heart attack and died.

George was a unique voice in Canadian literature. Whenever I find myself missing him, I can turn to *The Walls of India* and relive our time together.

Chapter 22

Views of Mount Fuji

In October 1988, Yukiko and I arrived in Tokyo on our fourth visit to Japan to find that Emperor Hirohito, the world's longest-reigning monarch, was slowly dying. His thin face haunted the cover of every newspaper and magazine at the airport. From our room on the thirty-second floor of the Asakusa Prince Hotel, Yukiko pointed out the pale green copper roof of the Imperial Palace and a wall of the moat that was strewn with flower offerings from the public. On TV white-coated medical personnel shuttled in and out of the compound and members of the royal family arrived in black limousines. Newscasters in dark suits reported on the Emperor's health as if it were the state of the nation—which it was, in a way.

We were there at the height of the Japanese "bubble economy." Tokyo real estate had an estimated value of more than all the land in the United States, absurd prices that soon tumbled more than eighty percent. But in the meantime, a hotel room that might have gone for $85 or $100 in Canada cost us $400 a night. A cup of coffee was six dollars; a bread roll, three. Yukiko thought me cheap when I tried to restrain her from shopping in Tokyo, yet wads of Canadian dollars seemed to vanish in the blink of an eye. Just to pay for a single week's accommodation and expenses in Tokyo would take the sale of a $5,000 or $6,000 oil painting.

Selling art was something I explored through Canadian embassy contacts. I handed out business cards that identified me as a former fine arts professor, and a member of the Royal Canadian Academy—

a distinction more impressive in Japan than in Canada. With the help of the Canadian cultural attaché, I met the director at the Parco Gallery. It was part of the Seibu department store, TV and publishing empire—a perfect combination for promoting art. But nothing came of the meeting. On a previous trip I'd met with the Gallery Art Park in Shinjuku, and nothing had come of that, either.

With a sense of resignation, we left Tokyo, taking the *shinkansen*, or bullet train, to Osaka. The 300-mile journey took less than three hours. The ride was so smooth on the welded track that I nodded off. Yukiko nudged me awake as we slid past Mount Fuji. The great pyramid-shaped volcano rose from the clouds, reminding me of the Hokusai woodblock print, "Summer Showers Beneath the Fuji Peak." Fujiyama is an almost perfectly symmetrical mountain. It would lack all tension if it were not for the gentle breaking of that symmetry by the raised lip of one side of the old crater.

My wife went to Japan every year to see her mother, Sumiko, who also travelled to Vancouver. But I hadn't visited Sumiko in Osaka since 1978, shortly before Yukiko and I were married. A slim, cheerful woman with short black hair, she waved at us from the arrival gate. "Welcome home!"

With a formal bow, Yukiko greeted her mother. "Are you well? I missed you," she said.

I tapped Yukiko on the shoulder. "It's been a year. Give your mother a hug."

She stiffened and glared at me.

"Sumi-chan!" I grabbed Yukiko's mother and kissed her on the cheek as only a *gaijin* would. She giggled nervously. I had even used the diminutive form of her name. Because of the twenty-one-year difference between Yukiko and me, at least I had the excuse that I was almost the same age as her mother.

Yukiko was livid. I had been to Japan before and should have known better.

"Your mother liked it," I said.

Angrily, she turned from me. The taxi driver opened the passenger door and she stepped into the car.

Had I gone too far? Trying to understand what Yukiko meant often felt like stalking shadows, even after she'd studied English for a few years. I still had to guess what she wished to communicate to me, but as soon as I was sure of it, the certainty vanished. In the absence of conversation, subtle gestures served as Yukiko's language: pursed lips might show her displeasure; a slightly parted mouth, that she was pleased. Whenever I asked Yukiko a question, I had to interpret her response because she committed herself so tentatively and indirectly, even though she now spoke English very well. Everything became clouded with a frustrating ambiguity totally at odds with the way I was accustomed to speaking. And I had to learn to be very careful of how I said anything.

Yukiko had once told me: "We Japanese say, 'Truth is a moving finger'."

"That's all very well," I argued, "but you reach a point when you have to make up your mind."

"You don't understand," she said. "Telling me something is true is very arrogant, Toni. You never hear me saying things like that."

"Yukiko, at some point, you have to drive your sword into the ground and declare, 'Here I stand'," I replied.

However, we are all prisoners of our culture, so Yukiko was as right in her way as I was in my own. Fortunately her anger at me subsided as quickly as it usually did. Sumiko, who was in the front seat, turned to Yukiko and teased her. The two women laughed, and I caught just enough of their Japanese to guess that they were discussing my beard.

To avoid traffic, the taxi detoured from the main road, by chance turning into the route through Itami, the town where Yukiko had grown up, now virtually a suburb of Osaka. "It's been years since I've seen the place," Yukiko commented. "Itami used to be very rural. There were rice fields everywhere." She pointed out her elementary school and high school. As we drove up a small forested hill she added, "Our old house is up there."

I imagined her home as an old wooden house with metal shutters to draw over the windows at night and a clay-tiled roof. The taxi crested the hill. "It's not there, anymore," I observed. Occupying the site was a massive apartment block with forty or fifty balconies and laundry hanging out to dry. "That's too bad, Yukiko," I remarked.

She seemed strangely unmoved. "Toni, I was born after the war. Things changed all the time."

Her answer surprised me. It reminded me how differently she and I thought. When we went to the Isle of Man in 1981, I had shown her my old neighbourhood and the different homes where my family had lived, from the first one on Albany Street in 1928 to the large brick house on Cambridge Terrace that we sold before emigrating to Canada in 1948. Each of the four houses was larger than the last as my father's fortunes had improved. Then I took Yukiko to see St. Mary's Parish school, the scene of so much of my childhood suffering. The school had been knocked flat for a government parking lot. Though I had loathed the place, I felt betrayed, robbed of some personal history.

Sumiko had separated from Yukiko's father years before, and she now rented an apartment. It had a few sparsely furnished rooms and a narrow balcony where she dried her laundry and stored her bicycle. When Sumiko first came to Vancouver and saw our house, she had been astonished by the contrast. Yukiko had translated for me, "You have separate rooms for sleeping and for eating in? What a waste of space! You could sleep a whole village here."

In the corner of the living room in Sumiko's apartment, not far from the TV, stood a small black-lacquered wood cabinet, a *butsudan*, or family shrine, with a figure of the Buddha. The shrine was new, I had not seen it before. A small gold silk bag tied with a white cord was displayed in the shrine. A candle burned beside offerings: a tiny can of Kirin beer, a cup of sake and a pear. An etching of mine called *Delta*, which I had given to Yoshimoto, Yukiko's grandfather, hung over the shrine, and a bonsai tree stood before it. I asked Yukiko about the gold silk bag and the offerings.

She looked up as she unpacked our bags. "It's grandfather's bones. The bonsai is from his garden, to keep him company."

My eyes misted over at this humble remembrance of him. He had died a year earlier. After his cremation, fragments of bone in a gold silk bag were all that remained of Yoshimoto, the one male in the family who had had no reservations about Yukiko marrying me. There had been an anniversary ceremony a week before our visit.

Sumiko's apartment was near the Osaka domestic airport, which closed around ten at night, then reopened at seven the following day. On the living room floor, Sumiko unrolled two cotton futons for Yukiko and me. The next morning I awoke with the roar of jetliners in my ears. The paper screens in the apartment rattled. The walls shook. Sleepily, I staggered to my feet. I saw that Yukiko had already risen, so I donned a *yukata*, a cotton robe, then retreated to the living room sofa where I leafed through a book, *Exotic Japan*. The morning air was cold, so I tried to cover my bare legs with the lower part of my robe. Sumiko, who had started breakfast, noticed my bare legs, came into the room and covered them with a down quilt.

Yukiko had dressed and was putting on some gold earrings. She scolded her mother. Sumiko smiled, her hand to her lips, and left the room.

I closed my book. "What did you say?"

"I told her not to spoil you because you're a lazy good-for-nothing."

"I'm an artist," I retorted.

Yukiko was wearing culottes, a white silk blouse with a bow, and a cashmere sweater. "Well, Mister Artist, Mother and I are going shopping." She put out her hand. "I need some money today."

I opened my wallet, took out some large notes, and then peeled off a roll of blue 1,000-yen bills, the note with the picture of the satirist Soseki Natsume, the Meiji-era author of *I Am a Cat*. "At least the Bank of Japan honours artists."

She dropped the roll of bills into her purse. Then she snapped it shut. "Why don't you get dressed and go painting somewhere, Toni?"

I shambled off to the shower. *Tekito*, the principle of suitability, ruled Yukiko's life. She had done our packing in Vancouver so I'd have almost no informal clothes to wear. And God help me if I spilled some soya sauce on my tie. On my last visit to Sumiko's apartment, I had borrowed her bike and cycled to Ina River park and painted there for a few hours. I had laughed when Yukiko had translated the sign in my picture. "The kanji just reads, 'Don't!'" On one of our visits to Tokyo, while we walked through the crowd of rush-hour commuters at Shibuya station, a crazy old man suddenly unbuckled his trousers and mooned the passersby. I nudged Yukiko. "Did you see that?" She completely avoided looking at him, took my arm and propelled me past the scene. "Face ahead. You do not see." I had glanced back anyway. Not one of the hundreds of people surging through the station looked at the naked old man, either.

Now I decided to paint Osaka Castle and I caught the train downtown. Glimpses of the five-storey gabled tower flashed by in the spaces between office buildings. I found it easily. Turning a corner, I saw the vast moat and enormous eighty-foot-high stone walls. The original castle had been built on the orders of Hideyoshi Toyotomi in 1583, then attacked with fire and seized by his archrival for the shogunate, Ieyasu Tokugawa. On a previous visit I had seen in the castle museum a poem Toyotomi wrote on his deathbed:

> Everything's a dream.
> Man's ambition is a dream of dreams.
> With a big Osaka in my mind,
> I must disappear like the dew.

The deathbed poem is a traditional Japanese art form. The Zen monks think of nothing else when the end is near. The most famous poems are quoted for hundreds of years. My favourite, like the poem above, reminds us not to take life too seriously:

> Birth is thus
> Death is thus,
> Poem or no poem,
> What's the fuss?

I tucked my paintbox under my arm. Only castle walls and art endure, I thought, as I entered the Otemon Gate.

The entire first grade of an elementary school had beaten me into the compound. Little boys and girls in canary yellow sun hats carried drawing boards and watercolour paints. Three or four classes of school children were yelling and running in every direction as their head teacher bellowed instructions over a loud-hailer. Other teachers sat the children down in groups and started them on their art work by drawing an outline of the castle, later to be filled in with colour, as if they were creating their own colouring books. This did not seem to me to be very Japanese. I positioned myself on a high wall above the students, to gain a relatively tranquil spot from which I could paint the castle. The day was so warm, it dried my watercolour as fast as I painted it.

In Japanese cities I constantly battled the crowds and the noise. The urban environment seemed to contradict the traditional aesthetics I so much admired. Instead of labouring for hours over a realistic depiction of a flower, the classical Japanese painter created a likeness in a few strokes. He looked at the flower once, then worked from his memory of his experience of it. The Japanese masters practised "the way of the brush," where one makes value judgements about the work as it proceeds and is free to make a change in midstroke. That was my ideal as well.

The sight of Mount Fuji from the train to Osaka had convinced me to try to paint it from all sides and in all light and weather conditions just as did the flamboyant *ukiyo-e* artist, *Gakyojin*—mad-about-painting—Katsushika Hokusai.

We rented a car, drove to Lake Yamanaka, and checked into the Mount Fuji Hotel on a high hill overlooking the lake. The day proved so cloudy that at no point did we see the famous 12,000-foot mountain, although from our room we had a splendid view of the lake. The trees on the surrounding hills, already touched by frost, were changing to fall colours. But instead of the brilliant oranges and reds of Canadian or New England maples, their leaves were the gentle umbers and rose madder of Europe.

Later, as we sat in the terrace restaurant facing the mountain, the upper half of Mount Fuji suddenly materialized with a pale yellow sunset behind it. To see it appear so precipitously, in such light and at close range for the first time, sent a shiver of delight through me. It was so much bigger than I had expected, even at this high altitude. We looked up, and up, to where it was crowned with a grey lenticular cloud. Then we watched silently as Mount Fuji slowly dissolved into darkness, vanishing into the night.

Yukiko said, "It really is something, isn't it?"

I nodded. "Mount Fuji is truly a wonder of the world."

About 6 a.m. the following morning, I heard the sound of windows sliding open. It was a cloudless day and I opened ours to look at the mountain, too. For some reason, the hotel's architect had faced the hotel to the lake instead of Mount Fuji. I could see guests hanging perilously far out of their windows like me and twisting at the waist to try to see the mountain. According to the law of averages, I reasoned, the hotel must have lost a few guests over the years.

Yukiko joined me at the window and we stared at Lake Yamanaka. Scarcely a ripple broke the surface of the water.

I turned to her. "Wouldn't it be great if I had my flying boat here? I could moor it at the dock and fly around the slopes of Mount Fuji."

She laughed at me. "If you tried that, Toni, they would throw chains around your plane and arrest you."

I sighed, "I'm sure they would."

For the next few days, our stay at the hotel followed a simple pattern. In the morning I would go to the terrace and try to paint the peak before the clouds obscured it. Then we'd drive partway up the mountain so I could paint there.

On the morning of the second day, the base of the mountain glowed pink in the light shifting through the moist layers of cloud. We drove above a cloud deck at 5,000 feet and parked at the treeline, at 7,500 feet, where I sat in a patch of sunlight and painted. Later we descended into a deep valley to investigate the two lakes, Kawaguchi and Saiko. From the valley road near Lake Kawaguchi, the view of Fuji in the light of late afternoon was almost too picture-perfect. I painted it anyway, concentrating on the glow that the sun, now only partially above the ridge, gave to the mountain.

On each of two days, I painted five watercolours. When I rose on the third day, the sky looked ominous, overcast and black. Mount Fuji appeared as a dark, overwhelming silhouette that cast a shadow across the earth. From the terrace of the hotel, I painted the fearful shape of the raging black mountain. With a loose, confident hand, I explored the nearly perfect shape on my paper, leaving the luminous white paper around it in the shape of clouds. To the black-green trees around the lake, I gave a rich velvety colour. The air was laden with moisture and my paper dried very slowly, allowing me to rework the highlights in it. Then I peeled the painting off my board and set it aside to dry.

That afternoon Yukiko and I drove to one of the base camps for climbers hiking to the top of the mountain. As I set up my paint-box and board, I heard a convoy of Self-Defence Force army vehicles rolling toward an artillery range on the barren flanks of the mountain. When I heard the guns rumble later, it sounded as if I were painting an active volcano.

When I returned to the car, Yukiko seemed to have plunged into despair. She hardly talked to me. I put it down to my neglect of her that day. As usual, I had painted instead of spending time with her. Our trips together were always like that for her, hours of tedium, watching me paint.

I learned it was even more than that. Yukiko reminded me about how much she missed Japan by living in Canada with me.

I tried to reason with her. "You go home every year. It was practically our wedding agreement."

"You don't understand me, Toni," she replied. "I don't know where I belong any more."

"Do you think you belong in Japan?"

"I've been away so long, I don't feel comfortable here any more, either."

Yukiko grew more upset. Our life together meant entertaining my friends, making public appearances where she felt little more than ornamental. I listened and hoped her mood would pass.

The next day I put away my brush for Yukiko. We rented bicycles and rode around Lake Yamanaka. Among the guests in the hotel restaurant that evening were two elderly Japanese couples. Evidently at least one of the party was hard of hearing, since all four people spoke loudly. Yukiko, who could hear what they were saying, interpreted for me.

One man spoke of the Japanese, "When business is good, no one can afford to leave it and take a holiday. Now that the economy is so poor, we have to work even harder."

It appeared to me that modern Japan had become a marvellous foundation for industrial growth. It had become the kind of no-nonsense society in which the Bank of England would invest. I turned to Yukiko, "When will people learn that you can buy everything except time? We need to learn how to linger over things."

Yukiko nodded. "No Japanese would stay a week at Mount Fuji."

"I wish we were staying even longer," I added.

The next morning was a cold and windy one. But the sky was very clear, and I painted from our hotel, peeking out from the windows, framing a scene in my mind, then committing it to paper. I could have stayed there all day looking, then painting. The clouds around Mount Fuji dissolved, then reformed into new shapes. Yukiko dragged me away for some breakfast on the terrace. I took my paintbox with me and stared at the mountain while eating. Then I started painting from the terrace.

At noon, the clouds rolled in. It was going to be our last full day at the hotel. We drove to Lake Kawaguchi and another of the climbers' base camps on Mount Fuji. Impulsively I put my paintbox under my arm and started climbing the mountain. As I brushed against some gnarled and stunted pines by the edge of the lava field, dead pine needles showered onto the Greek fisherman's cap I was wearing. I brushed them off and they dropped onto the ground, a brilliant mustard yellow against the black cinders.

The trail grew steeper. Soon, I could hardly see my goal, the con- ical apex of the mountain. After a few hundred metres, I stopped looking up and concentrated on my footing on the loose volcanic rubble underfoot. In an hour or two I was sweating profusely. I scratched my hands scrabbling up the rocks with my paintbox. I doubted that Hukusai had ever climbed up here. In his thirty-six views of Mount Fuji, the mountain is always in the distance.

Exhausted, I rested. Salty sweat almost blinded me. It seemed pointless to carry on to the summit when I had lost all sense of the mountain's beauty. Besides, Yukiko was waiting for me below. To her I had slowly become a tiny speck, and then disappeared. I climbed back down by following an old lava channel until I regained a view of the summit. I found a large weathered rock to sit upon and stared at the peak, which had emerged from the clouds. Working swiftly, I created one of those paintings that seems to come together by itself—the mountain and the clouds knitting together under my brush. I finished just before a cloud once again obscured the moun- tain. Happy about the painting, I walked down to our car where I rejoined Yukiko.

When I awoke at 6 a.m. on the last morning, I opened the window and let in the raucous cries of the black crows. There was Fujiyama, its black sides rising up through storm-grey clouds. The first snow- fall of the season had clad the summit in a brilliant white snowcap, and the peak shone like a diamond in a jet-black obsidian ring. I had time to make one more painting from the terrace as Yukiko packed.

Later, she met me on the terrace. "I have to try to live my own life, Toni. Sometimes I don't know who I am."

I remembered why she had come to Canada, fearing that she might not fit in with the life of a woman in Japan. She had desperately needed someone and, at first, she had pursued me more than I had pursued her. Then, I had been touched by her vulnerability, and had fallen in love with her youth and beauty.

Yukiko and I had been married twelve years. I was going to be sixty in November, and we faced difficulties that neither of us had foreseen. I glanced at the dark shape of Fuji again. For an instant, my whole world seemed ready to tumble into winter.

Chapter 23

The Tempest

The years from 1988 to 1994 were extremely difficult for me. In the fall of 1991, Yukiko finally left me. That was devastating. In trying to console me, my father, who had never overcome his prejudice against foreigners, remarked: "How could the marriage work out, Toni? She came from a different culture."

A few months later, in 1992, I learned that Dad had a problem of his own. He had kept the information to himself for a long while, but eventually I learned that he had cancer. As soon as I heard about it, I flew to Penticton.

I found him sorting through boxes of things he had collected over the years. He handed me the account book to his bank. He showed me the key to his safety deposit box where he had squirrelled away $10,000 in emergency cash. The gravity of the situation finally sunk in when he got out his Hardy split-cane fishing rod. He had never let me touch it before.

He passed me the rod, "Here, Toni, you might as well take it."

I almost burst into tears. That was as close as he could come to saying good-bye.

I guess Dad feared he'd lose control of his feelings. I know he would have avoided that. Our last visit reminded me of the time a twelve-year-old friend of mine on the Isle of Man was hit by a double-decker bus. My parents knew my friend's family and we went to the funeral together. The boy's father wept uncontrollably through the service. After we returned home, my father shocked me by remarking, "He should have pulled himself together and taken it like a man."

I suppose Dad's behaviour in my childhood affected my reactions to the deaths of my first wife and my daughter, Jennifer. From my father, I learned to avoid dealing with painful issues by suppressing my emotions. Not until much later did I realize how mistaken that approach had been.

My father never directly talked about dying to me, and he never discussed it with my mother, either. Instead, he spoke to her as if he were going to recover. They both knew better, although he probably convinced himself that he was protecting her. For her part, my mother knew better than to confront or contradict him. My father could be terribly overbearing when anyone else in the family disagreed with him. When my sisters and I were young, his bad-tempered tirades convinced my mother, a fairly easygoing woman, that they were temperamentally unsuited to one another. She'd confide in us afterward, "When you kids are grown up, I'm leaving him!" Of course, she never did. I doubt that she could have. She was party to one of those old-fashioned marriages that become a matter of habit.

For his part, my father worshipped my mother. I recall him telling one of his friends about how the family had immigrated to Canada in 1948 as a result of his appearing in the Service Players' amateur theatre production of the Rodgers and Hammerstein musical, *The Desert Song*. Because he had befriended a young woman in the show who had an uncle on the board of directors of the Cunard White Star Line, Dad was able to purchase our tickets to Canada even though passage was very difficult to obtain at the time.

My mother was weeding while he showed his friend their garden, and as he told the story, Dad walked over to her and sang the love song from the musical.

At first, my mother frowned, "Jim, don't be silly." But I could see she liked the attention. She rose to her feet. He took her hand and she smiled at him, the old charmer. And even at that age, well into his eighties, Dad had a lovely tenor voice:

> The desert song calling
> Its voice enthralling
> Will make you mine!

My career amazed my father and that always pleased me. He had never thought I would amount to much when I was younger. As related earlier, during my teen years on the Isle of Man I was first apprenticed to a printer, then articled to an architect. I was nineteen when we left for Canada, and shortly after arriving I was able to earn enough money to support myself. I always wanted to show him that I could make it on my own.

I remember Dad asking me during one visit. "Toni, do you remember your summers at Granddad's house? That was when you started painting. Your mother and I still have one of your first pictures, a sailing ship, HMS *Lightning*, berthed in Ramsey Harbour. You didn't know how to spell, so you painted 'Litning' on the bow."

I grinned. "I still can't spell."

"You were just a little kid, and you still spent all your time sketching or painting," he added.

In some ways, my father and I competed with one another. I was driven to do the things he would have loved to do. One of them was to travel. I learned how to fly my own plane and that impressed him, too, even though he feared small airplanes. When he and I went on fishing trips together, we spent most of our time in the car, driving up logging roads to high mountain lakes. We'd drive for hours until I'd feel the urge to say again, "Dad, we could have flown here in fifteen minutes. You know I keep an inflatable boat in the back of the plane. We could have gone fishing all day, caught our limit and flown home for supper. Now we've got to set up camp and be eaten alive by mosquitoes, and we must have put ten years on the Rolls getting here."

I finally convinced him to fly in my Lake Buccaneer flying boat. On our first flight, he couldn't wait to land. The second time he kept frantically directing me across Okanagan Lake. However, everything changed once I set the plane down. We were visiting one of his friends, a retired army colonel, so Dad went to great lengths to show his bravery—once we were out of the plane.

"It's great to go flying," he informed the colonel. "I fly with Toni every chance I get."

I think that my father lived vicariously through my experiences. He would have loved to travel to the Arctic or to Japan or India. He was never able to travel as much as he would have liked.

With my son, James, and my father, James Onley, 1987. Photograph by Yukiko Onley.

Most of all, he would have loved to have made some money in his life. Unfortunately, by the way he kept moving from one house to another, he frittered away what little capital he had.

The one time I thought he had made a good real estate investment, he lost it. He bought a house on the west bench above Skaha Lake, which had a view from Okanagan Falls on Skaha Lake to Squally's Point on Okanagan Lake. The house was a small one, but more than large enough for two people, and it was situated on a large piece of property. I used to sit out on the big lawn and paint. Mom was a tremendous gardener and in the summer she grew beautiful flowers.

But soon Dad was dissatisfied with the house.

"It's got dry rot."

"So fix the bloody thing," I replied.

The next time he visited me in Vancouver, I asked him about the property. He told me he'd up and sold it. I couldn't believe it. "You did what?" I asked. "How much did you get for it?"

"I got a couple more bucks than I paid for it."

"Dad, how much did you sell the place for?"

He didn't want to tell me at first. I persisted.

"I got $22,000 for it."

"Dad, you didn't!" I exclaimed. "You gave it away!"

Mom sat on the couch just shaking her head.

I told him. "If I had known you were going to settle for that kind of money, I would have bought it myself and you and Mom could have lived in it free for the rest of your lives."

Dad had moved them into a mobile home in Penticton. Manufactured homes can be moved, and Dad had such itchy feet that he likely believed he would move it to another location one day. In the meantime, he'd put it up on cinder blocks. To try to compensate my mother for the loss of her beautiful garden, he built a small, glassed-in addition where she could grow a few plants. He built it on the cheap with wood he had scrounged. When he showed it to me, he announced, "We call it the solarium."

At heart, Dad was always an actor. Late in his career, he appeared on CBC television on a series called *The Lectern Theatre*. He read parts from famous plays and passages from the classics in a booming voice, sounding a lot like Dylan Thomas. When my sisters and I were children, he read us bedtime stories. That was how I learned to read. Certainly, I never learned anything that important at St. Mary's elementary school. Dad started me reading by serializing *Treasure Island*. He'd read to the most dramatic part of the chapter, then announce, "That's enough for tonight." Eventually I became so curious about what was going to happen to Jim Hawkins that I read the book for myself.

During his lifetime, my father acquired a reputation as a great storyteller. There always proved to be some truth to his stories, which made it all the more difficult to unravel them. A family favourite was his visit to the *Titanic* as a nine-year-old boy. In this case, his maternal grandfather, Captain Tobin, had been in charge of HMS *America*, the mail ship at the *Titanic*'s last port of call in Ireland. Dad maintained that he had just happened to visit his grandparents in 1912, and that Captain Tobin had taken him out on the mail boat and shown him the great ship. He further claimed that while the mail was being transferred to the *Titanic*, Captain Smith had asked them aboard.

"The captain invited us into the officers' mess. And I remember him giving me a bottle of ginger beer," said my father. "My grand-dad had scotch. He and the captain had a couple of snorts. Then we walked on deck while the men finished bringing the mail on board. My granddad shook hands with the captain—he was a big man with a beard—and the captain leaned down and shook hands with me. Then we trotted down the companionway and it was hauled up. Our ship lay there with its engines stopped while the *Titanic* moved away into the darkness. You could see her lights. You could hear the band playing. Some passengers were leaning over the rails and waving to us. We were the last people ever to see her."

If that weren't enough, Dad also claimed that he met one of Hitler's top lieutenants, who he said had been imprisoned in Braeside, a walled mansion on Glen Crutchery Road in Douglas. Surrounded by a high wall, Braeside held internees, the German con-suls from Iceland and East Africa and several other dignitaries who had been in England or on Allied soil at the outbreak of the war. Dad's commanding officer, Major Daniel, is supposed to have sent my father over one day with a packet of Players Number 1 Navy Cut cigarettes and some scotch for this special prisoner.

"I saw a large man with a villainous-looking face and beetling black eyebrows," said my father.

"I see you have my cigarettes, thank you. Your name?" the pris-oner asked.

"Onley, Jim Onley."

Potterton, the British officer accompanying Dad, snapped, "Jim Onley, sir!" Dad refused to salute. The man was a German prisoner of war, to hell with him.

"Very well, Onley, thank you," said the prisoner.

The British officer clicked his heels and bowed. "Will that be all, Herr Hess?"

It was Rudolf Hess. Hess had flown to Britain in an ME-109 fighter in May 1941, then parachuted into Scotland to broker a peace treaty. The British arrested him. Hitler, infuriated by Hess's mission, repudiated him.

"Hess had a thick German accent, but otherwise he spoke excel-lent English," recalled Dad. "He didn't seem fanatical or stupid or insane." Dad added that he and Hess talked about classical music, particularly the German Romantic composers. "It was strange. Hess loved Mendelssohn," said Dad. "He played the *Hebridean Suite* on his phonograph all the time, even though Mendelssohn was a Jew."

When I revisited the Isle of Man many years after we had emigrated, I tried to verify Dad's stories. He and I had been to Dublin, but I don't believe that he went to Ireland as a small boy or rode the mail ship out to the *Titanic*. Not one person on the island, from the Manx Museum archivist to the librarian, had ever heard that an important prisoner like Rudolph Hess had been held on the island.

I found one of Dad's acquaintances from the Manx Amateur Dramatic Society, Frieda Standen. After she retired, she wrote two books about her life on the island. Because she was in her eighties and hard of hearing, I had to write down my question about my father's stories.

Frieda chuckled as she read my note, "Jim always was a storyteller. Did he tell you the one about the bottled water from the Sargasso Sea? He showed us a bottle of murky water that he insisted had come from the Caribbean. Florence put her foot in it by accidentally calling it 'bathwater'."

"Were you ever put off by any of my father's stories?" I asked.

"By no means. Jim was never the run-of-the-mill type that you find in a small place like the Isle of Man. Winters were pretty long here and he kept us well entertained."

Maybe I learned the power of a good story from my father. When I lived in Penticton and my paintings began to attract some attention, he was selling advertising for the local newspaper and used his connection with the paper to arrange a number of news stories about me. While he operated the Starlight Theatre in town, he always managed to get a story on a theatrical production instead of paying to advertise. That helped me to realize just how important publicity could be in my career and furthermore, that it could be free. I have come to believe that the media is just like a hungry beast. It needs to be fed news constantly. This is especially true of television.

Sometimes I think my father took refuge in other people's words instead of his own. He had a wonderful memory for lines and he knew something from almost everything Shakespeare wrote. During a telephone call that turned out to be our last conversation together, he quoted Ariel from *The Tempest*:

Full fathom five, thy father lies;
Of his bones are coral made:
Those are pearls that were his eyes:
Nothing of him that doth fade,
But doth suffer a sea-change
Into something rich and strange.

Yet Dad still had bouts of optimism about his illness, and during the phone call he insisted his health was growing better. He had been complaining of terrible arthritis in his limbs. "It's funny, Toni, all the pain is gone," he said. "I can move my hand. I can walk around. It's some kind of miracle."

I figured that Dad's condition had stabilized. I was supposed to give a painting workshop in the Fraser Valley and I had some appointments in Vancouver.

"Look, Dad, I've got to finish up here and clear my schedule. Call me if you get any news. I'll be back in a few days to stay with you."

Two days later, my sister Moira telephoned from Penticton. My father had suddenly had difficulty breathing on Sunday night. His lungs had filled with fluid and he had lost consciousness. The ambulance took him to the hospital where he died during the night of February 25. For the first time in my life, I felt that I was really on my own.

When my father died, Yukiko was very sympathetic. She offered to accompany me to the funeral and we drove to Penticton together. I guess we talked on the long drive from Vancouver, though I can't remember either of us saying anything of any consequence. She was moving on with her life. That day was probably the lowest point in my life.

The director of the Penticton Art Gallery lent us a room for the funeral reception. The gallery held a large collection of my work, much of it donated by the people in Penticton who had been my early supporters.

I painted a watercolour during the week I stayed there, and on it I inscribed Dad's quotation from *The Tempest*. The last three lines are the ones carved on Shelley's tomb. I created this strange, sad painting one morning as I looked out from my hotel window at the mountain basin that contained the broad waters of Okanagan Lake. The lake was the same colour as the overcast sky. There was a fire in Naramata on the east side of the lake; the smoke made me think of a funeral pyre. I added its windblown trail to my painting so that a gentle haze of grey drifted over Shakespeare's words.

I donated the painting to the gallery in memory of my father. He was eighty-eight when he died, and his life had spanned the Modern Age. He had seen two world wars and the dismantling of the British Empire. Halley's comet had visited the earth twice in his life-time. In 1911, when he was seven, he had seen the long tail of the comet in the sky, a sign some believed marked the end of the world. He had been terrified when he heard the comet might hit the earth and shatter it into pieces. It was the year George V, the grandfather of Queen Elizabeth II, came to the throne. He was eighty-two years old the second time the comet came, but the sky was overcast and he could not see it. This seemed to be a disappointment for him, as if he had been denied some obscure form of closure.

My mother would die seven years later, at the age of ninety-two. My parents' ashes are scattered together high on the mountain above Naramata where there is a wonderful view of the Okanagan Valley they loved so much.

After losing Yukiko and my father, I spent most of 1992 travelling. At first I thought that getting away from Vancouver would be the most effective kind of therapy. I flew to Whitehorse, then to the Bahamas. I even flew to Bali. I eventually realized that even if I had gone to the moon, my grief over losing my father and Yukiko would have remained. I took my sorrow with me everywhere.

I searched for some way to express my feelings and deal with my misery and found my salvation through my art. The emotional experience of the two terrible events in my life led me to the next turn in my work. I tore up my calligraphy practice sheets. Initially, that assuaged some of my anger and anguish. Then that reflective part of me—the artistic self—took over. I collaged copies of pages from the diaries and torn practice sheets. The process proved cathartic. In January 1994, I had a show, "Japan Remembered."

In one collage, *Rising Sun*, a blurred sun floated over a torn, sandy earth. In another, *Sanctuary*, I had sliced a copy of a page from my diary, folded it over and pressed it onto the paper, where it hung in an accordion fold over a grey form twisting into the earth below. Another work contained a handwritten fragment of "Intimations of Immortality" by Wordsworth: "Where is it now, the glory and the dream?" One reviewer said this work was the closest viewers would ever get to the artist as a man, to knowing his "thoughts that . . . lie too deep for tears." Not one landscape was exhibited among my pieces. The critics hailed the show as a profoundly personal and technically innovative break with my past.

I had returned to the art of collage, which had been so important in my early career. I still enjoyed working with random shapes and spaces. A breeze might come through an open door and shift the pieces into entirely new positions. That excited me. Yet my new collages were quite different from the abstract collages I had done in the late 1950s and early 1960s. I now worked in a small format and included calligraphy in the composition.

I still felt a great unhappiness about the break-up of my marriage. I consoled myself a little by recalling an old story from the Isle of Man. A farmer owned a wonderful dappled grey horse, which ran away to the other side of the island. Everyone said that was too bad. "Not at all," he replied. The next spring, the horse came back with a mare that bore him a colt. The man let his son ride the horse and the boy fell and was injured. Again, people sympathized. Again, he told them not to feel sorry. A war broke out and many young men were conscripted and killed in the fighting. Because he was lame, his son did not have to go to war. Like that Manxman, I tried to look on the positive side of things.

Gradually, I overcame my grief. I realized that I should have been more attentive to Yukiko. If you spend your life painting as I have, you eventually understand that you could have given much more of your time to your loved ones. Time and time again, I have held back from that. I never felt I had any choice. I couldn't stop painting. I couldn't take any time out. The deaths of my first wife and my daughter had brought it home to me that no one can count on a long life. Wasting an hour was a sin I felt I could not commit.

I also saw clearly enough to be grateful to Yukiko for the experiences I gained through our years together. My painting continued to be influenced by what I saw in Chinese and Japanese art. My approach of beginning directly with painting, instead of first drawing, as in the British tradition John Nicholson had taught me, was echoed there, while the Oriental aesthetic generally suited my temperament, for I am intuitive in my approach to life rather than logical. I like to think that a good painting almost paints itself. My marriage to Yukiko and our trips to Japan strengthened these aspects of my work.

I am optimistic by nature. I am, even so, surprised at and grateful for the success of my life's journey so far. My work is the true foundation and most serious purpose of my life. I have, I feel, been generously rewarded, most of all with the freedom to paint. I am happy that my work is enjoyed and appreciated by so many people.

I have pushed ahead in my work. Though at times there may not seem to be much difference from one exhibition to the next, over the long term the changes are there, sometimes subtle, sometimes dramatic. I moved from the landscape painting I learned on the Isle of Man to the abstract collages I did in Mexico. In Britain, I explored minimalism. Then I returned to the landscape with new insight. I have travelled the world with my watercolours, painting in the Eastern Arctic, in Europe, in China, Japan, and India, in Vietnam, New Zealand and Egypt, to mention some of the places I have visited. After Yukiko left and my father died, I spent a year and a half in absolute misery, but that experience, too, led me into a new kind of art.

Although it would be comforting to believe that there's a divine will operating in the world and an afterlife of some kind, I have never put much faith in that idea. I am quite sure that my only hope of immortality lies in the art that has been a driving force in my life. Major galleries, including the National Gallery, the Museum of Modern Art, the Tate Gallery, the US Library of Congress and most public galleries in Canada, have collected my work. The Vancouver Art Gallery has a complete collection of my serigraph prints, etchings and lithographs as well as many of my paintings and collages, making it their largest holding of an individual artist, including Emily Carr. The Victoria Art Gallery, the Edmonton Art Gallery and the University of Lethbridge all have a complete serigraph print collection as well.

I am sometimes asked how I can part with the paintings that mean so much to me. I reply that a productive creative artist always has a storage problem. The purchaser buys the right to store the work, to enjoy looking at it, and to resell it for financial gain, but the painting in another sense always "belongs" to the artist who created it and signed it. Most collectors share their art with the public through loans and donations to public art galleries. The visitor to a museum exhibition sees a work by me and says, "That's one of Toni Onley's paintings." Also, I own the copyright. So it never stops being "my" painting, in that sense. Art really belongs to the artist and the public. The purchasers and collectors are public benefactors who make it possible for the artist to continue painting and for the public to see the art, both at the galleries through which the art is initially offered for sale and at the later museum exhibitions. Thus the "commodity" use of art supports both the artist and the cultural value of the art.

In 1998, the federal government recognized my contributions to Canadian culture and my philanthropic efforts, and made me an officer of the Order of Canada. George Woodcock once remarked, when I asked him if I could borrow one of his many honorary doctorates, "At a certain age, Toni, they will all come to you." In June

The Isle of Man stamps, 2002.

2000, I was awarded the honorary degree of Doctor of Letters by Okanagan University College.

It is fitting that this story should end with my retrospective exhibition at the Manx Museum on the Isle of Man, which opened on June 28, 2002. To coincide with this exhibition, the Isle of Man post office issued five new stamps, images selected from water-colours of the island I had painted two years previously. Isle of Man stamps are much sought-after by collectors, so it amuses me to real-ize I will be appearing forever in countless tiny exhibitions in stamp albums around the world.

In 2001 I was unexpectedly invited back to where I started my life's voyage to share my art with the island. The term "coming full

Punting and painting, Oxford, 1998. Photograph by James Onley.

circle" springs to mind, but I don't like it because it seems to imply that my life is almost over. I am beyond three score and ten, but I still feel thirty-five. I jump into my flying boat and head out across Canada in search of subjects, and hope to do so for many years to come before I am anchored to the earth with a stone or drift around the globe with the wind.

It seems like only yesterday that I roamed over the Isle of Man, gathering mushrooms from the woodlands and seabird eggs from the cliffs while acquiring an intimate sense of the landscape that would eventually emerge in my paintings. The island is my ultimate spiritual home, a sacred place scattered with neolithic standing stones which, although severely weathered, have not moved in

4,000 years. The ancient stone circles that look as if they have grown out of the earth are still places where I go to paint and meditate. These are places that can foster both contemplation and determination. It is on the Isle of Man that I first looked to the eternal beauty of nature as a subject for my art.

Manx people are fiercely independent; on an island with few reliable economic opportunities they have had to use their wits, imagination and ingenuity. The island has been home to smugglers, pirate radio, and gambling casinos, and has lately become a tax haven. We are as well known for taking the initiative as was the Manxman Fletcher Christian, the first mate of the *Bounty* who seized control of the ship rather than die of thirst.

I am just one of the many who left to find a new life beyond the island. Rooted today in a psychic space that somehow contains both the tradition of the Isle of Man and the new world of British Columbia, I feel the need to paint more than ever. No matter how many paintings I have created, it's the one I'm doing now that thrills me. Art is my record of discovery, of places visited, of experiences, and of the sense that I have lived. As I paint, something new and exciting enters the world. It keeps me alive and I can share it with others. At my age, what more could an artist ask of life?

Epilogue, 2002

The reader may wonder what has become of the family characters in this drama of an artist's life. Lynn, my daughter by my first wife Mary, is an accomplished ceramic artist and watercolourist who lives in Vancouver and sometimes accompanies me on landscape painting excursions. Her son, Byron Bertram, the "Adventure Comic," entertains audiences around the world with his unique combination of juggling, Houdini-like escape acts and stand-up comedy. Gloria, my second wife, ran her own gallery and art publishing company in Vancouver until 1992, when she retired to devote herself to editing and writing. James, my son with Gloria, was awarded a Ph.D. in modern history from the University of Oxford in 2001, and is now teaching at the University of Exeter in England while awaiting the publication of his first book by Oxford University Press. Yukiko, my third wife, is a photographer in Vancouver.

—Toni Onley

Chronology

1902 Toni's father, Jim Onley, is born at Land's End, Cornwall.

1907 Toni's mother, Florence Lord, is born on the Isle of Man.

1927 Toni's parents marry.

1928 Toni is born on Tuesday, November 20, on the Isle of Man.

1936 Begins to spend the summers with his grandparents.

1941 Leaves school at 13, is apprenticed in the printing trade.

1942 Attends evening classes at the Douglas School of Art; goes on painting expeditions with his first painting teacher, John Hobbs Nicholson.

1944 Is articled to H.A. Thomas, architect.

1946 Paints in Liverpool with Nicholson on his first trip off the island.

1948 Emigrates with his family to Canada.

1950 Marries Mary Jean Burrows, May 27.

1951 Has a daughter, Jennifer, born on January 16.

1953 Has a daughter, Lynn, born on February 24.

1955 Is devastated by the sudden death of his wife, Mary, on June 15; moves to Penticton with his daughters and works in architecture.

1956 Receives a scholarship to the Instituto Allende in San Miguel de Allende, Mexico; auctions 250 paintings.

1957 Arrives at San Miguel de Allende in December with daughter Lynn.

1958 Starts making collages; meets Alvin Balkind, New Design Gallery, and Bob Hume, the director of the Vancouver Art Gallery; has a show at the VAG; returns to Mexico.

1959 Has a one-person exhibition at the New Design Gallery in December.

1960 Returns to Vancouver in May after Lynn's appendectomy.

1961 Marries Gloria Knight, September 12; works on a mural for the Queen Elizabeth Playhouse.

1962 Installs mural and faces a storm of controversy in February; is awarded a Junior Canada Council Grant; meets Clement Greenberg at Emma Lake Workshop.

1963 Wins Zacks Prize at Royal Canadian Academy exhibition for collage, *Polar No. 1*; spends nine months in London on a Canada Council grant; visits the Isle of Man; rediscovers nineteenth-century British watercolour painters; learns print-making in Birgit Skold's studio.

1964 While returning to Canada learns that his daughter Jennifer was killed in a car accident.

1966 Teaches at the University of Victoria; learns to fly; has a son, James, born on December 17.

1967 Joins the University of British Columbia Fine Arts Department.

1968 Begins making serigraphs with Bill Bonnieman; buys his first airplane.

1970 Flies across Canada to visit sculptor Bob Murray in Georgian Bay.

1973 Meets Pierre Trudeau in St. Andrews, New Brunswick, who later arranges his first trip to the Far North.

1974 Voyages to the Arctic on the icebreaker *Louis St. Laurent* in September.

1975 Buys a Lake Buccaneer flying boat; flies 6,000 miles to Cape Dorset; separates from his second wife, Gloria.

1976 Resigns from the University of British Columbia.

1978 Has a retrospective exhibition at the Vancouver Art Gallery comprising 314 works; visits Japan for the first time with Yukiko Kageyama.

1979 Marries Yukiko Kageyama.

1980 Sells 1,287 prints and paintings to the "Fraser Valley Phantom" for $929,000.

1981 Sees the publication of his first book, *Toni Onley: A Silent Thunder*, a short biography and commentary on his work with 62 large reproductions of his watercolour landscapes.

1982 Buys a ski plane and flies on painting expeditions onto the BC mountain glaciers; visits India with George and Inge Woodcock in December.

1983 Threatens to burn prints to protest the income tax reassessment of Canadian artists.

1984 Crashes on Cheakamus Glacier on September 7; is rescued with photographer John Reeves after 18 hours suspended over a crevasse, but loses his ski plane.

1985 Sees the publication of *The Walls of India*, illustrated with his paintings.

1986 Voyages to the Arctic on the icebreaker *Des Groseilliers*, from May 22 to June 5.

1988 Travels to China in the spring; travels to Japan in October and paints Mount Fuji.

1989 Sees the publication of *Onley's Arctic: Diaries and Paintings of the High Arctic*.

1991 Separates from third wife, Yukiko; has first Canadian art exhibition at new Canadian embassy in Tokyo.

1992 Mourns his father, who dies at the age of 88.

1998 Is made an officer of the Order of Canada.

1999 Mourns his mother, who dies at the age of 92; sees the publication of *Toni Onley's British Columbia: A Tribute*, a book of landscape paintings with commentary by the artist.

2000 Receives an honorary doctorate from Okanagan University College.

Big Sur, 2002. Photograph by James Onley.

Index

Bold type indicates illustration